MANTHA

Alchemies of the Cultural Turn

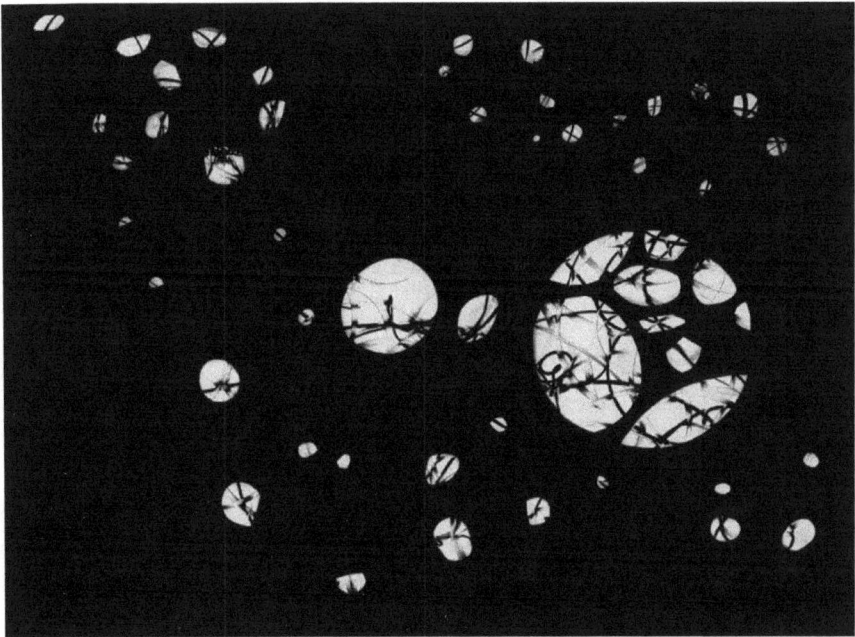

Mark K. Warford
SUNY Buffalo State University

Series in Language and Linguistics

VERNON PRESS

In the Americas:	*In the rest of the world:*
Vernon Press	Vernon Press
1000 N West Street, Suite 1200,	C/Sancti Espiritu 17,
Wilmington, Delaware 19801	Malaga, 29006
United States	Spain

Series in Language and Linguistics

Library of Congress Control Number: 2023941159

ISBN: 978-1-64889-905-8

Also available: 978-1-64889-733-7 [Hardback]; 978-1-64889-771-9 [PDF, E-Book]

Cover credit: Pollina, L. (2013, November). Noosphere No. 14. [Drawing in graphite]. Retrieved from: http://lorypollina.com/omegapointproject.shtml Original project completed in 2009. Used with artist's permission.

MANTHA (Sanskrit):

v. stir, churn, agitate

n. churning stick, stirred potion

Sources: McDonald, A. A. (nd.) A practical Sanskrit dictionary. Digital Dictionaries of South Asia: dsal.uchicago.edu; Narten, J. (1960). Das vedische Verbum math. *Indo-Iranian Journal, 4,* 121-135.

Table of Contents

Acknowledgments

First and foremost, I would like to recognize and thank Lory Pollina the artist whose drawing on graphite is featured on the cover- a major source of inspiration for *Mantha*. You can find out more about the collection to which it corresponds at lorypollina.com Several organizations were instrumental in the preparation of this book, including the Sanskrit study group of the Hindu Cultural Society of Western New York, the Centro Jung de Buenos Aires, and the Analytical Psychology Society of Western New York (APSWNY). In addition, I would like to acknowledge the invaluable input and feedback of colleagues: in particular, Northeast Modern Language Association colleagues Claire Sommers (Washington University) and Elia Jordan (Regis University) for their counsel in matters of Classical Studies and the (monstrous) feminine; Marko Miletich (Buffalo State University), for his input on content relevant to Translation Studies; APSWNY Vice-President, Paul Kochmanski; my father, Malcolm Warford, on various philosophical thinkers featured in the book, and my wife, Dana Warford, for her wide-ranging foundation in the Great Books and ancient Greek.

-M. K. W.
Buffalo
August 2022

Introduction

Regardless of one's intellectual or political inclinations, it seems clear that the Western psyche is off-kilter, polarized between a focus on the individual on one side and cultural consciousness on the other. What if this binary masks a deeper, emergent connectedness between psychological and social forces? In psychoanalytic studies, linguistics, educational research, organizational theory, Translation Studies, and other fields, there is a growing recognition of a reflexivity between human subjects (the learner, citizen, worker, etc.) and the vast variety of social network chains —both empirical and virtual— with which they engage. The epistemological ground of this perspective is the assumption of active, reflexive and often disproportionate dialogues between *cogito* and culture, mind and milieu, vestiges of an age-old metaphysical tension posed by the ancient Greeks: the One and the Many. On a related note, it was about halfway through this project that a dream image came to me through what C. G. Jung would call the transcendent function.[1] This dream image had both an auditory and a visual component. I share it here both to illustrate the core energies that drive this book and as a way to promote your own alchemical processing as you turn the pages.

"Holes" and "Wholes"

Regarding the auditory component, the verbal message of the dream was something about holes and wholes, and it likely was inspired by Lory Pollina's (2013/2009) *Omega Point Project and the Noosphere* series of drawings in graphite, one of which is printed on the cover. Inspired by the Jesuit paleontologist Pierre Teilhard de Chardin, this collection suggests to me that no vital system is completely sealed off. Pollina's method interchangeably layers and erases graphite, imbuing the circles with an analogous possibility for both orb-like volume and interiority: spheres and portals. Regarding the latter, my eyes are drawn to *holes in the whole*, finding there a portal that connects me to a rich, expanded field – a *whole* in that hole. Paul Kugler (2002), a Jungian analyst who has reclaimed a linguistic focus in psychoanalytic studies, asserts that psyche privileges sound over semantic connections. Accordingly, he might suggest that there is something archetypally rooted in the phonetic contiguity of hole and whole. This metonymic language play resonates somewhat with

---

[1] According to Jung, the transcendent function "facilitates the transition from one psychic condition to another by means of the mutual confrontation of opposites" (CW11, para. 780).

educationist Douglas Sloan's (1983/2008) notion of insight-imagination, a "participation of the whole person—in logical thinking, feeling and willing—in the act of cognition" (p. 69). Accordingly, over the course of this book, I challenge you, the reader, to find purchase in the play of these declarative statements, which respectively evoke two ways of perceiving the circularity of forms suggested in Pollina's work:

1) The individual psyche is the hole in the whole (the circles are portals) and

2) Culture is the whole in the hole (the circles have an orb-like substance).

There is something in the homonyms of whole and hole that evokes two fundamental drives in the psyche that may have propelled human evolution and have perhaps been driven to extremes in the rise of the West: the need to belong (the whole in the hole) and the need to slip out into our own pathway (the hole in the whole). Certainly the trajectory of Western cultures has centered on the latter, jettisoned by an apparently innate curiosity in the human psyche, what the theoretical physicist and transdisciplinary studies scholar Basrab Nicolescu (1994), describes as "a gaping hole towards the unknown, from where comes a fascination for laws. Laws of the unknown" (p. 111). There are those who would describe this hole-portal as a sort of rabbit hole, one that runs the risk of untethering the human subject from a healthy sense of "wholeness" – both in a cultural as well as an ecological sense.

Accordingly, the current project entertains the possibility that there is something of an emergent *whole* in the hole, a new cultural direction in the making, and conversely, something of a likewise emergent *hole* in the whole, a flaw in the collective container suggesting the need to find a patch from some proximal system. As the reader will see and hopefully experience, one needs the other.

A vision of the churn

The paleontologist-priest Pierre Teilhard de Chardin (1959/2008), who inspired the cover art of this book, visualized this phenomenon as a stable, *radial* force and off-shooting *tangents* in the trajectory of evolution. Both the Tao and Complexity Theory frame this phenomenon as a spiraling emergence fueled by the dance of attraction and repulsion. The move from the pervasive binary principle in Western culture to a blending churn, what I will refer to as a "mantha" a semantic borrowing from the Sanskrit *mantha*, depends on a change of preposition. Applying a bit of Jung's challenge to hold the tension of opposites, it becomes possible to confirm that the whole *and* the hole are interdependent. In other words, we need to value and cultivate blends of cultural stability and personal striving, substantive relatedness, and subjective space.

In bringing Jung's thought into the discourse on cultural studies, what has been lacking is an alchemy to forge the right key, and the dream presented this in a most peculiar image. Having reflected on the binary of Jung's inward-focused psychology set against more socially situated epistemologies, and by way of the transcendent function, the answer came vividly around 4:00 am in the form of a single dream image that provided much of the fuel for the work you are about to read. The image-symbol that materialized was a crucible mixing two substances: one light, one dark. Slowly the substances begin to churn one into the other, resulting in the emergence of the well-known symbol, the Tao, which blends these two energies: one stable and settled (Yin) and the other active and assertive (Yang). The questions posed by the images were clear and seemed to demand further exploration: Why does the story of the West seem perennially locked in polarized, binary thinking? Why the extremes? Speaking to ways out of the binary, Nicolescu (1994), suggests a sort of alchemical antidote: "One of the possible meanings of alchemy: transforming the binary structure of misunderstanding into the ternary structure of meaning" (p. 60). As we will see, this "ternary structure" is necessarily dynamic, pluralistic, and connective; in fact, one may argue it is not a structure at all but rather a sort of rhizome that branches into unexpected tangents. What if the A + B of this alchemy were not C but rather ∞?

On Alchemy and variations of (pra)ma(n)tha

So, as the title of this work suggests, all leads back to and forward from alchemy, not in the literal or Jungian sense, but in a more expanded, transcultural frame. The contours of this cultural turn reflect a similar turn (culture turn) in Translation Studies (see Bassnett & Lefevere, 1990) and more recently in post-Jungian studies. Certainly, the history of alchemy studies reflects this transcultural quality. Stanton Marlan (2021) has traced Jung's work in alchemy and the origins of his concept of the Self back to collaborations with Richard Wilhelm in preparing the translation of *The Secret of the Golden Flower* for Western audiences (pp. 12-13, citing Wilhelm, 1931/1962). In comparing Western and Eastern conceptions of development, Marlan (2021) cites Kaway (1996), who underscores a contrast between the West's emphasis on the individual and linear pathways, on one hand, and the Eastern focus on nature and circularity on the other. Ultimately, it is concluded that "It is possible to view these processes from either style of consciousness" (p. 30). The Jungian union of opposites, the coniunctio, arguably occupies a central position in both frameworks, at least from Jung's perspective: "For Jung, Taoist alchemy and his approach to depth psychology both sought renewal of psychic life through a reconciliation of opposites, leading to a sense of Self as a harmonious whole in intimate relations with the Cosmos" (Marlan, 2021, p. 103).

Returning to the dream, in the time leading up to the Tao image, my primary focus on bringing Jungian thought into conversations on personal and cultural change had centered on Prometheus, inspiration of educational innovations like *Promethean* interactive whiteboards, a figure who perhaps more than any other mythologem has concentrated meanings of human progress and striving. A deeper investigation led me back to depictions of the war between the Olympians and Titans and Aeschylus's *Prometheus Unbound.* In plowing through the old myths, I was surprised to find there a curiously overlooked and sublimely omnipresent Titaness, Themis. Depending on which version you follow, Themis was either portrayed as Prometheus's mother or wife, but in her own right, her contribution to the story of how Western culture emerged is of considerable (and arguably neglected) importance, illuminating the origins of this interplay of the hole and the whole and the One and the Many in ways that will be made evident in the chapters that follow. In direct contradiction to archetypal psychology's preference for Olympian psychology, it takes Titans to blend the binary, and the presence of Prometheus and Themis does not fade from chapter to chapter. Likewise, the monstrous is a compelling Greco-Roman trope that will be explored in-depth further on. The monstrous has a lot to de*monstra*te to us about the West's phenomenological binary of Self- Other.

Prior to the presentation of the dream image, I had also been reading Nicholas Gier's (2000) comparative study of Western and Eastern Titanism. Gier has reopened the Pandora's Box of the Prometheus's origins, from his Greek name, which translates to "forethought," to the Sanskrit *pramantha*, which is constructed on the root 'manth' (p. 63) and may be traced back to the Hindu Asuras, the Eastern parallel and possible progenitors to the Greek Titans, as sustained by Gier. We may easily ascertain that the *pramantha* is a sacred Vedic fire tool essential for performing the Agnyādheya (अग्न्याधेय) or "kindling of the sacred fire" one of seven sacrificial rites (Wisdom Library, 2021, February 27). The trail from pramantha to Prometheus, however, is a tricky one,[2] and it usually begins with evidence of a 'Zeus Prometheus' figure uncovered in the coastal Italian town of Thurii, which features the mythological figure holding a fire 'drill'.[3] Historian and author Robert Graves (1960), alluding to the Bhagavata Purana, posits that the brothers Pramanthu and Manthu are

---

[2] A. Nicholson casts doubt on such connections (personal communication, June 26, 2021). As we will see, there is no direct etymological or mythological path from East to West along the line of Prometheus.

[3] See Graves (1960, p. 9); Kuhn, 1859/2015) though Jung (CW5), working from Kuhn's analysis, suggests that the Thuric "Προ-μανθεύς" is not directly tied to pramantha but rather constitutes a cognomen (nickname) (para. 208). Later, we will further question the 'drill' interpretation.

prototypes for Prometheus and Epimetheus, but indologist F. B. J. Kuiper (1971, in Moore, 2015) demonstrated how the Prometheus connection can be traced to a tenuous connection drawn by nineteenth-century German scholar Rudolph Roth and more confidently asserted by Adalbert Kuhn.

In the twentieth century, Kuhn's research, in particular, was adapted by the early psychoanalysts, starting with Karl Abraham, and taken up by Jung and his mentor Sigmund Freud. Abraham (1909/1913) interchanges Pramantha and Prometheus as if the connection between the mythologems is a given, and his focus is decidedly phallocentric: "matha (=the male genitals,[4] compare the Latin *mentula*)" (193, p. 45), characterizing the Prometheus myth as "a pure masculine saga" (p. 62),[5] and minimizing any prominent role for the feminine in matters of creation. Not surprisingly, the common thread in this German line of thought is a focus on the "masculine firestick" (Jung, 1911-12/1952/2014, para. 208) sense of *pramantha*, focusing on variations of *bore* and *born* in German. Abraham is directly credited for Freud's corresponding analysis of a young male patient's fixation with a bath nozzle, noted by Jay Geller (1999):

> Perhaps, too, the word 'borer' ['Bohrer'] was not chosen without regard for its connection with 'born' ['geboren'] and 'birth' ['Geburt']. If so, the child could have made no distinction between 'bored' ['gebohrt'] and born ['geboren']. I accept this suggestion, made by an experienced fellow-worker, but I am not in a position to say whether we have before us here a deep and universal connection between the two ideas or merely the employment of a verbal coincidence peculiar to German. Prometheus (Pramantha), the creator of man, is also etymologically 'the borer.' (Cf. Abraham, *Traum und Mythus*, 1909, 98n.1, p. 368)

The full analysis is too involved to explore here, but Geller affirms Freud's conclusions, which center on an "entire network of Oedipal symptoms and phantasies" (p. 368).

---

[4] The comparison defies explanation. There is no such Greek or Sanskrit equivalent. In Sanskrit, a matha's meanings range from a hut to an educational center. See Monier-Williams (1988/1899, p. 730) for the full dictionary entry.

[5] The following quote offers some more context: "There can be no doubt (for reasons that I cannot discuss in this place) that the magic wand signifies the symbolic representation of the male genitals. A quite similar symbol, the rod boring in the wooden disc, is the nucleus of the oldest form of the Prometheus saga. The procreating man appears in it as well in the form of a person (Pramantha) as also symbolically. The woman is only represented by the symbol of the wooden disc and in the saga is only casually mentioned" (Abraham, 2013, p. 62).

Jung, for his part, filters pramantha through his particular revision of Freudian psychoanalysis. The Swiss psychologist does not discount the sexual connotations; rather, he deduces underlying, archetypal roots of the libido, as evidenced in *Symbols of Transformation* (1911-12/1952/2014):

> It is just possible that we owe the discovery of fire to some such regression to the presexual stage, where the model of rhythmic activity can co-operate effectively. The libido, forced into regression by the checking of instinct, reactivates the infantile boring and provides it with objective material to work on—fittingly called "material" because the object at this stage is the mother (*mater*). As I have pointed out above, the act of boring requires only the strength and perseverance of an adult man and suitable "material" in order to generate fire. Consequently, the production of fire may have originally occurred as the objective expression of a quasi-masturbatory activity.
> (para. 227)

Nicolescu (1994) warns: "Avoid at all costs the formidable trap of confusing the meaning of history with the history of meaning" (p. 57). Echoing this aphorism, Jung ultimately and astutely discards the established etymologies of pramantha, concluding that "the line from pramantha to Prometheus does not go via the word, but more probably through the idea or image, so that Prometheus may in the end have the same meaning as pramantha.[6] Only, it would be an archetypal parallel and not a case of linguistic Transmission" (para. 208). Though ultimately tethered to the phallocentric 'boring' line of inquiry into the mythological roots of Prometheus, Jung acknowledges the etymological complexities undermining a direct line from East to West, and he is quite a bit more attentive to the role of the feminine in pramantha, as evidenced in his explication of the *manthana*, the Vedic sacrificial ceremony that reenacts the birth of the fire god, Agni, through the union of a fire stick and a bored piece of wood. Jung (para. 210) appears to mistake the corresponding tools for their mythologems. The two components (my corrections in parentheses) consist of a masculine boring tool called the *uttararani* (which symbolizes the Sun King Puravas) and a feminine receptor called the *adhararani* (which symbolizes the moon nymph Urvashi). The resulting spark is mythologically represented in Urvashi's utterance: the birth of the fire god Agni. In this ceremony, he discerns the archetypal sacred marriage here, the Greek *hieros gamos* (para. 214), and, though he does not reference the parallel here, the assessment parallels the

---

[6] Jung inserts a rather lengthy footnote here, which features a churn and burn through various philologists and Greco Roman texts, extending the root, manth-, into everything from "mangle" [mengeln] to nouns like "mint" and a priapic "chin" and "mind."

wedding of Sol and Luna in the Western alchemical *coniunctio*, the union of opposites depicted in *Aion* (Jung, 1959/1979), the *prima materia* of his notion of psychological individuation, but it is important to highlight some crucial differences. Luna, for example, is objectified as material (*prima materia*) to be worked through. The same could also be said of Yin in the Tao: both alchemies portray the feminine with a passive, earthy, and decidedly dark quality. In contrast, Urvashi is a lively feminine figure with a voice and a talent for dancing. It also is worth noting, in contradiction to the typical Western trope of a sun-spirit-patriarch in the sky over the earth- and moon-bound matriarch, Pururavas is associated with the moon. Likewise, the butter "churn" sense of mantha offers a creamy, premium blend for the cultural turn that suggests something of the feminine, a reminder that the ingredients of change do not necessarily require the violent Hegelian sparks of upheaval.

And yet the mantha undeniably connects churn to burn, with all the attending phallic qualities of sticks and friction we have already discussed, though further analysis further attenuates this depiction and the associations with Prometheus. The German drill etymology of (pra)mantha, in spite of its compelling polysemy with birth and boring, requires a stop through Greece in order to complete the Pramantha-Prometheus connection. According to the classical Greek scholar Athanassios Vergados (2012), the Alexandrian philologist Hesychius attributed fire sticks —*pyreia*— to Hermes or Prometheus. Though there is obviously no direct etymology to connect the Greek pyreia to the Vedic (pra)math, there is a case for extending the Greek "to learn" (μαθ-) to "grasp, apprehend" (citing West, 2007, p. 273); this is a connotation noted by Jung that gets lost in the complex constellations of word associations inherited from his predecessors. On the matter of drill vs. stick, the main thread leading to the former seems to be rooted in Kuhn's (1959/2015) interpretation of Hesychius's reference to στορεύς, an option discarded by Morgan (1890) due to the association of the suffix -εύς with a person, although Vergados argues that there is room for this morpheme to denote a thing (presumably a drill vs. a driller). The more complicating factor, it would appear, is that στορεύς would have to encompass not only a drill tool made of laurel but also an "underlying piece" (p. 228) made of buckthorn. This "flat component" would have a non-drill referent in Greek "which would thus correspond to the 'flat' sea, rendered so by the γαληνοποιός"[7] (p. 228). Rather than denoting "drill," then, Vergados concludes that στορεύς "is the product of conflation" (p. 230), which further complicates a purely phallocentric perspective.

---

[7] For readers unfamiliar with Greek characters, γαλ η νοποιός a Google Translate phonetic transcription renders *galinopoiós*.

(Pra)Mantha Phonetics

At the risk of boring further into a boring discussion of all these 'sticks and dicks' variants of (pra)ma(n)th, it bears pointing out the difference an 'n' makes. Johanna Narten (1960) was the first to posit the divergence between math- and manth-, noting that the former has a connotation of "a violent snatching" ["ein gewaltsames Entreißen"] (p. 123), and that the 'snatching' has more of a sense of being whisked away by the wind (p. 127), a correction to the general view tentatively presented by Roth (1855) and uncritically incorporated by his predecessors, that Mätarisvan, the Vedic wind god and alleged forerunner of Prometheus, stole fire from the gods for the benefit of man. She questions this interpretation (p. 133), and, as Kuiper (1971, in Moore, 2015) has noted, he actually stole *for* the gods and for the benefit of man. What a difference a preposition makes! More importantly, regarding the latter, Narten discerns a distinction between the math- focus on "whisking away" (as opposed to the literal "robbing" ascribed to the Promethean connotation) and *mantha*, which points to "the churning [whisking] of milk and butter, the mixing of a potion, etc., cf., or *mantha*, a 'stirring potion'" (Narten, p. 121, citing e.B.).[8] It is also worth noting that Kuhn (1859/2015, p. 15) points out that the Greek μανθανο (ma<u>n</u>than<u>o</u>) means to learn, suggesting that the learning as grasping or apprehending holds up across the variants of ma(n)th.

So, after all this churn and burn and learning, a cursory glance at the notes in the appendix will confirm the mantha sense of butter churning in the dream image that launched this investigation, as well as a decidedly more feminine sense as the sort of churning ascribed to the fire ceremony,[9] and the inclusion of the nasal phone [n] clearly predominates. In fact, the removal of n from pramantha (pramatha) has a tremendous impact on the meaning. In addition to being a masculine noun, it is ascribed to "a class of demons attending on śiva" (Monier-Williams, 1883, p. 238). S. Joshi, of the Western New York Hindu Center affirms that "'Pramathas' are a type of nondivine forces which we call the beings of falsehood that belongs to the subtle physical/vital world, and they impair/ harass any divine work going on in this terrestrial world. They are very low level (not like intelligent asura) beings of falsehood" (S. Joshi, personal communication, June 28, 2021). Not surprisingly, the range of meanings listed

---

[8] Translation from German based on comparison of Computer-assisted translation technologies.

[9] Kuhn (1959/2015) shares detailed descriptions of butter churning (citing Wilson, 1850/1949, I.28.4) and fire churning (citing Stevenson, 1842, p. VII) in India, which confirm a similar technique involving ropes and sticks, the former involving a circular motion and the latter centering on wrenching the string.

in an online Sanskrit dictionary (sanskritdictionary.com) includes tormenting, torturing, raping, slaughter, and other nasty deeds.

While it entails a somewhat incautious extrapolation, I would argue that the mix of sound and visual images in the dream fragment reflects Kugler's (2002) assertion that psyche privileges *phonetic* over semantic patterns, a finding derived from the word association tests made famous by Jung and Freud. Tossing the words around, sounding them out to myself, the connections were clearly there in the common thread of clustering and metathesis (exchange of phonemes) between nasal consonants /m/ and /n/ and the voiceless dental fricative /θ/ (as in the 'th' sound in *th*ought):

Mantha

Pro**meth**eus

Themis

In addition to the phonetic blending, the potential archetypal meanings provide an even more compelling connection that the dream image likely incorporated: Themis and Prometheus, as fundamental, complementary principles of change, emblematic of an energetic, dynamic churning or blending (*mantha*), rather than structured along fixed binaries. Such is the nature of language, and a related premise of linguistics is the blending of synchrony and diachrony. While synchrony, with its colorful dialects and linguistic innovations, centers on the phenomenon of language variation, as it manifests itself in current usage, diachrony takes in the bigger, evolutionary picture of how language evolves over time, in dialogue with changing circumstances on the social plane. The blending of both perspectives in linguistics is known as *panchrony*, which recognizes the blending of both ways of understanding language emergence (Silva-Corvalán, 2001).

A Mantha Roadmap

Having ventured down the rabbit hole of mantha, there is undeniable promise in its alchemy. Without necessarily privileging it over its close associates, the Tao and the coniunctio, mantha is a compelling tool for navigating the cultural turn after Jung. Blending sound and image, masculine and feminine, the One and the Many, smoothing and agitation, its very nature is constituted by an East-West confluence. Moreover, there are compelling connections, however tenuous, that point to deeper knowledge: Prometheus, the Titan who is closely associated with knowledge creation and innovation, and math-as-learning; these are key ingredients for churning change, and they are always grounded in language and culture. While acknowledging the "no-pain, no change" agitation sense of manth, inclusion of the "n" offers the possibility of wholeness in the bored hole of the feminine, philologically and psychoanalytically speaking. The time has come to deepen explorations of the matriarchal feminine, so let us allow Urvashi, and her mythological counterpart, the Greek matriarch Gaia-Themis, to have their say. Taken together, the myriad phonetic and semantic, as well as diachronic and synchronic variations of *ma̱nth-* furnish us with the *prima materia* —in alchemy, the raw material to be worked upon— to fuel this journey into alchemies of psychological and social change, this timeless dialogue between the One and the Many. Marlan (2021), with a bit of word play, describes the philosopher's stone, the ultimate attainment of alchemy, as "chaosmos," a notion that invokes a synergy of the One and the Many (p. 243). Indeed, Jung's "unifying diversity into oneness, chaos into cosmos, and suffering into healing and wholeness" (p. 234) connoted in the *mysterium coniunctionis* is constituted in this ancient Greek metaphysical trope. The trope is likewise constituted in Eastern non-duality, which is at ease holding the diversity of the Many and the unity of the One.[10]

As may already be apparent, the approach I have adopted in this book is rhizomic, primarily rooted in Jung's spiral essay style, which Susan Rowland (2010) characterizes as a hermeneutic winding around text that "go[es] deeper and wider into historical origins and cultural analogies" (p. 32). This approach likewise blends intellect and imagination in ways that find favor with Camille Paglia's (2006) notion of imaginative academic critique and Douglas Sloan's (1983/2008) notion of insight-imagination. Insight-imagination not only informs the serpentine branches that unfold in the writing of the text; its reading constitutes an expansion of the rhizomes off the pages. To this point and invoking Jungian alchemy, Marlan (2021) argues that the act of reading constitutes a sort of alchemical prima materia, in itself, one that makes it possible for "imagination to play a greater role in the formation of our ongoing understanding and perception of the cosmos" (p. 1). Imaginative academic critique necessarily engages subjective speculation, and that subjectivity encompasses both inner and outer experiences. Consequently, we find intersections here with transdisciplinarity. As summarized in Declaration Three of the UNESCO conference on this emergent field, transdisciplinary studies seek "a dynamic exchange between the natural sciences, the social sciences, art and tradition" (Nicolescu, 2008, p. 258), and a central related focus centers on "an equilibrium between knowledge and being" (p. 63). A related notion is that knowledge cannot be arbitrarily excised from the knower.

---

[10] Nicolescu (2008), for example, notes: "The western idea of unity in diversity and diversity through unity is isomorphic to the eastern idea of non-duality. Why set them in opposition to one another?" (p. 37).

Of course, whenever the intellect and the imagination are in dialogue, there is always the danger of going to extreme, the greater risk perhaps being the latter. In this book, I will call attention to tragic consequences of failures of imagination, but flights of imagination are certainly equally perilous. Sloan (1983/2008) warns, for example, that uncritical analogy and association obfuscate otherwise serious scholarly investigation. In his defense of Wolfgang Giegerich's Hegelian discipline of logical negation, Greg Mogenson (2005) illustrates how Hegel's analytic and objective approach sought to correct Kant's synthetic and subjective path to truth: sometimes we take things into the subject that *may not be of it*. In my estimation, this is a risk worth taking.

In both my professional and personal life, this blended perspective on personal and cultural change has only recently come into full view, but it is at best a panchronous snapshot of an emergent process of being, knowing and growing: call it an *-ing* thing. *Being* human, we confront this opaque, deceptive presence of the Other, a phenomenon that Jungian psychology locates within the infinite Self and projected out into the milieu. As such, our connection to the Other may indeed be mirror-like, or as the phenomenologist of the Other, Emmanuel Levinas (in Peperzak, 1993) posits, perhaps we find ourselves overwhelmed by and subordinated to this overwhelming complexity and totality and infinity of the Other. The nature of our ego's relation to the Other may be, as Levinas suggests, an affinity to this alterity, or, as Teilhard de Chardin (1959/2008) asserts, the tether of Self-Other is tight and fluid as he alleged a continuity in all living things between the within and the without. In articulating his approach to transdisciplinary studies, Nicolescu (1994) likewise affirms: "Outside- great particle accelerators; within – the great accelerator of consciousness. 'Outside' and 'within' are merely two facets of one and the same reality" (p. 20).

The religious studies scholar Raimon Panikkar (1995), working from an ecosophical perspective, suggests that these syzygies of Self to Other, micro to macro, inner to outer, and other manifestations of what the ancient Greeks framed as the One and the Many[11] (a concept that will consume quite a few pages of this book to fully engage) are bound for a "radical metanoia" (p. 4), a profound transformation that highlights basic principles of relation: *sarvan-sarvātmakaṁ*: "all is in relation to all" (p. 15). Alluding to the Upanishads, he asserts: "A mutual relationship prevails between each and every person, considered as a microcosm, and the totality of the universe as macrocosm" (p. 58). One side of the scale is not necessarily privileged over the other. For

---

[11] Echoing Teilhard de Chardin, Panikkar (1995) posits a sutra that rejects "the dichotomy between the outward and the inward" (p. 17).

example, the Many also manifests itself in the Machine, a scale that dwarfs a more microcosmic valuation of the individual (Man, or for our purposes, the One). In fact, the dwarfing of Man under Machine consciousness is one of the cornerstones of Panikkar's criticism of technocracy. Throughout this book, we will uncover a range of manifestations of the Many, from its "feel good" aspects to the Many of mass media, mobs, and all matter of mass hysteria.

Regardless of where we stand on this matter, the fact remains that the engine of Western 'progress,' fueled by binary divisions, rests upon the desecration of this Other. From the subjugation of the feminine and the natural world to conquest and colonization, the Other, elusive as it may be in terms of pinpointing and defining, has played a primary role in the subtext of the Western metanarrative. We will examine the many faces of the Other, from its origins in the Greco-Roman monstrous to Rowland's feminist and post-Lacanian critique of the Other. To play upon the sign over the door of Jung's consulting room in Kusnacht: "Bidden or unbidden, the Other is always present."[12]

Over the past decade, I have begun to explore C. G. Jung's legacy in the context of sociocultural change, mainly in educational and organizational settings. As the reader will pick up, this is not easy terrain to navigate, particularly for me, given that the primary focus of my research and teaching has centered on ideas rooted in the Russian social psychologist, Lev Vygotsky, as well as grounded in the findings of social psychology and applied linguistics. Furthermore, my scholarship, to date, has more or less stayed within the conventional conceptions of research methodology: both quantitative and qualitative. Mainstream academia has left depth psychology behind, save for literary criticism, and even in psychoanalytic studies, C. G. Jung's thought lags far behind that of Sigmund Freud and Jacques Lacan. Modern higher education has primarily been driven by practical questions of *what* and *how*. Fundamental human questions of the elusive *Why?* are increasingly commonly relegated to Schools of Arts and Humanities, which have come under threat lately within the trend toward technical and vocational conceptions in academe.

The fundamental challenge posed in this work centers on putting the *why* together with the *what* and *how* of personal and cultural change. The more I have studied educational and organizational reform, the more my traditional rootedness in the dominant empiricist epistemologies of change has been offset by unexpected results that beg questions of why. In fact, where we look at questions of what or how, the data often point a trickster finger back at us: "Why?" Lines scramble into circles and spirals, small interventions produce

---

[12] Jung found this saying in Erasmus's *Adagia*: "Vocatus atque non vocatus deus aderit" (Bidden or not bidden, God is present).

huge changes, and in the case of teacher development, a tremendous amount of pre-professional development falls apart the instant teaching candidates sign a contract for their first teaching job. In the face of pressures to conform, I have seen many promising reflective practitioners cave into the more custodial concerns of school administrations.

Why is transformative change so elusive? There is a common cliché in educational research and methodology: "It's a mile wide and an inch thick." Shallow questions of how change occurs result in shallow constructs that paint impossibly reductive, linear, and usually confirmed ('data-driven') models that tell us extraordinarily little of the richness underneath the number crunches. In both qualitative and more complex statistical modeling, the data has been revealed to be in a dance; this dance of *emergence* seems to suggest deeper and more dynamic connectedness between the variables. Without getting too far ahead of ourselves, these dancers around the system, be it culture or cognition (or both), have been given such exotic names as 'strange attractors,' 'repellors,' and 'connected growers' that promote development and potential for growth and 'basins of attraction' draw us back to the status quo. Such terms, which recall the archetypes, suggest an imaginal richness normally shunned in the mainstream, and they point to an epistemological fullness that cries out for the depth of Jung's psychology.

At first glance, Jung's legacy presents promising and compelling answers to questions of why, and contrary to popular conceptions, they may hold the balance between the realms of fact and meaning. It is not accurate to write off Jung's interest in alchemy and religious traditions as originating from an uncritical perspective. A return to Jung, however, does present a number of complications. Jung was notoriously ambivalent about his legacy, and we will see this revealed in his fundamental distrust of all things *collective* that often led him to talk to himself rather than to submit his thought to communities of inquiry, save for the Eranos Conference and his admirable interviews with thinkers representing a variety of cultures and traditions worldwide, from yoga gurus to tribal elders. At the end of the day, Jung was an introvert who held the greater social milieu with a raised eyebrow, if not with utter contempt. The resulting binary between mind and milieu is currently being worked through in what I would call a cultural turn in Jungian studies, as evidenced in the rise of scholarship centered on cultural complexes and trauma. To stay with the Jung Classic brand will not do; it does not measure up to the emergentist move in natural and social sciences. Consequently, I will introduce the spirit of Jung to perspectives that are less hostile to socially situated approaches to cognition.

So, how do we re-vision Jung as blending the binary? According to Rowland (2002), in spite of the fact that Jung's thought emerged to compensate for binary thinking, a product of the Enlightenment's pervasive influence on Western civilization, he himself was bound to it. Rafael López-Pedraza (1990; 2000a), in analyzing Jung's particular variety of cultural anxiety, affirmed that Jung failed to hold the tension between his Swiss brand of Protestantism, and the pagan-polytheistic side of his psyche. Calling ours the Age of Titanism, López-Pedraza suggested that we are all tethered to this sort of polarized thinking, which is rooted in monotheism and taken to the extremes, thanks to this all-or-nothing vortex of excess and vacuity rooted in the Titanic. Nevertheless, a mantha of Titanism opens unforeseen gateways, holes in the whole, and we would not be honoring Jung's legacy without going into the areas of greatest resistance.

In light of the current dominant position of Marxist-materialist and postmodern critique, it may be rightly argued that Jung and his legacy no longer have a place in scholarly discourse (Jensen, 2004). To the contrary, Paglia (2006) insists that Jung still has academic credentials, arguing that "his archetypes constitute the universal tropes and basic structures of epic, drama, folklore, and fairy tale" (p. 7). Furthermore, she is critical of feminist critique in the Freudian line.[13] Whether we base our inquiry on concrete, material facts or rational deductions, I am open to both interpretations, and furthermore, my hope is that by the last page of this book I will have convinced the reader that the stances are not contradictory at all. As a scholar of Soviet social psychologist Lev Vygotsky, I could look back on my own development as carried along an empirically grounded dialogic of semiotic tools that have steered my socialization. Or, in a Jungian and Levinian sense, I could ascribe some sublime alterity beyond my ego that guides this mental handiwork. Strictly following the prevailing zeitgeist in Jungian and archetypal psychology, I would honor the image and not corrode it with such things as notions and concepts. Following Vygotsky and mainstream educational research, I would not hesitate a bit to submit the image to the full measure of logical reduction and reduce that image to a trope. Neither extreme will do. The archetypal material of psychological and cultural change rises to something more than clichés, but I make no pretense that it rises to the rigor of scientific inquiry in the strictest sense. By the time I finished drafting this book, it was clear to me that such pristine adherence to one extreme or another is exactly what was being worked out in its production. Imagination and logic, as with a billion other binaries that pervade the Western psychological and cultural project, are ripe for blending.

In invoking the *coniunctio*, it is important to point out that the scholarly ground on which the *mysterium* was advanced has shifted. For example, the feminine has rightly claimed its authorship principle of mediation from the winged-foot male Olympian, and the feminine, itself, has been wrested from

---

[13] "British and American academic feminists took up French Freud via the pretentiously convoluted Lacan instead" (Paglia, 2006, p. 7).

literal, biological reductions as the 'Male-Other' (Rowland, 2002). In agreement with Marlan (2005), the position adopted here is that the *mysterium* renders not empirically factual, static product; rather the emphasis is on dynamic, emergent process. In other words, the blending of opposites never renders a fixed product; it is always spinning, or in the Sanskrit sense of *mantha* as churning. In fact, because the Sanskrit *mantha* alchemy is free of the binary baggage associated with the *coniunctio*, it opens new hermeneutical spaces for this cultural turn after Jung. As with any growth, there must be sacrifice and pain;[14] accordingly, it is important to point out that both the *coniunctio* and the various morphological variations of *ma(n)th-* suggest a high price for transformative personal and cultural change: churn, burn, split, death, slaughter, whisking away… a metaphorical maze that reminds us that change is hard. Very hard. That said, as pointed out in the preface as regards the variations of ma(n)th (inclinations of math- toward the masculine and mantha toward the feminine), it does not have to be violent.

The tension of opposites inherent in the coniunctio and relevant to our sense of mantha necessarily leads to border crossings, collisions with the other sides of poles, a phenomenon Jung (1990/1921, p. 426) referred to as enantiodromia. Enantiodromia, the eruption into consciousness of one side's other, resonates with the pramantha, churning out a spark where the soul needs a "wake-up call." Enantiodromia is engaged whenever we step out of known ways of interpreting and negotiating meaning and into others. Anyone who has dedicated a significant amount of time and effort in adapting to another language and its cultures will attest to an onslaught of binaries: individualistic and collectivistic, conquerors and colonized, to name but a few. What is this fundamental binary that pervades Western psychology and sociology? The human species seems prone to go to extremes. As conveyed in the cauldron's Tao image and the *mantha*, this binary may not be driven by some tangible, stable structure, but rather an energetic, emergent process. Borrowing from the New Physics, let us call it that particle AND (as opposed to 'or') wave phenomenon. What if there really is no binary? What if alleged opposites, rather than constituted as fundamental, are instead seen as a *prima materia* in need of cultivation? As Jung asserted: "everything rests on an inner polarity; for everything is a phenomenon of energy. Energy necessarily depends on a pre-existing polarity, without which there could be no energy" (1966, pp. 74-75). There is a lot of generative energy in this *coniunctio*, and quite possibly, therein lies a way out of the decay and destruction that are the byproducts of a West lost to extremes.

---

[14] "There is no coming to consciousness without pain" (Jung, Baynes, & Baynes 1928/2006, p. 193).

In Promethean (or *Pramathian*?) defiance of warnings in analytical and archetypal psychology to the contrary, we dare to go through the door to the East opened by Gier and (pra)mantha this tension of belonging and branching off in Western narratives. By dint of enantiodromia, anywhere a polarity emerges, there is the perfect place for a mantha. Starting with the premise that there is still value in Jung's project, this work takes aim at the one-sided anti-Titanic, anti-collective threads in (post-) Jungian thought and supports emergent studies of cultural complexes and trauma. Those *ancestral elements* that Jung uncovered in his dream cellar[15] are still very much present and we need to follow those presences—the living archetypes—with fresh insight and imagination and open to the possibility that archetypes are not static structures but rather energies that emerge along the rhizome of psyche and culture.

An interdisciplinary hermeneutic is helpful as a de-centering tool, opening up a blending Other to rock the West's essentialist "Self-Same" binary off its axis. Likewise, we seek to expand and de-center Jungian and archetypal conceptions of psychological and cultural change, submitting them to the mantha. Whether it serves as a linguistic and cultural benchmark, given that this manth- morpheme and its variants are evidence that the Promethean engine of the West was, albeit errantly, fueled by Eastern meanings.

So, this *mantha* (churn) or blending of the Western binary follows a structure that reflects Teilhard de Chardin's (1959/2008) rhizome metaphor for evolution. Accordingly, having established the alchemical connections between East and West, the book is structured to subsequently reflect further on the cultural turn after Jung. Focusing on cultural complexes and traumas, we will broadly outline related symptoms in contemporary Western contexts because it makes sense, however imperfect, to 'do the work' prior to writing off any attempts to deepen our inquiry.

The following chapters then closely examine Western roots in Greco-Roman mythology, with a focus on the emergence of the first binaries, including Olympians vs. Titans, patriarchs vs. matriarchs, and heroes vs. monsters. A closer examination of Titans and monsters will reveal early cracks in Western binaries that continue to radiate through the rise of Western civilization after Greece and Rome.

From there, we will branch out into current epistemologies of psychological development, pedagogy, and ways to better navigate the increasing speed with which technology and innovation transform personally and culturally, sometimes blurring lines between creativity and innovation. Greco-Roman

---

[15] We will explore this material further on, in more depth; the term has origins in a 1925 lecture (Jung, 1925/1989, p. 36) and is based on a dream involving a cellar.

concepts like the One and the Many, Titanism, Mythos and Logos will likewise be paired with more modern academic concepts and constructs from a diversity of disciplines.

Finally, a Pratimantha (afterword of sorts) will broadly reflect on the major concepts we have subjected to the mantha. Accordingly, new directions will emerge, including a possible place at the table for depth psychology in the discourse on transdisciplinarity.

With the cultural turn after Jung in mind, this is a book about change in blended perspective. As you "churn" the pages, submitting your own experiences of personal and social change to the *mantha*, I have no doubt that new and unanticipated possibilities and directions for this discourse will emerge.

Chapter 1

Reflecting on the cultural turn after Jung

Building on the ancient Greek metaphysical paradox of the One and the Many, this is a book about change contextualized in the timeless tension between self and society, Descartes' famous *cogito*[1] ("I think...") and the cultural milieu ("*We* think..."). As this chapter is primarily concerned with culture, it makes sense to start with some preliminary explorations of the same. "Culture," defined for this cultural turn in depth psychology, conveys a sort of convergence, or as Teilhard de Chardin sees it, a radial orbit around a system; conversely, "Psychological," in analytical psychological framework of individuation, centers on a divergent "breaking away from the pack."

If individual psychological change is difficult, it is understood that cultural change, at least beyond fads and such, is even more daunting. Entire fields of study, organizational theory and diffusion of innovations, and research on teacher development, for example, have all arisen, in part, due to the persistent challenges of cultural change. Educational reform, for example, has been likened to moving a cemetery. Mindless change, however, is on warp speed, fueled by mass consumerism and social media. Jung rightly warned us about this almost a century ago.[2] Regardless of the Promethean virtues of its champions, change, as a virtue unto itself, has little to offer without the sanction of the collective, which Jung aptly characterized as unconscious. Of course, 'change is inevitable,' but in the interest of blending the binary, the West must confront its binary between cogito and culture. The "I am" and the "We are" are intricately connected and compensatory; they also subordinate to this larger tension of the One and the Many. Panikkar (1995), well-versed in both Greek and Indian philosophy, offers a description that, although it does not reference the One and the Many directly, is extremely well-suited to the core of this ancient paradox:

> A system is a multiplicity, somehow one, separate, self-sustaining (up to a point) in a way that at least unconsciously suggests this center of consciousness, this paramount unity, the "I" that I can utter and that in the welter of other experiences impinging on me at any given time

---

[1] *Cogito ergo sum*: I think, therefore I am.

[2] "We rush impetuously into novelty, driven by a mounting sense of insufficiency, dissatisfaction, and restlessness" (Jung, 2002, p. 141).

(synchronically) or over a period of time (diachronically) provides me with an experience and concept of oneness, and more specifically of oneness despite diversity. (p. 338)

Having defined and explored the core heuristics that guide the alchemies of this work (Mantha, Coniunctio, Tao, the One and the Many), and with a view to navigating the cultural turn, we will remind ourselves from time to time that extremes in one direction –toward the One or toward the Many— will not do. The *mantha* calls us to a conscious *cogitamus*. It is my hope that this chapter and those that follow will open up a critical re-examination of the Western metanarrative that withdraws cultural shadows and opens the possibility of global perspectives by sketching a bold individual and collective *Opus Contra Prima Cultura.* Jung's greatest adventure centered exactly on this transcendence of his Western European roots; it is up to us to learn from his failures and continue the work.

An overview of Jungian and post-Jungian conceptions of culture

Centered on these pernicious binaries in the Western metanarrative, we confront some related unresolved tensions in analytical psychology between individuation and the collective that are central to a cultural turn in depth psychology. While James Hillman's archetypal psychology is often credited with leading Jung's ideas out of the consulting room and into the culture,[3] the origins of a cultural turn after Jung lead further back to Jung's protégé, Erich Neumann (1994), who sought to develop a "depth psychology of culture and of a cultural therapy" (p. xi), and it is impossible to underestimate the value of López-Pedraza's extensive writings on cultural anxiety, which constitute a somewhat overlooked and essential component in shaping this cultural turn after Jung. We will add to this mix of the Western One and the Many the Vedic resonances of manth-, and submit Western binaries, fueled by a toxic alchemy of Titanism, Monotheism, and Patriarchy, to a long-overdue blend. This mantha manifests itself both in content and manner: the medium is the message. As we have already established, Jungian thought arguably is both founded on and at least partially informed by this mantha trope; it also registered some formidable failures in living up to its own ideals of alchemical churning, both on the personal and cultural planes. In the interest of informing a cultural turn, this

---

[3] As Hillman's (1975) archetypal psychology took Jung's work out of the consulting room and into the culture, this intensive focus on the individual and individuation was recalibrated into the cultural realm. As Hillman puts it, "Integration of the shadow is an emigration" (p. 225).

chapter will focus on both. The research on cultural complexes and cultural traumas is central in such explorations.

In addition to Neumann and López-Pedraza, the cultural turn owes much to the ideas of Jungian analyst Joseph Henderson. Likewise, Thomas Singer and Sam Kimbles (2010) may be credited with properly introducing a culturally engaged application of Jungian psychology, focusing on the notion of cultural complexes. The following excerpt from their introduction to a collection of essays on the topic offers some food for thought on the cultural turn, where it is now, and where it may be headed:

> One can think of the loose collection of separate theories that have grown up to become known as "analytical psychology" as being a bit ramshackle like an old New England farmhouse. Many additions to the original structure have been made over time as different needs emerged. Our theory of cultural complexes is just such a new addition and we like to think of it as being built in the style of a farmhouse addition – we hope as a "great room," although some may see it as a "mud room." Whatever scale and value is given to it, it is clear that we need a new room (p. 2).

As metaphors go, I am not convinced that a 'great room' addition to a New England farmhouse is a suitable place to start in these matters of connecting Jung to the cultural realm. In fact, in light of the perception of analytical psychology as elitist and cultish,[4] lacking diversity and inclusion,[5] the parlor imagery seems like exactly the wrong place. If we are to settle for a mudroom, arguably a no less gentrified architectural motif, then so be it; let us don our Wellies and venture outward into the muddy milieu of cultural complexes and

---

[4] Richard Noll's controversial *The Jung cult: Origins of a charismatic movement* (1994) has not gone unchallenged. Sonu Shamdasani, in *Cult fictions* (1998), casts doubt on Noll's documentary evidence. The fact is, there is a general tendency to privilege consulting room over scholarly knowledge and to set up an ecumenical hierarchy whereby members of Jungian societies, including trained mental health professionals, are considered "laity" under those who have trained in a select few training centers specializing in analytical psychology. It is not the author's intention to weigh in; rather, I am merely pointing out some potential justifications for shifting the rhetoric of Jungian scholarship in light of these fairly well-established public and academic perceptions of Jung and his legacy.

[5] Brewster (2017), herself a trained Jungian analyst, outlines the corresponding problem in Jungian circles: while the number of African Americans entering psychotherapy has generally been on the rise, the number of African Americans pursuing Jungian analysis remains "exceedingly small" (p. 9): "The stigma of being considered strange, different, primitive, or Other—the language of Jungian psychology, infused with the possibility of racism—greatly decreases psychological options for African Americans in the area of Jungian psychology" (p. 8).

traumas. Let us also do so fully aware of matters of power, privilege, and the very real need to revise Jung, and the Western psyche from the outside-in.

It would be wrong to write off the life and work of Jung as anathema to a cultural turn in depth psychology, and arguably, it is indicative of the monotheistic good vs. evil binary that drives Western cultural complexes that we must sort influential thinkers arbitrarily into demons or angels. Though he arguably muddied his Wellies in his attempts, no other thinker at his time was so adventurous in venturing past the post-Enlightenment eurocentrism of the era. He traveled all over the world to explore alleged universals in the human psyche (Orient, North America, Africa). Nonetheless, he failed to transcend Western 'primitivistic' projections in his writings (Morgan, 2010; Rowland, 2002), and in the case of American identity, African and indigenous influences were characterized as "racial infection" (p. 112, citing CW10, Para. 966).

Africans and African Americans endure the most of these racial projections. Fanny Brewster (2017) reminds us that an Africanized primitive trope infused Jung's conceptions of the Shadow and that it was continued by his followers[6] and of a dream he recounts in *Memories, Dreams, and Reflections* while in Africa, which involved an African American barber who had cut his hair years earlier during a visit to the US and the threat of his hair being kinked (p. 108, citing MDR, 1961/1993, p. 272). Brewster also outlines the hypocrisies that accompanied this Africanized cultural shadow, beginning with Jung's indignance at accusations of his "admiration" of Hitler:

> The mockery of it! My whole life work is based on the psychology of the individual, and his responsibility both to himself and his milieu. Mass movements swallow individuals wholesale, and an individual who thus loses his identity has lost his soul. (p. 100, citing Hull & McGuire, 1977, p. 195).

This preoccupation with individual identity apparently did not include those of African ancestry. Brewster recounts Jung's 1912 dream study of fifteen African American patients at St. Elizabeth's Hospital in Baltimore, highlighting the utter lack of interest in either the individual stories and associations of his interviewees or the significant and brutal cultural consciousness of slave-descendants. Ironically, Jung's intent in this study was to transcend the race biases of the time by demonstrating that his notions of archetypes in the collective unconscious transcended racial factors. The revelation of an image of a burning wheel was sufficient for Jung to establish a connection to a Greek mythological figure, Ixion, who is punished by being bound to a wheel and

---

[6] "The initial Jungian understanding of shadow was that it was negative, dark, and primitive and belonged to that of the primitive" (Brewster, 2017, p. 5).

spun down to Tartarus. Concluding that this was a story with which the interviewees would not have been familiar, he determined this to be sufficient evidence that the archetypes of the collective unconscious are universal. Brewster, however, underscores several flaws in his research: 1) ignoring personal meanings directly contradicted his own approach to analytical psychology; 2) ignoring the potential for a "cultural consciousness" driving the imagery of burning (KKK cross burnings) and the wheel's long history of associations with torture, leading up to and including slavery, and 3) potential archetypal connections between the interviewed African American dreamers and the themes of betrayal and kinship inherent in the story.

In addition to his primitivistic portrayals of colonized cultures, Jung's propensity for antisemitism[7] presents a concern we should address in this cultural turn. Welcomed into an almost exclusively Jewish cadre of psychoanalysts led by Freud, Jerome Bernstein (2014, citing Maidenbaum, 2013) recounts how Jung assumed the presidency of the German General Medical Society of Psychotherapy and swapped out the term 'German' with 'International' in the organization's title in order to circumvent the discriminatory practices of German chapters; he also welcomed many members of the Jewish faith into his analytical psychology society, including his protégé Erich Neumann. Paglia (2006) relates how Neumann was denied an internship in psychoanalysis in 1933 due to antisemitic laws, how he was taken in by Jung, and how he "eventually became Jung's anointed heir," though she acknowledges that their relationship was undermined due to "Jung's sporadic antisemitism" (p. 3). To the question of Jung's antisemitism, Rowland (2002) highlights references to a 'Jewish' psychology in the journal *Zentralblatt für Psychotherapie*, speculating that he was motivated by a desire to promote his brand of psychoanalysis at Freud's expense and that the trauma of fallout with Freud may have been a contributing factor. According to Rowland, Jung was eventually denounced by the Nazis, and it has been revealed that Jung was recruited as agent 488 by US military intelligence (Dickey, 2018, Oct. 22).

At least in Jungian circles, it is generally accepted that the Jung-Freud debate is a fundamental cultural complex in depth psychology yet to be fully addressed. Thomas Kirsch (2010) offers us a glimpse into the potential cultural

---

[7] A special thanks to Elia Jordan for the following clarification regarding the omission of the hyphenated variant of this term (E. Jordan, May 11, 2022 e-mail communication) offered by The International Holocaust Remembrance Alliance (https://www.holocaust remembrance.com/antisemitism/spelling-antisemitism), which states: "The IHRA's concern is that the hyphenated spelling allows for the possibility of something called 'Semitism,' which not only legitimizes a form of pseudo-scientific racial classification that was thoroughly discredited."

complex following the demise of this iconic collaboration in the origins of psychoanalysis. As a student of psychiatry, Kirsch, the son of Jewish analysts who studied under Jung, recounts being repeatedly admonished that his Jungian connection would undermine his career. According to Kirsch modern Jungians, themselves possessed by the opposite pole of this cultural complex, have learned to relish their marginalization with a "defensive superiority" (p. 191), though he asserts that "there no longer is the same stigma if one crosses the party line and sees an analyst from the other camp" (p. 191). Perhaps this détente can be explained by the fact that both branches of depth psychology have decreased in esteem within the field of psychology, as the author himself admits.

Jung passed down two important essays on cultural complexes that serve as bookends on the rise and fall of National Socialism in Germany. Rowland (2002) and López-Pedraza (1990; 2000a) characterize "Wotan," an essay Jung published in 1936 on the possession of the German psyche by an ancient storm god (Wotan), and "After the Catastrophe,"[8] an elaboration on that cultural complex shortly following the end of WWII, as impersonal, academic pieces devoid of clear denouncement or contrition. Regarding "Catastrophe," López-Pedraza highlights this piece as revelation of Jung working through his cultural anxiety: "He did not place the guilt with the Germans in a manipulative or guilt-making way; he placed it with all the honest anger and rage he was able to express in writing, and he moves us to accept our own anger and rage as a natural resource to psychopathic behavior" (1990, pp. 46-47).

A full exploration of Western cultural complexes ultimately must grapple with the complexity of Jung. To this point, Marlan (2021) comments:

> The complexity of our times demands that we transcend the simple one-sided judgments and enter into a broader vision, as well as entertain many ways of imagining. From critics and debunkers Stern and Noll to classical analysts Edinger and von Franz, Jung has been as devil and saint, Eurocentric racist and compassionate wise man. The sheer range of evaluation testifies to the sense that Jung carries a multiplicity of mythical projections and perhaps for this reason is an exemplary modern man, a man at the crossroads of cultural transformation. He deserves to be seen with no fewer sensibilities than those he gave to us with which to see. (p. 135)

Whether or not Jung ultimately advanced knowledge in his explorations beyond his White, Protestant, European male privilege, the fact that one who

---

[8] Both essays appear in Jung (1946/1970).

intrepidly ventured both inward and outward arguably failed to integrate such journeys should serve as sobering evidence of the extent to which we all may be entrenched in our own cultural complexes. It is likely important to point out that the incendiary nature of cultural complexes is not limited to the West. Nicolescu (2008), for example, argues that globalization presents the greater threat:

> Globalization is today a potential source of a new decline. The two extreme dangers of Globalization are, on one hand, cultural and spiritual homogenization and, on the other hand, the paroxysm of ethical and religious conflicts – as a self-defense reaction of different cultures and civilizations. (Nicolescu, 2008, p. 2)

Accordingly, there may be something much deeper and broader that needs to be worked through in this cultural turn.

Cultural complexes (Kimbles & Singer) and Cultural trauma (Gudaitė and Stein)

In framing the origins of the Cultural Complex, Singer (2010b) relates Jane Harrison's (1912/1974) investigations into the origins of Greek religion and the discovery of a stone relief depicting the Hymn of the Kouretes on Crete. In this scene, Rhea has entrusted her baby Zeus to a band of warrior *Kouretes*, who perform a protective circle dance around the child (*Kouros*), protecting him from being devoured by Kronos, his father. For Singer, these *Kouretes*, or *Daimones*, are the focal point for cultural complexes, and he offers the example of the struggle of Elian Gonzales' Florida relatives to protect the child from Fidel Castro to illustrate the Kourete-Daimones' choreography. In distinguishing the healthy vs. destructive aspects of these archetypal Daimons, Singer comments: "the *Daimones* can serve both a vital self-protective function and can raise havoc with the fury of their attacks directed inwardly in self-torture and outwardly in impenetrability, hostility and ruthlessness" (p. 17).

According to Singer (2010a), the cultural complex does not denote a healthy sense of cultural identity but rather a noxious, autonomous, and self-fulfilling possession characterized by a resurgence of archetypal Daimon-Protectors, the "original perpetrators of the trauma" (p. 7). Cultural complexes are "repetitive, autonomous, resist consciousness, and collect experience that confirms their historical point of view…" (p. 6), and he points out that "offending groups" (p. 7) are just as likely as the groups they oppress to be possessed by them. The activation of a cultural complex allegedly induces a psychic implosion, triggering in the ego what Singer (2010a) describes as an "auto-immune system…gone haywire" (p. 18), resulting in an inability to individuate or challenge assumptions. In addition, a sense of authentic self is allegedly reduced to "vulnerable, wounded child" (p. 18) under the "alternately protective and torturing" shield of the Daimon, leaving behind a false self that allegedly struggles just to get by, one that demands "love, respect, sexual pleasure, freedom and happiness" (p. 19).

Cultural Trauma, (Gudait & Stein, Eds., 2014), a volume of writings published a decade after the Singer and Kimbles' *Cultural Complex* collection and informed by Donald Kalsched's (1996) psychoanalytics of trauma, suggests a deeper level of engagement with the West's own cultural complexes, focusing on the lingering wounds of monotheism, authoritarian regimes, conquest, and colonization. Inviting us to consider the following quotes, Kristina Schellinski (2014) posits that religious monotheism contributed to skewed interpretations of the Old Testament that ensured a path toward intergenerational cultural trauma:

> Jeremiah 31:29- "The fathers have eaten a sour grape, and the children's teeth are set on edge."

> Exodus 20:5- "For I, the Lord your God, am a jealous God, punishing children for the iniquity of parents, to the third and fourth generation."

Within this context of Abrahamic monotheism, we might also consider what gets lost in intergenerational transmission:

> Leviticus 19:33- "When a foreigner resides among you in your land, do not mistreat them."

> Leviticus 19:34- "The foreigner residing among you must be treated as your native-born. Love them as yourself, for you were foreigners in Egypt."

Notwithstanding the obvious fact that polytheistic cultures have logged similar transgressions, as evident in Myanmar or in India today, or among the Pre-Columbian empires of Latin America, or for that matter, the heralded Greco-Roman foundations that infuse Jungian and archetypal psychology, the apparent incapacity to honor the other (foreigner) documented in countless wars and genocides, evokes the inadequacy of what Hillman (1975) pejoratively referred to as the "monocular lens" (p. 179) of monotheism. Likewise, the passages resonate with a cultural amplification of Jung´s iconic notion of shadow work as receiving the 'guest at the door.'[9] Reflecting on the religious

---

[9] Jung (1975) imagined the invitation to integrate the cultural shadow with anticipation, as an "awe inspiring guest who knocks at the door portentously" (p. 590). For Giegerich (2008), shadow work begins with the collective, cultural level. In such shadow

origins of Western cultural trauma, John Hill (2014) calls out "a religious attitude that is encased in literal and rigid traditions that uphold the norms and values of a bourgeois, outward-oriented culture" (p. 34), taking Western patriarchy to task for its alleged lack of feminine, authentic spiritual values and creativity.

Many of the writings in this volume focus on the trauma of state authoritarianism. As Nicolescu (1994) reminds us, totalitarianism is fueled by binary logic, with its "implicit hypothesis of absolute truth and absolute falsity," driving killings "in the name of ideas" (p. 84). As we will explore further in the next chapter, the patriarchal roots of such binaries precede monotheism, stretching way back to the West's Greco-Roman heritage, as immortalized in the infanticidal patriarchal Gods and their patricidal offspring, a vicious circle fueled by what Neumann (1994) calls the "paternal uroboros" (p. 15). Neumann also ascribed authoritarianism to the patriarchal tendency toward false dichotomies of a higher masculine lording over an inferior, earthly feminine:

> This horizon, [which] reduces and is itself reduced to the level of the mass; what is 'above' is in this case not only dictators and dictatorial states, but also the press, radio, films, advertising, etc., irrespective of the source from which the media are directed. (p. 186).

As suggested in the Old Testament and Greco-Roman references, cultural trauma appears to be a 'family matter' of sorts, and its effects are carried forward through the family line. According to Schellinski (2014), the reality of transgenerational trauma has been upheld in both Freudian and Jungian psychoanalytic traditions and passage through up to the third generation can be empirically, genetically verified, as with the case of families of holocaust survivors.

She admonishes the Jungian community for not fully grappling with the transgenerational transmission of traumas originating in Nazism, traumas that damage the descendants of the aggressors and victims alike. Intergenerational protection (parents shielding children from the dark truth or vice-versa), coupled with defense systems, which include identification with either the perpetrator or the victim, ensure the unconscious transmission of cultural trauma, inducing psychic paralysis: "Above all, cultural trauma becomes entrenched when its victims are unable to move from one cultural standard to another; inversely, cultural trauma can be healed when a successful transition has been accomplished" (p. 32). Based on clinical experience, Hill holds out hope "that the psychic wounds of inherited trauma can be healed, at least in

---

projections, he discerns a cultural other in "the uncanny guest's first knock at the door...The enemy shows up at the border of one's country" (p. 89).

part, by remembering what is 'dis-membered'" (p. 32), which evokes the iconic scene of Dionysus's dismemberment at the hands of the Titans, a trauma that is passed on to Pentheus.

In matters of the sort of cultural trauma inflicted under totalitarian regimes, Eleonore Lehr-Rottmann's (2014) account of the State's usurpation of parental roles under the Nazi regime and Kalinenko and Slutskaya's portrayal of Stalinist Russia (2014) share some intriguing similarities in terms of the effects of authoritarianism on the family, starting with the substitution and degradation of family heads by State and its satellites in the Fatherland (Lehr-Rottman, 2014) or in Mother Russia (Kalinenko & Slutskaya, 2014). In both contexts, we find fathers who are debilitated, lost to addiction, or turned in to the state, and angry, dark mothers who loyally serve up their children for the State Head. Generally speaking, there is a sense of constant siege and suffocation of the individual. Healing of such psychic wounds, according to Lehr-Rottman, necessitates a bold *contra naturam* move, a "betrayal of the unspoken dictates of the collective to not reveal its secrets or to make them conscious" (p. 73). Indeed, it is precisely this notion of working against one's cultural and psychological wiring that will be tested in a mantha of the One and the Many.

Alterations of the family dynamic also emerge in psychoanalytic studies of Latin American totalitarianism. Beas and Sánchez (2012), for example, describe a Chilean isolation complex rooted in constant threat of Pinochet's secret police. In this context, mothers guarded the family unit from outside intrusion, resulting in an increase in maternal authority at the expense of paternal authority. On a national level, the authors allege that this tendency to protect the family from outside intrusion has led to xenophobia and an overall decline of socialization beyond the family unit. Another well-worn archetype, that of the charismatic, macho *caudillo*, with its roots in Spanish machismo and chivalry, certainly constellates around Totalitarian complexes and traumas. From Peronism to the Argentine Dirty War, from Castro to Pinochet,[10] we find strongman-autocrat updates of Zeus and El Cid. Arguably, by the end of this book, we will have traced a patriarchal aspect that pervades the Western cultural complexes and traumas.

In addition to his case analysis of the Wotan cult surrounding Hitler's rise, Jung's own contributions to what we might call an authoritarian complex were likely also influenced by his equation of Marxism and Soviet Russia with the threat of the Collective, which features a touch of Mother Russia misogyny.

---

[10] These dictators are not randomly selected. Modern history has demonstrated unequivocally that this caudillo-strongman archetype runs deeper than clashes between Cold War iterations of Neoliberalism vs. Neomarxism.

Among the various products of his stone craft that adorn Bollingen, Jung's iconic retreat, there is a depiction of a bear rolling a ball, upon which Jung inscribed in Latin, "The She-bear moves the mass." In her interactions with Jorst Horni, Bollingen's curator, Pam Cooper-White (2015) informs us that Jung had two explanations for his depiction. The first was that this represented Ursa Major ("The Big Dipper"), who was thought by the ancients to maintain the steady roll the world through the Heavens. The second sense of the bear centered on the Russian sense of She-Bear who rolls out Marxist manipulation into the world.

Cultural complexes and trauma on the border

Velimir and Marijana Popovic (Popovic & Popovic, 2014) deconstruct the Serbian psyche around the term historically used to describe their land of origin, the outer borderlands of the Roman Empire, the *limes*, applying this liminal space in the psyche to the collective heritage and discourse of Serbian analysands. Limes, according to the authors, denotes a defensive wall, a point of entrance or egress, a boundary or limit, and finally, the elimination or discarding of a thing or person. The authors describe how, psychologically speaking, the limes, for the Romans, represented the limits of civilization, a boundary against the untamed, barbaric realms that "civilized human beings did not transgress" (p. 162). On both the empirical and mythical planes, the *limes* also represents official civic unions and divisions. Arguing that the limes, itself, is a place, a sort of psychological container, they situate Serbian existence on this "swarming crossroad" (p. 163). As a container, however, the *coincidentia oppositori* (meetings of opposites) manifests as skirmishes on a plethora of fronts (religion, language, ideology, identity, families, etc.). In their assessment, "the limes for the Serbs almost never served as an image of holding, embracement, enclosure, or encapsulation" (p. 163).

Within this purgatory of limes, Popovic and Popovic (2014) argue that Serbia has been "unable to symbolize the traumatic experiences and narrativize the painful events" (p. 164). Living on the limes, according to the authors, also makes initiation, a necessary crucible for processing trauma, impossible. Citing Turner (1969), they illustrate how liminality, this mid-stage between separation and incorporation in the initiation process, is a crucial space away from the collective where the initiate's identity may be transformed and returned to the collective with a new role and identity. The authors argue that their ·Serbian analysands are literally stuck in this waystation of constant cultural trauma.

The core of the cure allegedly resides in the liminal discourse of their Serbian analysands; it stands outside of narrative time, "fragmented into static, atomistic, rudimentary, meaningless units" (Popovic & Popovic, 2014, p. 170).

The 'who' is lost to abstraction and imageless, vacuous monologuing and enumeration, rendering any symbolic or meaning potential impossible. In the liminal discourse of Serbian analysands, the authors perceived possession by repetitive "archetypal master plots" (p. 171) borne of collective narratives of Serbian cultural trauma, and all of the potential personal material overwritten by these patterns.

Traumas and Complexes of Mexican Miscegenation: Moctezuma and Malinche

The Europeans conquered the Americans with a common missionary and monotheistic zeal emblematic of the One. Nevertheless, a lot of the impetus for the Renaissance was fueled by cultural cross-fertilizations with the newly conquered continents. Though undeniably fraught with titanic atrocities, miscegenation happened, and Jung noted slight north-south differences in this process: "The foreign land assimilates its conqueror. But unlike the Latin colonizers of Central and South America, the North Americans preserved their European standards with the most rigid puritanism, though they could not prevent the souls of their Indian foes from becoming theirs" (Brewster, 2017, p. 15, citing CW 10, Para. 103).

Traumas of Mexican mestizaje (miscegenation) lead back to the first encounters between the indigenous inhabitants and the Spanish invaders, and they center on the Aztec leader, Moctezuma and Cortez's interpreter Malintzín. Regarding the former, a Moctezuma Complex originates in the alleged paralytic depression of the Aztec leader in confronting Conquistadors. According to Luis Zoja (2010) and Patricia Michan (2014), Moctezuma's cultural trauma resulted from the cognitive dissonance between Spanish linear and Aztec circular temporality. Even if the Spaniards had been initially explained away as the return of expected gods, they were quickly revealed to be "cruel, greedy, and mean...*popolocas* [barbarians]" (Zoja, p. 84). The protecting daemon-archetypes of Montezuma's and ostensibly Mexico's collective Self, were blurred in the figures of Cortez and Quetzalcoatl. Michan describes the effect of the shock on Moctezuma thusly: "Moctezuma's expectation of avoiding bloodshed, rioting, and invasion, together with his ancestral guilt, led to a failure to appropriately use his power" (p. 83). Extending Moctezuma's psychic paralysis to the present, the resulting inheritance, according to Zoja, is "a truly monstrous cultural complex" (p. 88), which he describes thusly:

> The traumatized Mexicans may have experienced a wound even more lacerating than that of being betrayed and abused by a parent: they have been abused by their gods. All the symptoms that followed correspond to this original catastrophe and will remain petrified for centuries in a large number of descendants: loss of self-confidence, loss of initiative,

introjection of conflicts without any sign of visible aggressiveness, inclination to self-destructive behavior (addiction, suicide) and to reenactment of the abuse.[11] (p. 84)

Michan (2014) focuses more on the present symptoms, alleging patterns of conformity, enmeshed families, dogmatism, and binary norms she ascribes to her analysands' psyches, men and women alike. There is also a strong measure of toxic masculinity centered on two aspects of a negative father complex, one that combines the brutal Spanish machismo with the Aztec patriarchs known as the *tlatoani*, who "commands empowerment and respect, and he requires stultifying submission" (p. 81). This double-negative, she argues, assigns a bipolar alignment of a sadistic explosive conquistador set opposite a degraded, implosive, masochistic *tlatoani*. As a remedy, she offers the figure of Cuauhtémoc, the last *tlatoani*, as a positive animus of resistance.

What Jacqueline Gerson (2010) calls the Malinchista Complex is associated with preference for anything foreign and a sense of betrayal of one's own Mexican culture (citing Wood, 2000, p. 33), and it is rooted in the historical figure of Malintzín, whose Catholic name was Doña Marina.[12] Malintzín was sold into servitude to the Aztecs by her mother and eventually ended up as the interpreter-concubine[13] of Hernán de Cortez, playing a significant role in the initial encounters with Moctezuma. Gerson considers self-betrayal to be the most corrosive aspect of her legacy. In addition to herself, she was alleged to have betrayed the indigenous people of Mexico. Flipping the betrayal notion, Gerson suggests that Malintzin's creation of a mestizo (mixed) race ensured the survival of the Mexican people, a covenant consecrated in the legitimization of

---

[11] Reading Gerson, Michán, and Zoja, it is a bit surprising that Octavio Paz's extensive and celebrated *Laberinto de la soledad* does not figure more prominently as a common foundation in any study of Mexican cultural complexes and trauma. Thanks to my colleague, Marko Miletich for echoing this concern and for connecting alleged pathologies ascribed to modern Mexicans to Paz's notion of *hijos de la Chingada* –roughly equivalent to "children of the first violated indigenous woman"—, the misogynistic roots of which are detailed in the following footnote. For more background, the reader is encouraged to consult Paz's Nobel-prize winning work: Paz, O. (1995). *El laberinto de la soledad.* New York: Penguin Putnam. [Originally published in 1947]. Available in translation.

[12] It is important to point out that the root name of the complex, Malinche, carries these pejorative connotations, which have been passed down in the violent misogyny of the root ching- (chingar, chingada…) in Mexican Spanish. Consequently, except when quoting Gerson directly, I refer to her as Malintzín, the honorarial name given to her by the Aztecs. Source: Candelaria, C. (1980). La Malinche, feminist prototype. *Frontiers: A Journal of Women Studies, 5*(2), 1-6, https://www.jstor.org/stable/3346027.

[13] Thanks to colleague Marko Miletich for suggesting "concubine" as a description befitting of Malintzin's likely lack of agency in the affair.

her first son by Cortez, Martín, through a papal bull of the age. Ultimately, the author affirms a balanced portrait: "Malinche's story represents the creativity in the psyche that allows a historical trauma to become a cultural complex, with both light and dark aspects" (p. 41).

According to Gerson (2010), "the malinchista complex operates to polarize and splits our vision for ourselves. On one side of the polarity, we feel that no one should or can know better than we Mexicans how to rule ourselves; on the other side, we believe that everyone manages to do everything better than we do" (p. 44). Pointing to the continued oppression of indigenous people in Chiapas and the atrocities committed against women in the border town of Ciudad Juarez, Gerson states: "We turn our back on our own even as we care for the global other, and in the process we have no eyes, no heart, no mind for our own cruelty or for our own beauty, our value, and selves" (p. 38).

African Americans and Traumas of Slavery

As with the cultural traumas inflicted by Authoritarianism, Brewster (2017) sustains that the mass enslavement of Africans during the Middle Passage resulted in immediate and enduring transgenerational disruption of the family unit, the most violent manifestation of which is rooted in the wrenching of children from their mothers. According to Brewster, post-traumatic slave syndrome includes a lack of self-esteem, intense anger and "racist socialization" (p. 69, citing DeGruy, 2005), pointing out that "one of the long-term effects of American slavery is that it severely damaged the natural line of maternal instinct" (p. 67). She points to the prominence of the *Mother of Sorrows* side of the Madonna, which intersects with the African goddess Erzulie Ferda (p. 74). For their part, African American men carry the threat of castration as punishment for reading, a history of being used by the colonizer as an economic or military pawn, and the constant accusations of raping white women, which often led to lynching. She notes that, as in the case of authoritarian regimes, the African American father was displaced, in this case literally as the slave master or overseer usurped his patriarchal role. A consequence of this transgenerational trauma, according to the author, is the serious problem of absent fathers, and the overall modern picture is devastating: "The relationship between African American women and men has been strained and damaged by slavery. The separation of families caused African American couples to distrust, betray, and abandon their partners and children" (p. 105).

A wound of invisibility pervades the trauma of African Americans. We have already referenced Brewster's (2017) account of the Baltimore study, which ostensibly rendered the African American individuals in that study invisible. On the myth of invisibility and its dehumanizing potential, Kimbles (2014) comments: "the unconsciously supremacist 'white' could, simply by averting his or her gaze, arrogating the right to direct it as he or she chose, destroy the 'person of color' as someone who didn't deserve being looked at as one would a fully human subject" (p. 27). Both Brewster (2017) and Kimbles reference Ralph Ellison's *Invisible Man* (1952) as evocative of this sense of identity erasure. It is worth pointing out, from a Jungian perspective, that the novel was criticized for not unequivocally portraying the African American subject as erased by Whites but rather implicating mass movements in African American resistance (in the novel, this is portrayed as the Brotherhood) to racism as a part of an overall threat to individual identity.[14] Within a Jungian frame, however, the work serves as a compelling allegory of individuation. Furthermore, it may also be argued that such simplifications run counter to the need for deeper critical perspective required for a cultural turn after Jung.

Cultural Anxiety

Perhaps the most important scholar in this cultural turn –and perhaps the most neglected— is Rafael López-Pedraza, who delved across history and global humanities in his explorations of the core complexes of the Western psyche. His notion of cultural anxiety is guided by a somewhat idiosyncratic view of culture. In contrast to the aggression of nature, culture has a cruel aspect, and he finds this cruelty to be exacerbated by a failure to cultivate and sustain psychic images. To this latter point, he quotes the Maestro, Argentine writer Jorge Luis Borges: "The boy who can't take the other's perspective. That has to be the origin of all cruelties. All cruelty must originate in a lack of imagination," (author's translation of Borges, in Bioy Casares, 2006, p. 1009, footnoted by López-Pedraza, 2000a). The cruelty of culture, for López-Pedraza, finds ammunition in two dominant forces in the Western psyche: Titanism and Monotheism, which allegedly serve to undermine the psychically balancing, image-rich quality of the Greek polytheistic pantheon.

Defining cultural anxiety precisely is somewhat difficult given López-Pedraza's general disdain for submitting psyche to conceptual abstractions. Nevertheless, I will attempt to outline the phenomenon-concept here. Cultural anxiety essentially stems from two opposing forces in the Western psyche: one centers on "our access to archetypal images and consistent life-forms, making

---

[14] In Ellison's defense, Denby comments: "Ellison's hero is "invisible" because no one has much interest in seeing him as he is in all his ornery individuality. Virtually everyone— blacks and white alike—wants to use him, to make him over in their own image, to turn him into a portent, a warning, a threat, a possibility." Denby, D. (2012, April 12). Justice for Ralph Ellison. The New Yorker, https://www.newyorker.com/books/page-turner/justice-for-ralph-ellison.

possible psyche, emotions and feeling, values, and marking our inner processes. The other is a lack of images, a vacuum, a lacuna, out of which come excess and the madness of power" (1990, p. 7). As previously noted, he alleges a conflict between a polytheistic foundation and a monotheistic layer. The latter allegedly has progressed from religious to more scientific and ideological varieties, a stance generally espoused in Hillman's revision of Jung. Regarding the latter, we have already explored the insidious nature of ideology in European manifestations of cultural trauma. To this point, the transdisciplinarity scholar Basrab Nicolescu (1994), raised in Soviet Romania, warns us of "Ideology disguised as philosophy, religion or science – one more ruse of binary thought" (p. 46).

As Rowland (2020) puts it, "Hillman's archetypal psychology pivots away from Jung's attempt to reconfigure Christian and monotheistic structures to a polytheism that he based on the Greek gods and goddesses" (p. 11). Suggesting that the Swiss psychologist suffered a "conflict with the scientific world so distant from his pagan soul" (1990, p. 44), López-Pedraza, presents Jung as a classic case study in the monotheism-polytheism tension purported to drive cultural anxiety.

In order to better understand the split between the monotheistic and polytheistic sides of the Western psyche, let us examine several points of comparison. With regard to the image, Judeo-Christian monotheism, according to López-Pedraza, focuses on "one all-powerful imageless God" (1990, p. 31). In contrast, he portrays the Greek pantheon as image-rich, permitting psychic differentiation. With regard to the Logos-Mythos continuum, the monotheistic side follows logical being in the world from the Christian Neo-Platonists to the Enlightenment philosophers and culminating with the rise of natural sciences and technology. In contrast, the polytheistic side stays within the realm of Mythos, of narrative, belief, and feeling, all rooted in the Pantheon, though he also makes room for Celtic, Nordic, Pre-Columbian and Afro-Caribbean pantheons as well, and certainly all and many others merit more consideration in navigating the cultural turn. Additionally, there is a different quality of affect to consider. López-Pedraza associates monotheism with guilt inflation, cruelty, fear of freedom. In contrast, he assigns broader sense of tolerance and range of feelings to the polytheistic side of the Western psyche. Consequently, monotheism is allegedly prone to flights of purity and ideological extremism where polytheism is arguably more tolerant.

To the tension between monotheism and polytheism, López-Pedraza (1990) adds another element of cultural anxiety: Titanism. Based primarily on the work of Friederich Georg Jünger during the throes of World War II, Titanism is alleged to be a core characteristic of the West´s predicament: The War on Drugs, Prohibition, Machismo, the Spanish Civil War, for López-Pedraza, are all manifestations of "titanic madness" (p. 73). Ascribed to a pre-civilized, pre-arquetypal part of the psyche, López-Pedraza states: "I prefer to view them [the Titans] as mythological figures representing mimicry and excess, for they are not archetypal configurations" (p. 14). Reflecting on his own Titanism, he confesses that it "may appear in preconceived theories, missionary attitudes, techniques, manipulation fantasies, cunning schemes, and in the basic destructiveness of human nature" (my translation of López-Pedraza, 2005, p. 17).

Echoing the prior allusions to re-membering in the writings on cultural trauma, López-Pedraza explores this Titanic-Dionysian opposition (2000a, 2000b) in childhood, adolescence, and medicine. In childhood, he measures this in the distance between "accepting childhood trauma as the appearance of the Titans with the intention to dismember and devour Dionysus" (2000b, p. 26, my translation) and helicopter parenting, the sort of overprotection that breeds "a presumptuous and brilliant psychopath, devoid of emotions" (p. 27, my translation).[15]

He associates Titanism in adolescence with puer, Dionysian excess (2000a, 2000b). Accordingly, he contrasts acceptance of Dionysian mortality and weakness is alleged to contrast with the anesthetized and repetitive suffering of Titanic (Promethean) medicine characterized by "avoidance of the constant reflection which death plays alongside life – the value of life that comes from the reflection of death" (2000b, p. 21).

Reframing individuation and collective: A mantha of Cogito and Culture

In view of the cultural turn, Jung's polarity of individuation vs. (cultural) identification with the collective poses an untenable polarity that must be worked through. In spite of his introversion, the Swiss psychologist engaged extensively with the outside world. In this way, the transcendent function was at work within his theory of individuation; it just needs to be worked through, and his ample body of work lays the groundwork for a more nuanced *coniunctio* or *mantha* of the individual and their cultural milieu. Jung (1921/1974a, 1954/1974b), for example, in an address to educators, informed his audience that in the child "consciousness rises out of the unconscious like an island newly risen from the sea. We reinforce this process in children by education and culture. School is in fact a means of strengthening in a purposeful way the integration of consciousness" (1921/1974a, p. 42). On the need for organization by the collective as a precursor to re-organization through individuation, he further states: "Before [individuation] can be taken

---

[15] Original text: "un psicópata, presuntuoso y brillante, vacío de emociones" (López-Pedraza, 2000b, p. 27).

as a goal, the educational aim of adaptation to the necessary minimum of collective norms must first be established" (Jung, 1921/1990, p. 449). Nevertheless, Jung meant these statements primarily within an innatist view of cognition, envisioning the cultivation of something that was meant to unfold in its own way, which is not far from Noam Chomsky. Recognition of the importance of both inner *and* outer work in integration, as will be emphasized in this book, is central to the work of blending binaries. If our goal is to compensate the rule of the Western cogito, then we need to transcend traditional focus on the former (inner work). Integration, as Hillman (1975) taught, should not be lonely, existential isolation or narcissistic self-absorbed 'self-work' associated with ego-based psychology. In view of cultural complexes and trauma, perhaps a more radical shaking up of the individual psyche is in order- more radical *Contra Naturam* work makes sense, as Schellinski (2014) advocates, in order to shake off the sediment of intergenerational cultural trauma. Accordingly, an additional step is required, an *Opus Contra Prima Cultura*, only by critically confronting one's first culture in deep exploration of a second (or third, or fourth...) will we truly engage what Jung called an education of the soul. There is a Hungarian proverb attributed to Charlemagne: "To have another language is to possess a second soul," but in light of Jung's *coniunctio* and the Vedic mantha, that is not quite all the way: it is in the alchemical Third between selves and societies where we find psyche's true treasure. There are many facets of this Third, including the Greco-Roman feminine and the Hidden Third Transdisciplinary Studies, but in matters of cultural complexes and trauma this thirdness that is not quite the first or second language and cultures is best captured in Homi Bhabha's (1994) notion of Third Space, a notion that he explores in post-Colonial contexts.

As an innatist, and contrary to common notions of culture, Jung held up the image of the Cultured Man as the end product of individuation, one who has done and continues to do the challenging work of working out his inner polarities. Rather than satisfying ourselves with this image of an inner Petrie dish, the implication is that we need to understand that this achievement of individuation is one of sculpting and refining shared meanings by integrating one's own innate and first cultural meanings with those of other cultures. Of course, the more different the better, so it makes sense to move beyond the end of the county line or from this club to another; the deeper the exploration into other languages and their cultures represents the crowning achievement of a Cultured Man as we define it in the cultural turn.

Another seed for a cultural dimension in individuation is connoted in Jung's concepts of the Shadow and its close companion, the Other. In analytical psychology, individuation is focused like a laser on integration of the Shadow. The Shadow, for Jung, indexed a psychic repository for all of the aspects of the

Self that are deemed unfit for integration into the ego, and its contents are determined, in large part, by the culture in which the ego of person is formed. These contents are arbitrarily assigned as *Other*, consequently, shadow work, the main work of individuation, is about un-Othering, a constant testing and tempering of positions that he deemed particularly essential to compensate for the unilateral nature of the Western Psyche. As Jung stated:

> Nothing in us ever remains quite contradicted, and consciousness can take up no position which will not call up, somewhere in the dark corners of the psyche, a negation or a compensatory effect, approval or resentment. This process of coming to terms with the "Other" in us is well worthwhile, because in this way we get to know aspects of our nature which we would not allow anybody else to show us and which we ourselves would never have admitted. (1963a/1955, p. 706)

Shadow work has its many forms. The importance of integrating the inferior function in typology, for example, extroversion for introverts and the reverse for extroverts, as well as the puer-senex opposition are two prominent examples. Perhaps one of the most fundamental aspects of shadow integration centers on gender. Men carry, according to Jung, an anima, the sum of all things feminine, both experienced and fantasized, both personally and transpersonally through archetypal symbols. The female equivalent is the animus. As Clifford Mays (2005) affirms, "Learning how to integrate one's contrasexual elements without forfeiting one's primary gender identity is a major requirement of individuation" (p. 67). Likewise, Neumann (1994) invokes the Quaternity of Man-Woman, Anima-Animus as the focal point for a final stage of psychological development in women: accepting her partner's and her own contrasexual nature (p. 52). This was an important door to open, but a deeper look at the complexities and somewhat arbitrary nature of gender identification is now quite literally a matter of life or death for millions of LGBTQ youth who live and die the reality of blurred lines between male and female, suffering the day-to-day torture of rejection and bullying. López-Pedraza (1991) was the first Jungian to unshackle the Jungian tradition from its tendency to pathologize anyone outside of traditional, heterosexual conceptions of gender, and he, in fact, opened border crossings, invoking Hermes, father of Hermaphrodite, as a way to promote *movimiento psíquico*. Singer (1976, in Rowland, 2002), working from a feminist critique, has raised attention to Jung's affirmation of androgyny as a way to psychic wholeness. Reflecting on Jung's life and work, we discern some promising steps forward and acknowledge the work to be done.

As has been established in the discussion of cultural complexes and trauma, the most significant and yet-to-be-worked out aspect of shadow integration centers on the cultural Other. One of the limitations of Jung's psychology was his struggle to hold the tension between the alleged inner work of individuation and identification with the collective, this vague abstraction of culture that connoted conformity to mass thinking. Perhaps owing to his introversion and Protestant-Enlightenment individualism, Jung's writings emphasize the primacy of the individual and the potential threat to individuation inherent in his or her milieu.[16] Jung's commentary on the collective suggests a "banking model"- that there is no engagement with the collective that does not come at the expense of individuation. Jung also expounds on a 'ransom' the individual must make with his cultural milieu for withdrawing from the collective, a 'guilt' exonerated by the products of this inward turn: "values which are an equivalent substitute for his absence in the collective personal sphere" (Jung, 1977, Para. 1095), the alleged blessings of a 'cultured man.'[17]

The overall impression of Jung's affiliation within the mind vs. milieu debate is one of preference for individual cognition, but this preference is not unqualified; Jung was, like all of us, pursuant to his own particular contradictions. He argued with himself constantly, and he would perhaps be the first to agree that his own individuation depended on losing those arguments. This is the alchemy of the transcendent function, the dance of the *mysterium coniunctionis*: a polarity presents itself by way of its opposite: enantiodromia. *Cogito* and *Cultura*, Self and Society, Mind and Milieu- these are references that will be explored as two intricately connected and basic forces in the Western psyche: the One and the Many.

As noted in the introduction, the metaphysical notion of the One and the Many is a through line in the West, and it dates back to the Greeks. The central idea is that a fundamental concern in any culture involves reconciling a diversity of manifestations through reduction into a central, unifying concept.[18]

---

[16] Following are some corresponding quotes from Jung's *Collected Works*: "The individual is obliged by the collective demands to purchase his individuation at the cost of an equivalent work for the benefit of society" (1977, p. 452); "If the individual is worthless, the nation will be worthless: and if the individual does not flourish, the whole will not flourish" (1911-12/1952/2014, p. 11); "Who looks outside dreams. Who looks inside awakens" (1928/1972, p. 188); "The individual is the only reality. The further we move away from the individual toward abstract ideas about Homo Sapiens, the more likely we are to fall into error" (1964, p. 45); "To find out what is truly individual in ourselves, profound reflection is needed; and suddenly we realize how uncommonly difficult the discovery of individuality in fact is" (1928/1972, para. 272).

[17] To this point, Jung also stated: "To find out what is truly individual in ourselves, profound reflection is needed; and suddenly we realize how uncommonly difficult the discovery of individuality in fact is" (1928/1972, para 242).

[18] Hooker, R. (1996). The one and the many. World Cultures General Glossary, http://www. faculty.umb.edu/gary_zabel/Courses/Phil%20281b/Philosophy%20of%20Magic/Dante. %20etc/Philosophers/Idea/www.wsu.edu_8080/~dee/GLOSSARY/ONEMANY.HTM

Singer (2010b) sees these tendencies as characterized by positive and negative aspects: the "many can denote a harmonious diversity or a fragmented sort of Balkanization and the 'one' may either lead to an integrated whole or a sort of reductive homogenization" (pp. 16-17). In terms of psychological and social subjectivity, Kimbles (2014) addresses the core of the concept of the One and the Many in the context of cultural complexes:

> The group has its own dynamism and unity that is separate from the individual but mysteriously linked to each person's individuality. We develop through our relationship with, and through our encounters with, that other dimension that is both living within and without. This relationship is organized by cultural complexes. (p. 9)

Though it is not altogether outside of these conceptions of the One and the Many, my own sense of it draws primarily from Prometheus and Themis, as a related propulsion of a singularity out of a system, a linear trajectory into some new terrain of psychological or cultural being-in-the-world (the One), which is matched by a fundamental circularity borne of belongingness:[19] an equally fundamental need for psychological and cultural coherence or 'systemness' (the Many). The One and the Many have a quality of Jung's *coniunctio* as 'third': they retain their core features, but they are always in dialogic constellation, one around the other. As Singer (2010b) suggests, the One and the Many may be engaged consciously and constructively, or destructively through the Shadow.

In matters of the One and the Many, there is just as much evidence in his work that suggests Jung's appreciation of relatedness in what he often refers to as the "milieu" (the Many) and its value for individuation (the One).[20] Nevertheless,

---

[19] To this point, Kimbles (2014) expounds on *kinship libido*: "As humans, we learn to lean on and are symbiotically tied to the need to feel that we belong, are held, and are respected by our reference group of related others within which we develop our individual identities" (p. 53).

[20] Likewise, some corresponding quotes from Jung: "Individuation has two principal aspects: in the first place it is an internal and subjective process of integration, and in the second it is an equally indispensable process of objective relationship. Neither can exist without the other, although sometimes the one and sometimes the other predominates" (1954/1998, Para. 448); "Collective relationships must be based on individual relationships, for an individual cannot exist without relatedness, for we are each cells in an organism. When we make individual relationships, we lay the foundations for an invisible church" (Jung, 1923, p. 20); "As the individual is not just a single, separate being, but by his very existence presupposes a collective relationship, it follows that the process of individuation must lead to more intense and broader collective relationships and not to isolation" (1921/1990, para. 758); "It is possible to participate in the unconscious with other persons, with animals, and even with objects, through an unconscious abaissment

in spite of his acknowledgment of connection and the collective, the trajectory overwhelmingly favors the individual and his individuation project. One can imagine some profit to the pecuniary bartering between the inner and outer sphere as a necessary by-product of an interface between psychological and the cultural work, but it is not possible, particularly from a Vygotskyan standpoint, to imagine depths of differentiation to which Jung committed without comparable breadth of experiences in the collective, especially with regard to collective ways of being that are different from one's own. Perhaps Jung's own introversion and Eurocentricism held him back from a full appreciation of the diverse cultural contexts of development. Accordingly, we should be on guard against an *opus contra naturam* that reduces the sociocultural Other to a fetish for individuation or, for that matter, the development of the Western ego, with all the attending issues of binary thought. As Nicolescu (1994) reminds us, "Complete actualization is annihilation of the other, which is why binary logic lies at the root of the new barbarism" (p. 83).

Traipsing out into the milieu, there are many cultural aspects of shadow integration still waiting to be addressed by Jungian Studies. Analytical psychology, as is the case for mainstream cognitive psychology, has been somewhat slow to concede the active role one's culture places in psychological development. When Singer and Kimbles (2010) characterize cultural complexes as "the essential components of an inner sociology" (p. 4), such phenomena have already been eloquently elucidated and empirically verified by Vygotsky and his colleagues, who viewed development as the integration of cultural into psychological meanings—from the intersubjective to the intrasubjective plane (Vygotsky, 1932/1994). Likewise, Giegerich's (2012) post-Jungian approach concedes "that everything comes from within is an illusion...what is (consciously or unconsciously) in individual consciousness must before have been in a cultural institution or work" (p. 183). There is, however, one marked difference in their epistemologies of social cognition. Contrary to Giegerich's dialectical approach, Vygotsky's sociocultural theory of mind views such processes as inherently and actively dialogic in nature, so the individual has some agency in appropriating what he or she learns in the social milieu. Accordingly, it makes sense to turn the work of individuation toward Western Shadow work, that of the cultural ego. There, fueled by patriarchy and Titanic monotheism, the Western Cultural Complex manifests its potential for projection onto a Cultural Other. As Kimbles (2014) suggests, cultural complexes are specifically driven by the monotheistic binary: a "tendency to black-and-

---

du niveau mental. Connection is made and something may happen. I may, for example, verbalize what the other person intended saying. But even the clouds, or a glass, can reflect the inner psychic situation' (Evans, Jones & Jung, 1964, p. 51).

white thinking, again fueled by an unexamined fear of differences" (p. 62). So the work begins, starting with the case study of Jung's life and thought.

In working through a Western cultural complex, it is important to bear in mind that Jung, in spite of failures in owning his own Western shadow, was nonetheless keenly aware of Western civilization's shadow. Rowland (2010), for example, recounts how, following his sessions with James Joyce and reading his famous work, *Ulysses* (1922), Jung became keenly aware of European culture's inability to integrate the cultural Other. Furthermore, the vacuous babble of the work and its ill effects on Jung, for López-Pedraza (1990), constitute classic symptoms of cultural anxiety.

Reflections on the cultural turn

In matters of confronting a Western cultural complex Helen Morgan (2010) pronounces the challenge before us:

> We cannot put aside the embarrassment of our founder's words and call him a man of his times, and we are indeed looking back at a man who is speaking from the first half of the twentieth century from a dialogue that has changed. But by doing so we are accepting that thought and image are constructed, contingent, and changeable, and how do we square that with the timeless, universality of the archetype. (p. 219)

Let us consider that quote in the context of deep psychological and cultural change. More concretely, what is this place and time, in general, and in the evolution of Jungian thought? If these are Titanic times, then we need to better understand how we got here and, as Giegerich might ask ourselves: What is this logic of being in the world?

Regarding questions of place, a great room will not do, and neither will a mudroom, for that matter. According to Jane Harrison (1912/1974), the Titaness Themis rules the *agora*, the open-air arena for public meetings; it is not the time to be agoraphobic. This cultural complex facing Jung and his legacy has to be worked out in this open space, where individuation may be engaged on both the personal and the collective level. Jung's antipathy toward the collective as a threat to individuation is well-established. In his own words, "very special attention must be paid to this delicate plant 'individuality' if it is not to be completely smothered" (Jung, 1953/1972, para. 241). Just as Jung and Jungians need to delve into this Collective Complex, this inability to fully engage with the cultural milieu perhaps fueled by the obsession with what Hillman (1975) dismissed as the individuation *fantasy*, there is also a need for the eurocentric West to take back its own shadow, to dig deeper into its own cultural complexes and their devastating effects. Accordingly, it makes sense to transfer this mantra to a cultural level of individuation. To this point, Singer

(2010a) states: "an understanding of the individual psyche through its consciousness will not be enough. The group itself will need to develop a consciousness of its cultural complexes" (p. 32).

In the chapters that follow, we will apply a coniunctio-manth of the One and the Many and its complex array of constellations, starting with the corresponding premise that individuation means nothing without social justice and inclusion. A true education of the psyche must be as broad and expansive in its exploration as it is deep in introspection: expanding outer circles need not spiral upward but rather downward where real personal transformation and integration is possible.

The corresponding agora should be as fully open to the present as it is mindful of the past. Consequently, shadow work starts with fully recognizing Western patriarchy and colonialism's role in inflicting cultural trauma and skewing narratives. Rather than contributing to othering by pathologizing oppressed groups, the cultural turn calls us to withdraw the projection and re-member lost narratives, re-learning the old stories with fresh insights into the archetypology of patriarchy, matriarchy, titans, heroes, and monsters. As we consider current conventional wisdom on how we know and grow, how we grapple with the velocity of technology and innovation, we will spiral back to a more expansive knowledge of the West's archetypal inheritance and possible futures.

Chapter 2
Raising the Titanic

"Where there are no gods, there are titans" (Jünger, 1947/2006, p. 108, author's translation.)[1]

Huge! Bigly! Epic! Such are common hyperbolic expressions these days. We live in an era of super-sized snacks, monster trucks, clickbait, bots, and absurd memes. Voicing an archetypal psychological perspective of our times, López-Pedraza (1990; 2000a), as alluded to earlier, marked the moment as characterized by Titanism, a cultural phenomenon he borrowed from Jünger. This chapter, in part, responds to his call for more investigation into this psychological phenomenon and to temper it with a more blended perspective of patriarchy's Greco-Roman origins, including these larger-than-life, inflated, and brazen entities known as the Titans. Indeed, a deeper psychology of Titanism is essential for this cultural turn in depth psychology.

To condense López-Pedraza's progression of cultural anxiety in the Western psyche, it would essentially situate the Titanic within three stages: a pre-civilized, extreme, Titanic level of the psyche over which was written a more cultured and polytheistic Olympian order that in turn was eventually subjected to a dominant monotheistic layer of consciousness. As established, this culminating monotheistic realm is characterized by the sublimation of an originating religious (Judeo-Christian) source into ideological and technological varieties (Giegerich, 2007). Often the lines are blurred between modern day monotheism and Titanism. For example, in classic archetypal psychology, as conceived by Hillman (1975) and López-Pedraza (1990; 2000a), both monotheism and Titanism are ascribed various measures of ego-inflation, male-dominance, binary ways of knowing, either an incapacity or unwillingness to cultivate images, and an overall sense of vacuity or excess, pathologies that allegedly have no place in their vision for a polytheistic psychology based primarily on Greek mythology. It is easy to get lost in archetypal psychology's *ad hominem* assaults on titanic excess here or titanic vacuity there. Consequently, it makes sense to apply Jung's alchemy-inspired *mysterium coniunctionis* (1955/1963b), the union of the opposites, to this tendency to exalt polytheism, on one hand,

---

[1] Henceforth, all direct quotes from this source reflect the author's translation from the Spanish version of this work.

and pathologize monotheism and the titanic on the other; it suggests a facile binary in need of a thorough mantha, in the sense of churning.

The goal of this chapter is just that: to "churn out" a more balanced and comprehensive analysis of Titanism, tracing its origins in ancient polytheistic Greece to contemporary, monotheism-infused Western culture. Several sources of post-Jungian scholarship figure important in this endeavor: López-Pedraza's notion of cultural anxiety, Susan Rowland's post-modern feminist revision of Jungian psychology, and Wolfgang Giegerich's Hegelian rebuttal to Jungian and archetypal psychology. In addition, the mythological scholarship of Karl Kerényi, Jane Harrison, and Friedrich Georg Jünger furnish a relevant foundation in Greek religion, one that highlights Prometheus and Gaia-Themis, Titans who constellate in ways that illuminate perennial tensions between patriarchal and matriarchal forces in the West, problematizing long-held assumptions about mono- vs. polytheism and binary stances on gender.

Origins of the Titans and Titanism

According to Kerényi (1997), the origins of the Greek Titan mythologem can be traced back to a larger-than-life, pre-civilized cult of first men, the Kabeiroi, which originates on the island of Lemnos. Like their predecessors, the Titans share the same reputation for excessive masculinity and an exile narrative. As related in the Titanomachia, the Titans were cast out by Zeus and the Olympians. In a similar fashion, these Kabeiroi, were, depending on the account, either annihilated or exiled by the women of Lemnos. Murray Stein (2020) describes one account according to which they are the product of a union of Hephaestus (a pre-Olympic variant) and *Kabeiro*, a variant of the Great Mother, creating the Kabeiroi. Jünger (1947/2006) sustains that, in addition to the Kabeiroi, Hephaestus has a special kinship with a similar proto-Titanic brotherhood, the Dactyls, who share a common interest in kiln craft. Their names actually index the world of blacksmiths: Damnameneus (hammer), Acmon (anvil), and Celmis (foundry worker). Considered sons of the Titaness Rhea, the Phrygian Dactyls were regarded as magical artisans gifted with nature's "secret powers" (p. 31). Pointing to the Dactyls, Jünger asserts that technology's origins are inherently Titanic, though Stein argues that Hephaistos rules *techne*, defined by Aristotle as "acting as nature asks" (p. 20, citing Panofsky, 1962).

Though Jünger (1947/2006) sustains that the origin of the term Titan begins with the union of Uranus and Gaia (it is the name Uranus bestows upon his offspring), he broadly categorizes the Titanic to include the Titans, their parents, as well as their monstrous cousins, the Gigantes. As the leader of the Titans' rebellion against Uranus, Kronos's patricidal severing of Father Uranus literally splits time and space, setting in motion the binary wheels that would spin the West. In response to the relatively uncritical lauding of Zeus in archetypal psychology, Giegerich (2008) offers the following challenge: "would there have been a Zeus at all, for whom Hillman takes up the cudgels with so much verve, or any of the Olympic gods for that matter, without Kronos's act of separation?" (p. 327). In a sense, Kronos indexes the origins of psychological differentiation. Against the nebula of chaos, elemental laws are set to Kronos's clock, and Jünger affirms that Kronos´s veneration by the Greeks persisted into the Olympian order, that the Greeks continue to honor the Titans and the elemental laws they represent.[2]

A closer look at these elemental laws tells us quite a bit about a Titanic psychology, particularly when compared with the cultural laws of the Olympians. Jünger (1947/2006) points out the following distinctions that demonstrate the greater differentiation of the latter:

- unlike Okeanos, Poseidon is not "identical to the sea" (p. 36);
- unlike Helios's agitated flame, Apollo's is more sublime and centered;
- in their shared lunar aspect, Artemis's agility and vigor contrast with the profound silence and somnambulant stillness of Selene;
- as an ideal of individualism, Apollo demonstrates more "maturity and splendor" (p. 75) than Prometheus, who demonstrates a "darker and more savage fire" (p. 76).[3]

An overidentification with their respective repetitive labors renders the Titans dour and dismal figures. Imagine having to ebb and flow, circle the Earth, ride the Heavens, etc. on Kronos time: twenty-four hours a day, seven days a week, ad infinitum. For Jünger (1947/2006), Cyclopes and Prometheus exemplify the insidiously mechanical and repetitive sort of labor associated with the Titans. Accordingly, there is something stoic yet fossilized in the Titanic. As Jünger recounts the petrification of Atlas into a mountain at the sight of Medusa's head, one gets the sense that nothing much has changed. Atlas literally carries

---

[2] "In the reign of Zeus, in which the majority of them continue dominating, their dignities are assured; they continue to be indestructible figures who cannot be exterminated" (p. 72). Jünger likewise affirms "their legitimate mode of acting. They are not insatiable usurpers of power nor are they the opposition to the legal order. Rather, they are the sovereigns of a legality whose need is never in doubt" (p. 95).

[3] Though Gier (2000) dismisses the dwarfish, savage figures, the Pramatha, as a red herring in connecting Indian and Greek Titanism, their similar connection to a "savage fire" merits consideration as a parallel here.

the characterization of the Titans as "bearers of loads...destined to 'sustain the weight and carry on under pressure'" (p. 58). This rigidity, in the case of Kronos, means that, in spite of his advanced age, he lacks maturity. As Jünger reminds us, he has no center, no capacity for personal or cultural growth.

The cheerless labor and self-absorption of the Titans finds its nemesis (or complement?) in exuberant, party-going Dionysus. To this point, Jünger (1947/2006) dotes on Dionysus as "a god of progression, of change, and of perpetual transformation" who opens "access to the atemporal present" (p. 61), singular moments of numinous connection inspired in moments of leisure lost in the beauty of arts and letters, which contrasts with the chronic daily grind of mechanical necessity associated with the Titanic. As Jünger puts it, "Time seems to have stopped; it will only begin to speed up under Kronos. When all is conceived as necessary, freedom does not exist, not even the need for it" (p. 63). For López-Pedraza (1990; 2000a; 2000b), Dionysus's weakness and death-accepting, soul-making nature likewise contrasts sharply with the Titan's hubris, death-defiance, and soul-numbing pharmaceuticals.[4] It bears repeating that the Titans dismembered Dionysus,[5] an archetypally feminine deity; consequently, our work will be to re-member and mantha subjugated scraps of the feminine on the male-dominated editing floor of the West. In fact, though the coniunctio and the mantha are quite similar, the latter offers a more active role for the feminine. Whereas Luna of the coniunctio occupies a rather passive role in alchemical processes, Urvashi of the Vedic mantha is ascribed agency in the form of speech and dance.

Titanism psychoanalytics

The basic physics of Jungian psychology predict that whatever is encouraged into the light of day has an opposite bound for the darkness (Shadow), and a similar dynamic drives Jünger's hypothesis that "when the Olympic gods become the drivers of human destiny, all things titanic recede into the shadow" (1947/2006, p. 95) and that "the gods dislike the titanic side of Man" (p. 57). Following are some corresponding characteristics that he relates:

---

[4] "This whole pharmaceutical arsenal is the product of technical specialists who think of the human body as a machine" (Jünger, 1946, p. 146).

[5] Jünger describes the scene thusly: "The Titans pursue Dionysus in all of his phases of epiphany and ultimately pounce on him. He becomes defensive and uses his art of transformation, as lion, serpent, or tiger, until he succumbs to them in the form of a bull and is dismembered" (p. 64).

- A lack of boundaries.[6]
- An inflated (Promethean) love of liberty.[7]
- Narcissism (the Titan is only preoccupied with his or her elemental law).
- Elemental (or binary) thinking.

Elemental thinking merits closer examination. In some ways it represents an excess of will,[8] but it also conjures a sort of vacuity or vegetative state:

> When we are seated on the banks of a brook or river and we watch the advance and retreat of the water, when we hear the eternal, monotonous whisper and murmur, this movement cradles us, it cradles us in atemporality and in the lack of destiny of the element that transmits to us the movement and sound of water. On the shores of the sea this sensation is even stronger. When we contemplate a flame, the fire, it can become so powerful that it acts as a sort of spell or compulsion. We cannot turn our eyes away from the movement of the element; we lose ourselves in the gaze, we are transfixed and enraptured. Face to face with this sort of movement, the man not only rests, but he finds himself dragged into it. He loses his individuality, his consciousness, and his memory. (Jünger, 1947/2006, p. 103)

It is worth pondering whether the Walden's sort of reverie is that far from "vegging out" on smartphone games. There is certainly an elemental quality to both experiences. Accordingly, we should not rule out a restorative, soul making quality in these moments of Titanism.

Prometheus and the Titanic Nonbinary

While Jünger and Kerényi buttress much of archetypal psychology's portrayal of Titanism, from vacuity and excess to hypermasculinity, a closer examination of Prometheus and Themis uncovers a more nuanced portrayal. At first glance, the defiant, freedom-loving Prometheus strikes us as emblematic of the

---

[6] "It is unfettered will that snares man in the titanic essence...he seeks to manifest the unattainable and succumbs in the effort" (Jünger, 2006/1947, p. 107). "The man without measure has something of an unfinished character" (p. 108).

[7] "Man's lust for limitless liberty and independence is titanic, and it is there where this desire imposes itself that its regulating precept appears, necessity, which acts mechanically and is precisely what arises to compensate this stuff. Such is the end of all that is promethean, all of which Zeus is well-aware. The new world Prometheus creates is not inextinguishable; its resources are also extinguished" (Jünger, 2006/1947, p. 109).

[8] "pure will is elemental, and it extends to all that is elemental" (Jünger, 2006/1947, p. 109).

hypermasculine Kabeiroi roots of the Titan mythologem. Likewise, his brand of rugged individualism gives him a sort of Clint Eastwood outlaw mystique, what López-Pedraza (2002) would call a "hecaterean charisma" (p. 31). The combination of individualism and freedom also distances Prometheus from his Titan brethren, particularly since he transcends the clockwork grind of Kronos. As Jünger (1947/2006) puts it, "he is attentive to change and, in contrast to Cronos, he points toward the future" (p. 75). Jünger also ascribes to Prometheus "an isolated and isolating energy" (p. 74), which is not at all surprising as he is the consummate innovator, a historically marginalized (if not crucified) occupation. Prometheus, for Jünger, symbolizes "a confidence in inventions, in mental tools. ...an artisanal force" (p. 76). As evident in the ubiquitous "mad scientist" trope, Prometheus's invention tends to overreach. As Jünger reminds us, "Prometheus is proud of the works of his mind and hands, and this pride is repeated to the point of deformation in the promethean man" (p. 78). As heroes go, Prometheus is generally revered in the contemporary West as an existential champion of sorts.

In spite of a number of the patriarchal anthropomorphisms that constellate around Prometheus, the Titan is very rooted in the feminine. As depicted in Aeschylus's *Prometheus Bound*, he is our conduit to the Great Mother. Prometheus has a moon-like nature that carries an aspect of the feminine, whether through his kinship with the Moon-Titaness Selene or the Olympian, Hera. Kerényi (1997), echoing Jünger, recognizes a darkness here, describing the Titan as "a moon-like being, but not a luminous one, embodying the darkness of the dark moon...a wounder and a wounded one" (p. 55). Regarding the moon nature, Neumann (1994) offers a more nonbinary perspective, reminding us that there is evidence of male moon deities (and female sun deities), ascribing a hermaphroditic aspect to the moon (p. 68). He does, however, allege a special connection between the moon and feminine consciousness:

> While patriarchal consciousness is by nature quick-moving and overtakes the long processes of transformation and development in nature with the arbitrary action of experimental calculation, matriarchal consciousness stands under the sway of the moon's growth time. In luminescence and its light-knowledge is bound to the course of time and to periodicity, as is the moon. For this form of consciousness time must ripen, and with it, like the seeds sown in the earth, knowledge matures. (p. 94)

Metaphorically, Neumann (1994) suggests that a moon consciousness centers on grounded knowledge that is inherently rhizomic, a brooding or sprouting into fruition from a concept- as-a-conception frame. I would add to this the fundamental law of relationship, *a spiritus mundi*: the rhythm and respiration of everything, from cognition to culture and, by extension of the moon's diverse influence, from tides and menstruation to the totality of the cosmos. I would further posit, and I think Neumann would as well, that people of all gender classifications have equal access to such consciousness.

Regarding Prometheus as a wounded wounder, Kerényi (1997) further alleges that Prometheus shares this feature with Hera and his Titan brethren: the darkest wound of pride. He also notes the potential significance of Prometheus's wound, his liver, which for the Greeks was the dark organ and the seat of passions. According to Kerényi (1997), again echoing Jünger's characterization, "The darkness of Prometheus signifies precisely the deficiency of one who needs fire in order to achieve a more perfect form of being. In obtaining this higher form of being for man, Prometheus shows himself to be man's double, an eternal image of man's basically imperfect form of being" (p. 78). While Kerényi is speaking to human striving, it is reasonable, in light of the patriarchal preoccupation with father-birth in ancient Greece, a point that we will explore in more depth later on, that there is perhaps a primordial male insecurity, perhaps even hysteria, imbued in the figure of Prometheus.

Nevertheless, Gier (2000) suggests that Prometheus is our best hope of reconciling the rift between *animus* (masculine principle) and *anima* (feminine principle).[9] Irritable and intolerant, the Prometheus immortalized in *Prometheus Bound* (Aeschylus, 1961) is the classic Jungian portrayal of the male possessed by the dark depression of a wounded anima, so such a feat might be considered a tall order. To Gier's point, I would argue that gender reconciliation begins with the archetypal image of mother and son and a deeper exploration of matriarchal Titanism.

The Matriarchal Order and Titanism

In matters of matriarchal Titanism, there is no clear empirical evidence of an actual matriarchal order, which is perhaps why Neumann (1994) preferred to speak of psychological strata in Greek mythology that are loosely bound to historical events,[10] though classicist Davide Salvo (2020, October 6) is more convinced that Zeus-worshipping invaders displaced the Hera worship of Greece's original inhabitants. Barbara Creed (1993), whose research on the

---

[9] "If bringing together Jungian anima and the animus represents the overcoming of Titanism, then it is Prometheus, ironically, who embodies this reconciliation, a Greek Titan rather than Zeus the chief Olympian" (p. 76).

[10] Neumann (1994) acknowledges "fundamental conflicts triggered by the clash of the pre-Greek matriarchal mentality and the invading patriarchal Greek peoples" (p. 47). Likewise: "The patriarchal order is the precise inverse of the earlier matriarchal order in which the Feminine predominates" (p. 69).

monstrous feminine will be discussed further on, ascribes to Freud's (1953-1966) account regarding the history of matriarchy, which situates the Great Mothers at the side of their future patriarch-sons at the time of its decline, alleged to be "a compensation for the slight upon the mothers" (p. 24). Regardless of the lack of historical or anthropological evidence, in mythological perspective, we may glean from Mnemosyne's weight of the past and the infinite grief of Gaia and Rhea for their children the vestiges of a lost Titanic matriarchy, which is always guided by a greater concern for maternal rather than spousal obligations. The myths also set the roots of a way out of patriarchal oppression in stories of intergenerational rebellion. To this point, consider the passage from the Titans to the Olympians. Something pulls forward in the Titaness Themis who, like her son, successfully transitions from the Titanic to the Olympian Order. According to Jünger (1947/2006), "There is a difference between Gaia-Themis and the wife of Zeus. Gaia's suffering is great because she is a titaness lacking measure and center. Eternal suffering is titanic" (p. 50). Themis carries the weight of the seer's suffering, but the Zeus order empowers her with a yet unrealized executive role in the Olympian order. As a result, "her dignity is considerable as wife of the supreme god; even after separating from him she continues being his advisor and confidante. Like Zeus, she maintains balance, signifying supreme power" (p. 50). Rather than a displacement of her Titanic identity, Jünger viewed the Olympian transformation of Themis as a full maturation of her titanic nature.

Jünger (1947/2006, p. 30) also credits Rhea with a sense of stepping out of Titanism. Alluding to the protective lioness nature of Rhea, he asserts that "she is tired of the Titanic progression, she fills with nostalgia for maturity; she wants to be mature, above all, as a mother. She looks for her maturity in maternity, and for that, Zeus is put to the task" (p. 97). The Hymn of the Kouretes is an iconic visualization of this desire to transcend the rigidity of patriarchal Titanism, though one could say it lacks the full compensation fulfilled in the figure of Themis.

As we pass from Rhea, Zeus, and their entourage of shield-wielding warrior dancers to the skene of Aeschylus, we are presented with a proximal stage of matriarchal empowerment and progress through (Gaia-) Themis. Her phantom presence evokes the sublime feminine in Rowland's (2002) exploration of the nineteenth century Gothic literature, which haunts the masculine Logos of the Enlightenment, seeding a post-modern feminism: "The Gothic challenges the Enlightenment suppression of the other yet serves to restore existing norms by expelling the terrifying sublime by the end of the work" (p. 152). Additionally, the Gothic feminine sublime evinces "the nightmare of technology and its assault upon the modern self" (p. 152). The gothic feminine sublime is perhaps better suited to a forthcoming discussion of the monstrous feminine and the

Gaia aspect of the Great Mother. Likewise, the sublime ghost-like presence of Themis does not convey a sense of horror wherever she is invoked in myth and on stage. In any case, perhaps the sublime quality is driven by matriarchy's relegation to the periphery, behind the *skenes*, so to speak.

On the stage, we are presented with the protagonist, Prometheus, bound to a rock but supported by a diverse *thiasos* (entourage) that includes the Titan Okeanos and his Okeanids, two Olympians (Hephaestus and Hermes), and poor Io, wandering in her sojourn after incurring the wrath of Hera through no fault of her own, having been raped by Zeus. Unbeknownst to Zeus, however, Themis has passed along to her son the secret prophecy of a challenge to the Olympian ruler's reign at the hands of one of Io's progeny (Herakles). In this liminal space, we have all the clues regarding a potential reconciliation of epic proportions, as the characters are openly engaging in empathic dialogue in support of one who has stood up to the patriarchal order. I would argue that Themis has convened this agora and that her authority in the Zeus Order is significant albeit sublime. Harrison (1912/2010), commenting on how the religious flows from social currents, asserts that "a matriarchal society will worship a Mother and Son, a patriarchal society will tend to have a cult of the Father" (p. 28). While the Hymn of the Kouretes undeniably indexes the passage in Greek culture from matriarchy to patriarchy, the through line taken up by Aeschylus intricately blends matriarchal and patriarchal authorities. There is some prolepsis in his configuration: an emergent *coniunctio-manth* of the aforementioned orders similar to what has been suggested by Gier and Neumann. One of the locations of this blend is temporal, centered on the proper placement of the human subject in relation to the future.

Futurism vs. Ordinance

Where the future is concerned, Prometheus and Themis demonstrate distinct perspectives: Prometheus's futurism and the oracular ordinance of Themis; however, these stances need not be fixed to poles of opposition but rather in a more compensatory arrangement. Jünger (1946) traces the futurism-as-mechanical-utopia trope back to Thomas More: "The utopian tale demands an image capable of rational development and expansion, and the most serviceable image of this nature that can be found today is the machine" (p. 24). Jünger (1947/2006) also asserts that "the titanic feminine is imbued with a singular power of prediction. In Earth Mother Gaia this faculty is related to maternity, which is reflected in Uranus's sentence [to be overthrown by his children]" (p. 49). The latter orientation to the future has an air of grounded pronouncement. As "Prometheus" translates to forethought, there is the sense of something seen, not said.[11] In contrast, Themis fore*tells*; as one of the first deities worshipped at Delphi, she *speaks* the oracle.[12] According to Harrison's (1912/2010) interpretation of Aeschylus, Themis represents "the oracular power of Earth" (p. 30), and of her prominence at Delphi she notes:

> Within the [Delphic] temple is the tripod and seated on it is not any particular Pythia, but Themis herself, the spirit, the projection of the oracle. Gods might come and go, Gaia and Phoibe and Phoebus, but Themis…who is below and above all gods abides there seated. (p. 480)

In Greek mythology, there are layered arcs set along patriarchal vs. matriarchal timelines, but "high-born"[13] Themis, "who is the beginning and the end of councils"[14] above and below is held constant. For all the distinctions drawn in archetypal psychology exalting the arc of an alleged victory of Olympian civilization over an allegedly wild and chaotic Titanic psychology, time reveals that these lines are ultimately blurred and that the Titanic feminine plays a pivotal role in setting the blueprint for sociocultural advances in Greek culture. Contrary to López-Pedraza's (1990; 2000a) assertion regarding relative dearth of cults dedicated to the Titans, Harrison (1912/2010), pp. 480-481) notes several religious sites dedicated to Ge Themis and her Themides.

Themis, Ordinance, and Pandora's box

Regarding questions of orientation to prophecy, Harrison (1912/2010) draws a distinction between earlier and later connotations. In her assessment, Themis, as an extension of Gaia, is the personified "prophetic powers of the Earth" (p. 482), but the sense of prophecy is more akin to notions of utterance in the sense of *ordinance*, prediction as a form of pronouncement. Similarly, Jünger emphasizes that Themis "speaks the oracle," having inherited "the prophetic charge of the

---

[11] Jung (1911-12/1952/2014), through a complex philological web of associations, including a strand among German philologists suggesting a fire drill (*bohrer*) connection to Prometheus, arrives at a connection between foresight and the wily Titan: "The only thing that can be established with any certainty in this complicated situation is that we find thinking, precaution, or foresight somehow connected with fire-boring, without there being any demonstrable etymological connections between the words used for them. In considering the etymology, therefore, we have to take into account not only the migration of the root-words, but the autochthonous revival of certain primordial images" (para. 209).

[12] Harrison (1912/2010, p. 385) alludes to the Prologue of Aeschylus's Eumenides (1-8), which recognizes Gaia, Themis, and Phoebi as the first divinities worshipped at the Oracle of Delphi until the torch is passed to Phoebus-Apollo.

[13] An epithet from Homeric Hymn 5, card 75.

[14] Homer, *Odyssey*, 2, card 1.

word, its sacred and ominous power" (Jünger, 1947/2006, p. 49). Though any connection may be accidental, it is worth pointing out the potential Promethean connection between utterance and sacred fire in this excerpt from *Symbols of Transformation*.

> [T]he Brihadaranyaka Upanishad, the most important discovery ever made by primitive man, the discovery of fire, came out of the mouth. As we might expect, there are texts which draw a parallel between fire and speech. The Aitareya Upanishad says:
>
>> Then he drew forth a Person (purusha) from the waters and shaped him. He brooded upon him, and when he had brooded him forth, a mouth split open like an egg. From the mouth came speech, and from speech fire.37 [Cf. pl. XIIIb.]. (Jung, 1911-12/1952/2014, para. 229)

Likewise, Panikkar (1995) proclaims: "The spoken word is always more powerful than the written phrase" (p. 24). In contrast to the power of utterance, the Jesuit philosopher Walter Ong (1977) ascribes to the written word and its separation from the embodied word as a sort of death or "mortification" (p. 235). This matriarchal notion of utterance leads us back to the iconic notion of 'mother tongues' and a neglected arc in the trajectory of Western discourse that merits closer analysis.

Ong's (1977) "technological history of the word" traces the move in world languages from verbal to written form and its consequences for "men's and women's presence to the world and to themselves" (p. 17). Epistemologically speaking, Ong argues that this transition resulted in a schism between "knower and known" (p. 18), a detachment that paved the way for the growth of arts and sciences but also led to the current situation of personal and social alienation in the modern world. Accordingly, Ong maintains a fairly balanced stance, recognizing the "discomfort and promise" (p. 19) of the move from oralism to literacy. For Ong (1977), the continuity and connection constituted in the uttered word are inextricably tied to the mother tongue, "to our mother's feminine world" (p. 23), and he adds to this a related neo-Freudian blending of language as "tongue" with the primordial act of suckling from the mother's breast (p. 24). The iconicity of this maternal oralism, Ong asserts, was displaced by the rise of Learned Latin, and its related shift to the printed word. Suggesting a more paternalistic sense of literacy, he writes:

> Latin was distanced—alienated—not just from day-to-day life, for it was the substance of daily life for lawyers, physicians, academic educators, and clergymen, but from the psychological and psychosomatic roots of consciousness. It no longer in any sense belonged to the mother. It did not come from where you came from. (p. 28)

On a more global scale, Ong demonstrates generally how modern languages, including Arabic, Hebrew, and Mandarin, established written rules and standards that absorbed languages under Latin's regional influence while remaining largely orate. Still, the overall shift, for Ong, may be situated in a shift from mother tongues to the detached, presumably patriarchal world of the written word.

Like Prometheus, the visualized written word is distant, isolated; however, the lonely world of the One is not without its advantages. As Ong notes:

> Alienation, cleavage, is not all bad. To understand other things and themselves, to grow, human beings need not only proximity but also distance, even from themselves. Out of alienation, and only out of alienation, certain greater unities can come. (p. 47)

For Ong (1977), there is a very particular division of the senses between the patriarchal and matriarchal realms:

> Vision has a paramountcy among the senses corresponding to that of the male sky god in a pantheon. For father sky and mother earth as modes of knowing or coming to terms with the universe around us can be related in terms of the economy of the senses we have earlier described. Mother (earth) and father (sky) are related to one another as tactile to visual. Mother and earth are close to us, ground our sense of touch (which develops in contact with the mother), and deeply involved in subjectivity; father and sky are more remote, more object-like, apprehended more by sight than by touch which, when attesting to existence of objects attests to our own subjectivity at the same time—I feel myself feeling something other than me. (p. 143)

Karin Littau (2000), a Translation Studies scholar, offers an important feminist revision of patriarchal notions of language and translation, as well as a more complete examination of 'mother tongues,' one which offers unique perspectives of the One and the Many in the context of feminine utterance. In her article, "Pandora's tongues," she revisits two myths of critical importance to Translation Studies: the Old Testament tale of the tower of Babel, which centers on the Abrahamic God's retraction of the gift of language by creating a confusion of languages, as well as and the Greek myth of Pandora, whose name contains a polysemic paradox: she "speaks in (at least) two tongues" (p. 24): hope or ills, and pharmakon as remedy or poison. In tracing the origins of the Pandora mythologem, Littau points out that "following the non-Hesiodic tradition of the myth, Pandora is Gaia, Mother Earth, the first woman, and wife to Prometheus, who created her out of water and earth and brought her to life with fire" (p. 23). The Hesiodic strand, in contrast, allegedly focuses on a femme fatale characterization that revolves around the famous box, an alleged symbol of female sexuality, out of which all the troubles of humanity are unleashed.

Littau (2000) primarily draws from Jacques Derrida's (1985) discourse on translation, which challenges notions of a pure, unitary source language. In the discourse of the One and the Many, and with implications for Translation Studies, there is no "one" source language; it is foreign to itself (p. 25, citing Johnson, 1985, p. 146). Extending Johnson's point regarding the West's repression of anything foreign that might disrupt its "sameness," (p. 25), Littau suggests "we might extend this argument to include also the repression of that which is foreign to man, that which is other to man: woman" (p. 25). She invokes Irigaray's (1985a) notion of "hom(me)ology" (p. 134): all roads in the West lead back to the same (homo) and to the man (homme). Extended to translation, there is a related drive to conserve the "sameness" of the original text, protecting it from allegedly inevitable loss.

Seen from Pandora's perspective, Littau (2000) argues to the contrary: "an excess rather than a loss" (p. 26), with each translation enriching the fundamentally unrealized potential of the text of origin. This rhizomic (as opposed to reductive) "unfolding" affirms the fundamental polysemy of language. As she puts it,

> Pandora's name and her tongue —the mother tongue— is not so much divided from within but must already be seen as multiplied. The many translations of Pandora's name engender her many different tales, and illustrate not a lack at the source, but an excess which is played out with each and every rendition. (p. 27)

Revisioning the phallic focus of Freudian psychoanalysis, Littau (2000) frames the figure of Pandora from the perspective of female sex, as postulated by Irigaray (1977, pp. 64-65):

> The female sex should no longer be conceived as lack, as a wound, or a black hole or "dark continent," but as the embrace of "two lips" by two more, and two more again (the lips that speak and the vaginal lips that touch). (p. 28)

Archetypally speaking, the configuration depicted by Ong and Littau is analogous to the tension between the patriarchal binary of the One and the blended pluralities of the matriarchal Many; moreover, it highlights the primordial quality of matriarchal utterance (ordinance). Similarly, in the Vedic texts, we find the matriarch Urvashi, who both speaks and births the fire god Agni in the Yajna fire ceremony surrounding the mantha. In the philological foundations of pramantha, we may confirm these rich rhizomes and polysemic slippage of the Many recast by feminist postmodernists, which discerns an overarching coherence in the Babel of sticks and pricks, bores, and birth. If we were to visualize the cover art of this book as spoken or written discourse, we might imagine the complex, apparently fixed constellations of spheres transform into porous portals, a mantha into new meanings, wholes into holes.

We might also say that the mantha and the coniunctio are reflected in this linguistic excess, and the overall sense is one of production that contrasts with reductive strains of rationalism, which target the essential One. In revising the Lacanian and Derridean sense of *le dit*, what is spoken (or written) does not vaporize at the moment it is manifested; we might rather say that it is stirred into the organic admixture of the mantha-as-churn. Accordingly, the excess of the Many even extends to translations (transmutations) of the iconic poster boy for the One, the rebel individualist Prometheus; one name with many meanings, from "humanitarian hero" to "technological engineer," which owes its rich panoply of meanings to the multivocal Great Mother, of "one form" and "many names." [15]

In matters of the One and the Many, Littau (2000) accordingly embraces Irigaray's (1985b) multivocal sense of the feminine: "we were always already several at once" (p. 209, cited on p. 29). The resulting richness of the portrait sheds the sense of void and lack around Pandora and her box. As she retells the myth, "Pandora definitely exceeds the pharmakon, because the box lacks nothing" (p. 29). Turning the tables and speaking within Irigaray's (1985a) idiom of hom(me)ology, the retelling of the Pandora myth highlights the lacuna in Western patriarchy and its roots in psychoanalytic studies:

> Since patriarchal culture, a culture based on the homme, can only function if he is its model, and others are modelled on him, it necessarily has to reduce woman to the other of the same (homo/same = homme/ man); and rather than account for the difference of femininity, her sexuality is explained as nothing other than a mutilated copy of his. (p. 30)

Not surprisingly, hom(me)ology is characterized as thriving on the binary, essentially reducing all to the one and its other (Littau, 2000, p. 30, citing Irigaray, 1985a, p. 134), and Littau connects this procedure to traditional approaches to translation, which are based on assumptions of an immaculate, univocal original that "must be matched by its self-same translation" (p. 32). Rather than being reduced to the self-same One, the series of (re)translations that follow it are destined to subject it to the rhizomic accretions of the Many:

> Just as Irigaray demonstrates a morphology of woman's body and her speech and writing, the lips which are not one, too complex, or several,

---

[15] "though one form, she had many names" (*Prometheus Bound*, l. 211).

to be reducible to the one, what Pan-dora, her name exposes is a seriality, not just that there never was "one," but that there is always "one" more, and so on. (p. 32)

There is much more to be explored regarding matriarchal feminine perspectives of language and translation, and we will return to these threads in the context of the monstrous feminine and integrative approaches to psychology and pedagogy.

Themis, "wonderful counselor"

In addition to her association with language and foretelling (ordinance), Themis, the goddess of "civility and community" (Singer, 2010, p. 14), has vast powers of administration. To illustrate this executive function, she points to excerpts from Homer's *Iliad* (xx. 4-6; xv. 87-95) and *Odyssey* (II.68) that clearly delineates her charge in matters of convening and adjourning meetings. Zeus may be the Chairman of the Board, but Harrison (1912/2010) reminds us that he answers to Themis in matters of basic organizational operations. Harrison also reminds us that Themis also rules the *agora*, the iconic ancient Greek public meeting space, where everything is literally "out in the open," so we should be open to the possibility of her behind-the-scenes orchestration of the scene at the rock in *Prometheus Bound*.[16] Certainly, the agora precedent would have been common knowledge to any Athenean around the time the play was written. In answering the rhetorical question of why such a straightforward charge was not conferred on one of the existing Olympic heralds, namely Hermes or Iris, she asserts: "she [Themis] is the very spirit of the assembly incarnate" (p. 485).

As portrayed by Harrison (1912/2010), Themis's quality of ordinance is more proleptic than prophetic, rooted in the notion of Doom connoted in her name, one that extends a long arc, from the cultural to the divine. She explains:

> *Doom* is the thing set, fixed, settled; it begins in convention, the stress of public opinion; it ends in statutory judgment. Your private doom is your private opinion, but that is weak and ineffective. It is the collective doom, public opinion, that, for man's common convenience, crystallizes into Law. Themis like Doom begins on earth and ends in heaven. On

---

[16] Prometheus's own bad behavior may also account for his mother's absences. As Davidson (1949) points out, his intelligence that lacks the far-seeing wisdom of the matriarchal feminine. We may further draw a connection to Themis in Davison's assertion that the play establishes that Prometheus has not fully recognized his "*Adrasteia*" or judgment (l. 936, cited by Davison, 1949, p. 71). In short, she has not abandoned him; he has strayed from her.

earth we have our Doomsday, which projected into high heaven, becomes the Crack of Doom, the Last Judgment. (p. 483)

Creed (1993), writing in a Freudian-Lacanian vein, challenges the predominant feminine-masculine dichotomy that excludes "the possibility that the mother can be identified with the law" (p. 161), presumably in the sense of Jacques Lacan's phallic Symbolic, alleged to govern language and institutions. In the broadest sense, Themis literally translates to 'law' in Greek. Accordingly, Themis, herself, is constituted by the distillation of the jurisprudence of the ancient Greek social order. As evidence, Harrison points to worship of Themis "in the plural" (p. 483) as Themides at the altar of Trozen and the *themistes*, which denote "many dooms, many public opinions, many judgments" (p. 483) as consolidated into one divinity to represent the Greek *gemeinschaft*: Themis. This plurality, as we will see, sows the seeds of the Many.

As Themis passes from Greece to Rome, Ovid (1/1995-2009), offers a perspective of Themis that evokes a sublime sense of ordinance, proleptically proclaiming a path to salvation for her children, and it echoes Aeschylus's portrayal of Themis's counsel to Prometheus: 1) that he should side with the Olympians rather than the Titans in a war that would be won by wits rather than by brute force (*Prometheus Bound*, 206 ff), and 2) that he will be delivered by the progeny of Io (869 ff). While Prometheus's reputation as the savior of humanity, whose ruses saved us from succumbing to starvation (tricking Zeus out of the choice cuts of sacrifice) and cold (gift of fire), Ovid develops similar savior credentials for Themis in his account of the only survivors of a great flood that has all but vanquished humanity at the hands of Jupiter (the Roman equivalent of Zeus), Deucalion and Pyrrha (Bk I: 381-415). The despondent couple enter the temple of Themis and entreat her for some sign of hope. She responds with the following ordinance: "Leave my temple, veil your heads, loosen your robes, and cast behind you your great mother's bones." While this seems a rather dubious and disrespectful gesture, the couple complies, and the bones (stones) are transformed into men and women. While Ovid concludes from this tale, "Hence we are hard, we children of the earth, and in our lives of toil we prove our birth," an alternate, post-modern feminist interpretation would affirm a maternal sense of augury bourn of the timeless devotion and nurturance of a long line of mothers, a point that will be developed in greater depth later on in this chapter.

Prometheus's futurism, in contrast to Theman ordinance, carries the mechanical time of Kronos, without whose scythe, we would apparently still be somnambulant, adrift in Uranus's amorphous space.[17] As with Kronos, there is a repetitive aspect of Prometheus's labor, in this case a vulcanic sort of artisanship that Jünger associates with the Cyclopes. However, Jünger also concedes that, unlike Kronos, Prometheus carries the forward momentum of liberty and will.

Prometheus's futurism also carries the Christian monotheism that refashioned the wily Titan as a sort of Christ-like savior figure. This resonates, though not symmetrically, with Giegerich's (2007) commentary on the Old Testament Covenant, a milestone that marked a transition from an eternal present in Mythos, marked by pagan cyclical time, to a present characterized by pent-up anticipation of a "deferred ending: apocalypse" associated with the coming of the Messiah (p. 142), a tension he likens to "jet propulsion" (p. 144) for the linear move toward logical being-in-the-world. As noted by López-Pedraza (1990; 2000a), the Romantics further fueled a futurism around promises of revolutionary change. This overall pivot reminds us, to a certain extent, of Prometheus delivering Humanity from nature's cyclical shackles through the gift of fire; it also prefigures the jet propulsion of technological innovation and the move from present to screen time. Perhaps Prometheus also figures into Hillman's (1975) warnings against the "flight into futurism and its technologies" (p. 28).

In fashioning our orientations to the future, we should perhaps also draw a distinction between the sort of technology[18]- and patriarchal, power-driven futurism, on one hand, vs. the matriarchal oracular arc, which bends toward justice and the cross-generational, global good. Perhaps drawing from his political maneuvers behind the scenes in the Titanomachia, the dominant position in archetypal psychology casts Prometheus's futurism as a sort of opportunistic, crass gamesmanship, as an a-moral, psychopathic manipulator.[19] Arguably, as an innovator, Prometheus is more mimetic than creative, a point we will revisit later on. In any case, his orientation to the future is undeniably

---

[17] Jünger (2006/1947) and Giegerich (2007) point to the conflict between Uranus and Chronos as the splitting of space and time.

[18] Hillman (1975) distances archetypal psychology from "Flight into futurism and its technologies" (p. 28).

[19] Hillman (1989) connects the Titanic to an allegedly psychopathic education in manipulating others at work in the US; López-Pedraza (1990) characterizes Prometheus as mimetic, a quality he equates with psychopathy; points to Prometheus playing the saviour (p. 18) as a major source of modern-day Titanism.

tethered to issues of power and patricide, angling the cyclical rise and fall of patriarchs.[20]

Promethean futurism is also inextricably tied to theft. To this point, Kerényi (1997) draws some intriguing comparisons with Hermes. Hermes, like Prometheus, is also a thief, with one crucial difference: the humble herald of Mt. Olympus created the craft of making fire, not the fire itself, suggesting a creative faculty, though he acknowledges some text fragments suggesting that Prometheus taught the humans how to use fire in craftwork. Ultimately, however, as the author puts it, Hermes' theft "springs from a creative art, which enriches the divinity of the world with playful magic" (p. 46). In contrast, he alleges: "Prometheus…was a cheat and a thief" (p. xxii). For Jünger (1946), Prometheus's theft constitutes a sacrilegious pilfering of the sacred sun-fire:

> Without sun-fire life is unthinkable. The wrath of the gods, then, cannot have been provoked by the fact that Prometheus had tried to bring this fire to man as a life-giving element, for as a life-giving element the sun had always come to man; there was no need to steal it. No! The wrath of the gods was provoked by something different, namely, by the enslavement of the sacred fire which Prometheus dared to perpetrate. This was an act of desecration, a most dangerous undertaking. (p. 289)

Likewise, Jung (1911-12/1952/2014) notes that "In many myths fire-making is something forbidden, a criminal act of usurpation which can only be accomplished by cunning or violence, but mostly by cunning," and incorrect use of fire, Jung alleges, met with "severe penalties" in early Hinduism (para. 248).[21]

---

[20] In relishing the eventual fall of Zeus, Prometheus states: "immediately the curse his father Kronos invoked as he fell from his ancient throne, shall be fulfilled to the uttermost" (*Prometheus Bound*, 907 ff).

[21] Jung, as is typical of the eighteenth century German mythological and philological scholars, sustains a connection between Prometheus to Vedic traditions through the trope of stealing *from* the gods; however, in matters of etymology, Narten (1960) deems the various meanings of "ma(n)th-" insufficient to account for the myth of Mātariśvan's bringing the fire from the gods for the benefit of mankind (p. 127). With respect to the mythological roots, neither is there a convincing case for a one-to-one mythological connection between Prometheus and Mātariśvan. Kuiper (1971), in investigating the alleged connection between the Vedic Mātariśvan and the Greek Prometheus, demonstrates how this initially attenuated match sketched by Rudolph Roth (1855) was upheld, unhedged, by Adalbert Kuhn (1859/2015). He notes an additional complicating factor centering on blurring between Mātariśvan and the fire deity Agni (Confirmed by Abraham, 2013). Adding additional layers of complexity to any potential parallels, Kuiper alludes to I.93.6 of the Rigveda, highlighting Mātariśvan's "fetching" of Agni and an eagle

That said, the theft of fire, as well as the ruse through which Prometheus tricks Zeus into ceding the lion's share of animal sacrifice to Humanity, are generally regarded as virtuous acts of defiance on our behalf that are ascribed a sort of savior status, lifting us out of a hapless, vulnerable stance in Nature (Kerényi, 1997). López-Pedraza (2000a; 2000b; 2002), however, sees these acts as part of the wily Titan's pathology, which is allegedly rooted in an inability to stay within the healthy boundaries of the present: an unhealthy futurism drives his self-righteous idealism and general ego-inflation. Regarding Prometheus's egotism, the dialogue between Prometheus and Hermes in *Prometheus Bound* presents us with an archetypal opposition between Promethean hubris and Hermetic humility, as Prometheus scoffs: "Better no doubt to be slave to a rock than be the Father's trusted herald" (Aeschylus, 1961, p. 94). It is not without a large measure of prideful projection that the Titan casts Hermes in a puer light, writing him off as "childish" and "foolish" (p. 50), in light of his own issues with boundaries.[22] Still, spiraling back to the theft question, I would argue that there is hidden wisdom in his defiance of the patriarch. Contrary to depictions of Prometheus as a player in patriarchal clashes, he may instead represent a blended figure in this frame, stealing not from the Great Mother—a trite trope in the hero's journey— but rather from the Great Father, thwarting the repetitive senectitude of the paranoid patriarch who perceives the sharing of consciousness as a threat to his control. Subjecting these portraits to the *mantha*, it may even be the case that Prometheus's futurism and theft were informed by matriarchal ordinance.

(śyena) that steals Soma, a divine elixir, from "the rock" (p. 86). An alternate account has Agni and Soma being born to the Asura Vrta as a necessary precursor to Indra's defeat of this primordial dragon (Cf. TS. II. 5.2.2-3). Consequently, there is no "theft" from the gods for the benefit of mankind; Soma and Agni's acts of procurement were carried out "for Indra and the Devas" (p. 90). Furthermore, Kuiper argues that Agni's trajectory is far from a simple migration from 'high heaven' (i.e., Olympus) to the earth: "He (Agni) is said to have been brought 'from heaven,' 'from afar,' from 'the womb of the waters,' or have freed himself 'from darkness' (p. 93). Indeed, according to the Rigveda "heaven and earth were not yet separated" (p. 94). Concretely, then, Mātariśvan is not cut from the rogue rebel cloth of his alleged Greek counterpart (Prometheus): "nowhere in the Rigveda is Mātariśvan said to be an enemy of the gods. He rather cooperates with them to fetch the fire for men" (p. 95, citing X.46.9dc from the Rigveda). Though "theft," in the most abstract sense, does hold for both, Mātariśvan's act of theft is ultimately directed by (citing Narten, 1960, p. 133) and for (Kuiper's translation of III.9.5cd) the gods. According to Narten (1960, p. 127), the Sanskrit *mātarisvan* connotes theft in the sense of wind-as-robber.

[22] Though he does not make the explicit connection the puer archetype, Davison (1949) highlights Prometheus's juvenile aspect, noting Okeanos's description off him as a "new-yoked colt" (l. 1048).

In weighing Promethean prophecy, the overall picture is mixed as we consider his associations with technological progress. Gier (2000) underscores the dark, dystopian prescience of Prometheus's factory of humanity: Prometheus's kiln as forerunner of smoke-belching factories, though he acknowledges the strand of the Greek account taken up by Goethe in which Athene collaborates with Prometheus in the creation of Man. According to this mythological strand, Prometheus just fashions the shell; Athene breathes life into it. Karl Kerényi (1978), however, sustained that Athene is perhaps the archetype *par excellence* of the patriarchal Zeus order. Consequently, this could all arguably fit neatly into the patriarchal arc, and it is far from clear that such projects meet with the blessing of the Great Mother.

In assessing whether Prometheus is the Titan of plutocratic and patriarchal futurism, on one hand, or matriarchal feminine ordinance on the other, we are reminded that Prometheus draws his gifts from his Titaness mother, Gaia or Themis, depending on the account. As the following extracts from *Prometheus Bound* suggest, the line between one and the other is a bit blurred:

> My mother, Themis (Divine Law), or Gaia (Earth), one person, though of various names, had many times foretold to me, that not brute strength, not violence, but cunning must give victory to the rulers of the future. This I explained to them, with reasons--which they found not worth one moment's heed. Then, of the courses open to me, it seemed best to take my stand--my mother with me--at the side of Zeus, willing and welcome. It was I who gave that counsel through which ancient Kronos and his crew lie buried now in the back abyss of Tartaros. (Prometheus, addressing Okeanides, *Prometheus Bound*, 204ff)
>
> O Earth, my holy mother,
>
> O sky, where sun and moon
>
> Give light to all in turn
>
> You see how I am wronged! (Aeschylus, 1961, p. 52).

The plurality of Gaia-Themis to which Prometheus alludes resonates somewhat with López-Pedraza's characterization of the Titans as undifferentiated beings. According to Harrison (1912/2010), Themis, as well as her daughter Dike, mark the genesis of the social order, when it was still fused with the religious realm, adding to it a note of the "social and collective" (p. 28). While Dike governs human justice, Themis, as we have already established, represents the longer arc of divine law, and Aeschylus reminds us that her name translates exactly to that phrase: divine law. As portrayed by Hesiod, Themis is the honorable counselor and wife to Zeus, critical to the triumph of Zeus and the Olympic order. Pindar and Homer, likewise, set her at the top of Zeus's regime. While the

Gaia (Earth) nature of the Great Mother is well-known, it represents only half of the equation, a continuum of primordial matriarchies known as the Moira, whereas Themis represents an "evolution" from the natural to a social order. Henderson (2005), working within a Jungian framework, speaks of this Moira-to-Themis archetypal continuum: "Moira, representing a sanctity older than the gods, signifies social order as a Way of Nature, while Themis, representing behavior dictated by social conscience, signifies the Way of Civilized Man" (p. 210). The ascription of Themis to 'Civilized Man' suggests Themis as a tool of father-right; as will be made clear further on, this depiction fails to capture her rootedness in the matriarchal feminine.

In the staging of *Prometheus Bound*, Aeschylus presents us with a sublime mantha that deftly stirs together all these significations and the result is that Gaia-Themis is depicted not as a binary but as a premium blend of the Many of the matriarchal feminine.[23] In modern Western culture, just as we are accustomed to seeing statues of Prometheus holding the divine fire of knowledge and innovation, Themis's image is ubiquitous in the legal system, blindfolded, holding up the scales of justice in one hand and the sword in the other in a posture meant to evoke impartial judgment. Also, like Prometheus — and unlike her counterpart Athene— she is instrumental in bringing Zeus to power, but she is not just an unwitting tool of the patriarch; both Themis and Prometheus are the keeper of the prophecy that foretell the end of Zeus's reign, thus illuminating a titanic feminine check on the Zeus-order. In particular, it highlights a prophetic art and arc that is not limited to the cycles of plutocratic paranoia, a chain of tyrannical, devouring patriarchs, from Uranus to Kronos to Zeus. There is something more sublime than protecting one's power base that drives this prophetic mantha of Theman ordinance and Promethean vision, and arguably it is exactly what differentiates foresight from futurism, conceptualized in a mythological sense, or in the sense of modern political and economic Titanism.

In appraising the relative value of foretelling vs. foresight, we find an unexpected connection between the Great Mother and post-modern feminist critique. In the work of Julia Kristeva (1986), Rowland (2002) finds a more grounded form of augury in the maternal feminine, which seems appropriate to apply to Themis, and it resonates with Jünger's (1947/2006) portrayal of the titanic feminine: "mothering allows her to think of psychically evolving subjectivity as *prospective* (like Jung's). Women desire to have children *in the future* and imagine a future for them" (p. 122). On the surface, Prometheus, almost smugly, derives confidence from his foreknowledge; he, and arguably

---

[23] As Kerényi (1997) puts it, Gaia-Themis is: "Earth whose form is one, whose name is many" (p. 100).

Aeschylus himself, is perhaps oblivious to the larger, maternal container that sustains this sense of security. To this point, it is worth penetrating deeper into the clichéd expression "cradle of civilization" in light of the Hymn of the Kouretes. Shall we credit Rhea? As Aeschylus points out, the lines between Greek matriarchies are a bit blurred, and there is something of the Many in this. In any case, it suggests exactly this sort of nurturing matriarchal ordinance that makes cultural being possible and grounds it in communal connection.[24]

Themis, the post-modern feminist Many compensating the Western One

The titanic matriarchal principle of connectedness and plurality constituted in the Many inverts the patriarchal epistemology of logical negation into the One: for every analytical reduction, there exists a complimentary synthesis, informed by the jurisprudence of the *themistes*. As Kerényi (1997) reminds us, alluding to Aeschylus, Gaia-Themis is: "Earth whose form is one, whose name is *many*" (p. 100). Perhaps, then, we should reconsider López-Pedraza's characterization of the Titans as undifferentiated, at least with regard to the Titanesses, and Greco-Roman femininities, in general. Concretely, to call them undifferentiated negates a sense of sublime plurality constituted in the Many. It is precisely this plurality that contrasts most sharply with patriarchal binaries. Gaia-Themis, at her core, embodies a sense of continuity between nature (Gaia) and culture (Themis), a stance that is upheld in transdisciplinary studies. As Nicolescu (1994) argues, "The opposition between nature and culture is absurd. For nature, the womb of all wombs, engenders culture. Without nature, culture is merely a forlorn word that deserves to die" (p. 128).

In matters of feminine plurality in Greco-Roman mythology, it is worth highlighting the many groupings of feminine figures, most often in threes: in addition to the Moirae continuum, there are Themis's three disciples, the Themeides as well as her daughters, the twelve Horae (Hours) and three Moirae[25] (Fates). Harrison (1912/2010) notes the blending of Luna, Themis, and the Inacchian cow in III. 657 of Ovid's *Fasti* and *Metamorphoses*. We could also add the triumvirate of Aphrodite, Hera, and Athene whose competition over the Golden Apple drives the plot of *The Iliad* (Homer, 800 BCE/1995-2009) and Hades' abduction of Persephone also triggers the triad of Demeter-Kore-

---

[24] Harrison (1912) (in Henderson, 2005) uncovered the "Hymn of the Kouretes" on Crete, which ascribes Rhea to this account; however, what separates Gaia from Rhea and Themis is often blurred.

[25] According to Neumann (2015/1955) the moirae are "associated with three dimensions: birth and beginnings, marriage, and death and ends" (p. 231); it is not clear that there is a one-to-one correspondence between Neuman's Moirae and Henderson's (2005) Moira, though the notions are clearly illustrative of the Greek matriarchal Many.

Hecate. It is worth noting that Hecate, herself, is constituted triadically. According to Jünger (1947/2006), Hecate, who is revered by Zeus, rules over earth, sky, and sea. He also alludes to a frieze in Pergamon that depicts her with three heads and three pairs of hands (p. 45). Marlan (2021), speaking to a potential Hecatean third, comments:

> Perhaps the cool eye of Hecate's perspective, familiar with the underworld, knows more. Trained in the logical life of the soul, she can see beyond the mother complex, beyond life and love, and has a calm wisdom that exceeds what Hillman derisively calls the 'flap of Persephone' (citing Hillman, 1979)" (p. 185).

As Littau, Kristeva, and Irigaray have suggested, the feminine is always at home in subjectivit*ies* (plural emphasized).

Choreographing her Kouretes and support cast of *Prometheus Bound* around the analytical reduction, Gaia-Themis spins a multifaceted cultural complex, a cultural *myth*, borne of ordinance and pronounced in an agora. As with any myth, there is all of the potential for identity affirmation and entropy, emancipatory change and mass hysteria. As caretaker of the cultural Many, Themis may be empirically absent, but, to borrow from Rowland, the ghost of her feminine Otherness is arguably everywhere in *Prometheus Bound*, orchestrating the circle of support for her son, while maintaining the 30,000-altitude view of emergent social and cosmological change.

As we open a discussion of a dialogic *Many*, inspired by a Titaness and infused with post-modern pluralism, it should not be conceived in binary opposition to the One: Themis is, as previously mentioned, the distillation of many themistes. Furthermore, if we accept Prometheus, that wily nonconformist, as that One, his singularity is a healthy extension of the Many, much in the same way any dynamic system would stagnate and decay without a strange attractor in the periphery, scouting out new ways to adapt and revitalize, a pattern that has been empirically verified in both natural and cultural contexts of change.[26] In Teilhard de Chardin's (1959/2008) approach to evolution, this is construed as a sort of dance between radial and tangential forces in evolution. In social psychological terms, a similar connection might be drawn between needs for autonomy and homonomy; as Teilhard de Chardin sustains, we, like all organisms and ecosystems, are driven by tangential and radial forces. Henderson (1984) depicts the dangers of going to extremes thusly: "If one becomes too individualistic, the effect is psychic inflation and isolation from one's fellow man. If one lives too collectively, one becomes uncomfortably deflated and

---

[26] See Warford (2017) for a full discussion of dynamic systems theory in the context of innovation diffusion and educational change.

subtly depressed" (p. 23). Harrison (1912/2010) situates a period in ancient Greece precisely in this crucible, a move from religious experience as "spiritual and individual" to a more "social and collective" (p. 28) variety, with the latter being constellated around Themis, though the misanthropic presence of Prometheus is also arguably situated here as well. In the last chapter we will explore this interplay of the One and the Many in the context of innovation and creativity.

In philosophical terms, the classic Cartesian stance or, for that matter, Husserl's Self-Other dialectic, fail to fully meet the Many on its own terms, relegating it as an extension of the cogito-subject. In a way that conjures the patriarchal paranoia of Uranus, Kronos, and Zeus, Levinas (1972/2006) leads us to question the West's Self-Same panic in its encounters with the totality of the colonized Other. That said, his discourse on the Other likewise does not satisfy this notion of a dialogue between the One and the Many. Instead, it simply runs out to the "Other" extreme and this Many does not necessarily engulf the self-same subject like a devouring mother; neither the Moira nor the Gaia-Themis mythologems fit this mold. This Many is not necessarily the soul-crushing collective of Mother Russia, such as the Bollingen stone craft alluded to earlier, or, for that matter, any manner of matriarchal monotheism. Neither, for that matter, does the One necessarily entail a sort of fascistic Vaderland.

The origins of the One trace back to the rise of hero narratives in Greek religion. Harrison (1912/2010) asserts that "Homer's conception of the hero as the gallant individual, the soldier of fortune or the gentleman of property, is secondary and late" (p. 335). This Homeric individualism, according to the author, crystallizes in the trope of man slayings (*androktasiai*), the one-on-one showdowns that predominate in the *Iliad*. At their source, however, they are merely recasts of tribal conflicts (p. 335). Tribal conflicts loosened the association with daimon cults associated with tribal conflicts and were altered in such a way that "local daimons, eponymous heroes and the like become individualized Saga-heroes" (p. 335). One might argue, then, that the Cartesian One of "cogito ergo sum" might not have been possible, if not for Achilles. To the contrary, Freud (1939/1967) points to erosion of Homeric heroism: "The bravest heroic deeds of our days are no longer able to inspire an epic; Alexander the Great himself had grounds for his complaint that he would have no Homer to celebrate his life" (p. 89).

In any case, the binary One that drives the Western male ego belongs to the dialectic; no mantha is possible in the dialectic as everything on the other side of the polarity is ingested through logical negation into the One. Giegerich's (1999) sense of the One as a Hegelian distillation of the soul fits well with patriarchal monotheism. According to Giegerich, male and female, as constituents of a syzygy, are reduced to the notion of a "unity of unity and difference… [in which] the soul tautologically speaks about itself, its own (selfsame) nature" (p. 208). A core aspect of this notion centers on breaking out of the *unio naturales*, a trajectory centered on the subjugation and desecration of the Great Mother, indigenous peoples, and for that matter, the glue of Mythos. Giegerich further argues that these have all been *seen through*, logically subsumed under the move into (techno)logic; from a post-modern feminist stance, the epistemology is more rhizomic than reductive, though a mantha-coniunctio of the One and the Many necessarily should be open to both. As Panikkar (1995) reminds us: "Myth represents the most powerful of forces that guide human footsteps—and at the same time the weakest, indeed the most false, thing in human existence" (p. 3). In the following section, we will explore this dynamic as constellated through Prometheus and Themis.

The Fate of Foresight and Imagination in Titanic Times

In navigating between opportunistic futurism and ordinance, it is worth considering the fate of the image in the Age of Titanism. This century began with what has come to be regarded as a "failure of imagination," a phrase that originally was ascribed to the lack of foresight regarding the 9-11 attacks, arguably a Titanic vacuity that met with Titanic excess; the same phrase and dynamic re-emerged in the January 6th storming of the Capitol.[27] Both Hillman and López-Pedraza warned us *to stick to the image*, and the latter was unequivocal in distinguishing the imaginal richness of the polytheistic Olympic Order with the *carencias* of the same in titanism, psychopathy (2000a), and monotheism (2000b). Working from the opposite angle, Giegerich's (2007) stance, as previously mentioned, centers on seeing *through* the image. The core of his dialectical path depends on monotheism in its various manifestations (religious, scientific, technological) as instrumental in the sublation of the personalistic, imaginal (illusory) stance of Mythos to more logical being-in-the-world. His critique is compelling, pointing out, for example, that technology and monetization have hastened the erosion of the image, reducing it to a statement of pure *prestige* (my image): the immaculate "selfie." The advent of the 'deep fake' in digital imaging adds further weight to Giegerich's argument.

---

[27] Source for 9-11: National Commission on Terrorist Attacks Upon the United States (2004). The 9-11 Commission Report: Executive Summary. Retrieved on 3/2/21 from https://govinfo.library.unt.edu/911/report/911Report_Exec.htm; Source for 9/6 event: MSNBC. (2021, January 6). [video]. Wallace: 'Brainwashed Americans' pose domestic terror threat in 'staggering failure' to predict riots. Retrieved on 3/2/21 from https://www.msn.com/en-us/news/us/wallace-brainwashed-americans-pose-domestic-terror-threat-in-staggering-failure-to-predict-riots/vp-BB1cx6jD

Perhaps somewhere between these binary stances there is room to consider the image and the word as renewable resources, and it is likely this more dynamic perspective that is exactly what is needed in order to transcend the short-selling near-sightedness of futurism. Ironically, if the West looks to a blindfolded Titaness whose presence has been relegated to the ethers of the gothic feminine for guidance, foresight is not the way as hers is the way of oracular fore*telling*. Accordingly, perhaps we need to shift our focus from the eroded image to the regenerative power of language? Moving from allegory to post-modern feminist criticism, what we are trying to manifest is that pre-Oedipal maternal imaginary highlighted by Rowland (2002), which organically infuses language with proleptic meanings to be realized by future generations. This sort of imaginal and linguistic renewal expedition finds its perfect scout in Prometheus.

While we ponder that point, Prometheus has yet to tend to his bride. Pandora has opened the box. All the chaos is out; this is plain to see in any news headline, and one might argue that Faith and Hope remain trapped inside. Bound to that rock in the Caucasus Mountains, on the margin of East and West and only marginally cognizant of the complexities of connectedness, Prometheus pines for his mother. As Freud allegorized Oedipus, it is not unreasonable to speculate that each of us moderns, in our individuation journeys, enact the same narrative of this traumatized Prometheus. On a more sublime level of this trope, we see that there is a complex interplay of the individuation journey with the need for communion with the collective. To this point, Hillman's revision of Jung's psychology anchors 'self-creation' or 'soul-making' to correspond to the cultural domain, which I would argue is archetypally rooted in the figure of Themis and the more connected ways of knowing to which she points.

Concluding thoughts

I have presented in this chapter the case that there is value in raising and reexamining the Titanic. Furthermore, I would suggest that the Theman-Promethean archetypal strata remind us that the greater arc is not the passage from polytheism to monotheism in the Western psyche but rather the greater struggle with patriarchy in politics, arts, and letters. This arc stretches back to the hyper-masculine Kabeiroi, and we should not lose sight of the relevance of this mythologem in light of toxic masculinity and the epidemic of mass shootings committed by men, most of them of a younger age, and highly susceptible to Titanism.[28] Still, the arc of the feminine creation and foresight is as old as the planet, and it may be argued that a commensurate Titanism in the matriarchal feminine has served to compensate the excesses of patriarchy that pervade the rise of Western hegemony: the resistance of the women of Lemnos, Gothic horror, the rise of feminist and post-colonial criticism, the Me Too movement, and similar movements bear out this archetypal trendline.

We should also bear in mind that the Titanic feminine was instrumental in the rise of the Zeus Order, as iconically captured in the image of Rhea's Daimons dancing around the baby Zeus, Singer's ground zero for the Cultural Complex, or in the instrumental role Themis plays in helping Zeus win the Titanomachia. History shows how wagons of the Many have often corralled and subdued the strongman One; the Many have likewise subsumed themselves into the One's hecaterian cult of personality. In any case, the complex valence of the One and the Many is ready to shed its gendered shell. A closer examination of the tales, trials, and trails of Gaia-Themis and Prometheus ultimately reveal an anthropomorphic through line that transcends the primordial gender binary. Rather than limiting ourselves to the outdated discourse of feminine this or masculine that, by dint of the coniunctio and mantha, more connected ways of knowing are accessible to all regardless of biological gender, a dynamic interplay, respectively, of tangential and radial forces that are manifested both on intra- and inter-psychological planes. Prometheus and Themis remind us that there is a time to branch off and a time to come together, a lesson many of us have yet to master in managing cognition and culture, Self and Other, the One and the Many.

---

[28] "If men vastly outnumber women as mass shooters, those perpetrators are often a model for the next male shooters, who 'see themselves in them,' Peterson said, a phenomenon that she noted is particularly true among young, white men. Violence Project data show that white men are disproportionately responsible for mass shootings more than any other group." Source: Martin, M., & Bowman, E. (2021, March 27). Why nearly all mass shooters are men. National Public Radio. NPR.org. Retrieved on 3/28/2021 from https://www.npr.org/2021/03/27/981803154/why-nearly-all-mass-shooters-are-men

Chapter 3
Demonstrative Monsters

In addition to a deeper understanding of Titans and Titanism, a cultural turn after Jung necessarily leads back to Greco-Roman monsters and the Monstrous. Accordingly, we turn from the Titaness Themis to her monstrous half, Gaia, as well as from the narrative frame of the Titanomachia to the Gigantomachia. Given the holistic plurality of the Great Mother, it is impossible to extricate one from the other; it is exactly this sort of splitting of the matriarchal that she has undergone across the patriarchal arc that needs to be compensated. Likewise, the monstrous furnishes a sort of funhouse mirror to the patriarchy that de*monstr*ates its distorted Othering on many planes, gender, and culture in particular. What is the Other, if not a monster? Is there such a thing as Othering that is not monstrous? Wherever the patriarchy has imposed its One, the monstrous, intricately woven into the feminine, posits pluralities of the Many. In fact, in matters of the cultural turn and confronting cultural complexes and traumas, the monstrous is the perfect mantha to lift the West's many veiled binaries.

Greco-Roman origins of the monstrous

In Section 10 of *De Curiosite*, The Greek philosopher Plutarch denounces the sort of trivial inquisitiveness of the *busybody*, referencing the *terata agora* or "monster market." Whether the disabled victims of these carnivalesque scenes were paraded for perverse entertainment or actually sold into slavery is not clear (Felton, 2012), but we do know that the monstrous was more than just a minor preoccupation for the ancient Greeks, starting with Hesiod's references to 'Monstrous Gaia' or to Echidna, 'Mother of Monsters.' The feminine association with the monstrous was an aspect of daily life in ancient Greece, and *Teras* persists today in medical textbooks as the root word for the study of birth defects: *terato*logy. The Gigantes, Gaia's monstrous children, likewise are part of this etymological inheritance. In the Age of Technology, we measure data in both *tera*bytes and *giga*bytes.[1]

Having established the patriarchal tendency to associate the Great Mother with earthly materia (matter), the connection takes on a teratological turn for the ancient Romans, for whom *monstrum* connotes a 'divine omen (with

---

[1] See source consulted https://mashedradish.com/tag/teras

negative connotations) or abomination and the more familiar etymological branch of *monere* (teach, warn) or *demonstrare* (as in de*monstr*ate).[2] Lefkowitz and Fant (2005), for example, reference Pliny the Elder, who marvels with horror at the dark magic and "monstrous power of menses" (#451, citing Pliny, *Natural History*, 28.23, Excerpt L).

As a forerunner (and arguably driver) of cultural complexes and trauma, the monstrous reaches far back into the ancestral level of the psyche, representing the earliest initial stages of archetypology, with hybridities that often blend in something of the feminine. To this point, consider Neumann's (1955/2015) commentary:

> In the early phase of consciousness, the numinosity of the archetype consequently exceeds man's power of representation, so much so that at first no form can be given to it. And when later the primordial archetype takes form in the imagination of man, its representations are often monstrous and inhuman. This is the phase of the chimerical creatures composed of different animals or of animal and man—the griffins, sphinxes, harpies, for example—and also of such monstrosities as phallic and bearded mothers. (p. 13).

This hybrid aspect will be explored in more depth later in the chapter. For now, it suffices to recognize hybridity as a fundamental feature of the monstrous.

As has already been established, the monstrous points back to Hesiod's epithet 'Monstrous Gaia.' Uranus, by some accounts, is so disgusted by Gaia's monstrous offspring that he shoves them back into the cavity from which they were birthed by the Earth Mother. Nevertheless, according to Jünger (1947/2006) Gaia is the first deity to attract a cult following among the Greeks, often depicted as a sad and suffering mother who has weathered two wars among her children: The Titanomachia between the Titans and the Gods, and the Gigantomachia, between the Gods and Monsters. Like her daughter, Rhea, she demonstrates a greater concern for her children than her spouse (Uranus). In addition to this key feature of matriarchal Titanism, Jünger further underscores her favoritism toward her Titans and Monsters (against the Olympians), both groups succumbing to Zeus's authority in their corresponding wars. In this sense, Gaia's suffering is double.

---

[2] See sources consulted www.etymonline.com/word/monster; https://www.cam.ac.uk/research/discussion/what-is-a-monster; https://en.wikipedia.org/wiki/Monster#Etymology

The Gigantomachia

Like the Titans, the Gigantes are depicted as the haughty Tartarus-bound progeny of Gaia, yet they are mortal and allegedly bear no traces of Uranus's paternity (Jünger, 1947/2006), which suggest a predominant matriarchal association, though Jünger reminds us that Zeus cultivates the alliance of the Cyclopes and Hekatoncheires in his war with the Titans. Sharing a vulcanic association with the Kabeiroi and Dactyls, their temperament is alleged to be wild and savage. Neumann (1994) also connects the Titans and Gigantes through a common tendency toward hybrid-animal forms:[3] "We recognize the figure of the man with snake's body, for example, in the Greek myth of the Titans and Giants, the lower part of whose bodies were depicted as earth serpents" (p. 60). Though they are rather ambiguous and nameless, Jünger points out several Gigantes who make important appearances in the myths, including Alcioneus and Porphyirion, who are thwarted by Zeus and Herakles in their attempt to rape Hera.

Considered the aggressors in the Gigantomachia with the Olympic gods, the Gigantes, according to Gaia's oracle, cannot be killed by the gods, making Herakles a key confederate. Jünger (1947/2006) describes how, in faithful service to the Zeus Order, Herakles strives to eradicate the "chthonic monstrosity and excess" of the Gigantes and restore "limits and moderation" (p. 67). According to Jünger, "the gigantesque is not only a threat to mortal man but also a temptation to exceed limits…an aspiration to the colossal" (p. 71). Among the matchups, Apollo battles Python and Zeus contends with the greatest of Gigantes, the fire-breathing, many-headed Typhon-Teras. In the Homeric accounts, Typhon is depicted as Hera's "most monstrous offspring" (Stein, 2020, p. 69, citing Hymn to Apollo II. 351-2), whose very existence compensates the insult to "her essential telos" (p. 69) constituted in the birth of Athene from her husband's head: the right to motherhood.

Jünger (1947/2006) posits that, in comparison with the Titanomachia, "the opposition between the gods and Gigantes was more fruitful for Greek art" (p. 72), yielding renderings in which "the impious are rocked, annihilated, cowering under islands and mountains, as if the watchful eye were checking to make sure they will never reemerge" (p. 73). As we will see, patriarchy thrives on this tension between what is embraced and discarded as monstrous in the social order.

---

[3] This matches Oxford English Dictionary's first meaning of monster: "A. n. 1. a. Originally: a mythical creature which is part animal and part human, or combines elements of two or more animal forms, and is frequently of great size and ferocious appearance." See https://www.oed.com/viewdictionaryentry/Entry/121738.

Patriarchy and the monstrous feminine from poly- to monotheism

It bears repeating that the longer arc of interest in blending the binary is not so much the passage from Titan to Olympian, but rather the steady creep of patriarchy in the emergence of Western archetypology. On a related note, the patriarchal lens highlights flaws in archetypal psychology's assumptions about the Titanic vs. the Olympian. Let us start with the obvious fact that patriarchy is edified in the Zeus Order. If we stick to the myths, Gaia and Rhea's successful attempts to overthrow Titan patriarchs (Uranus and Kronos, respectively) ultimately come up short; the vulnerable Jupiter Puer shielded by the Daimones has grown into the patriarch that will be edified not only in Greek religion but in the deep structure of Western culture.

Nevertheless, beyond the myths, we lack a concrete historical context for the rise of the Greek patriarchal order. In anthropology, the jury is out regarding an originating matriarchal order that was displaced by patriarchy. Still, there was an undeniable effort to subvert the matriarchal feminine, as evidenced in efforts to promote Father Right and Father Birth and to cast women as inferior and monstrous. Setting aside historical and anthropological skepticism, praise for Zeus as the great polytheistic patriarch abounds in archetypal psychology, as previously noted. López-Pedraza (1990; 2000a) heralds him as the father of culture. Stein (2020), working from a more classic Jungian perspective, comments: "Under Zeus, consciousness is flexible enough to integrate all but the truly revolutionary ideas and futures. Emerging is the Greek ideal of exercising creativity within a framework of balanced order and harmony" (p. 12). Jünger (1947/2006), indirectly tied to archetypal psychology through his influence on López-Pedraza, lauds the Olympic patriarch's skills in maintaining equilibrium, declaring "Above him there is no one who merits greater respect" (p. 115).

In the shift from poly- to monotheism, patriarchy in all of its misogyny gathers momentum, laying foundations for a modern monstrous feminine. Neumann (1994) notes concerted attempts in Abrahamic religions to "'recognize' the Feminine and women as evil" (p. 39), with a similar tendency noted in Hinduism. Neumann also identifies the binaries that would fuel patriarchal monotheism's rise,[4] including a core polarity that developed in Abrahamic monotheism, which situated a higher, masculine Heaven set over an earthy, feminine "fallen" state that must be cast off (pp. 169-170).[5] Neumann captures

---

[4] "The patriarchally reinforced opposition of Masculine and Feminine, day and night, consciousness and unconsciousness" (p. 43).

[5] In Christianity, this binary reaches its height in the Middle Ages: "During the Middle Ages, the Christian patriarchal image of the Earth was unambiguously negative, while the positive archetype of Heaven was dominant. This means that the Earth, as the dark and

the essence (absurdity) of this mindset in a translation of Pope Innocent III's *De contempt mundi*, which declares his contempt for Earthly things, which are allegedly:

> Formed from filthiest sperm, conceived in the prurience of the flesh, nourished by menstrual blood, which is said to be so loathsome and filthy that after contact with it, the fruits of the fields no longer germinate, the orchards wither . . . and dogs, if they eat of it, become rabid. (cited in Neumann, 1994, p. 170).

Neumann (1994) is sensible to the patriarchal roots of this pathological disdain for the Earthly:

> Devaluation of the Earth, hostility towards the Earth, fear of the Earth: these are all from the psychological point of view the expression of a weak patriarchal consciousness that knows no other way to help itself than to withdraw violently from the fascinating and overwhelming domain of the Earthly. (p. 171)

On the fulfillment of this overall arc of disdain of the earth, Panikkar (1995) comments: "Modern Man has created a 'fourth world': the artificious world, in which the divine is banished from the earth, the human tamed and domesticated, and the material subdued" (p. 10). This artificious world evokes a sense of the Western One, and it reverberates in his own characterization of the same: "the august dominion of the will, whether it be the will to power, to conquest, or to go to heaven" as "one of the most stubbornly rooted dogmas in modern western culture" (p. 9).

Eventually, as pointed out by Wilhelmsen, in his Foreword to Jünger's *The failure of Technology* (1946), this disdain for the Earthly in religious monotheism takes a secular turn, fueling the rise of technology, "a hasty baptism of the machine by men eager to absorb the new world into the ethos of our Christian inheritance" (p. 10). This rhetoric of voracious patriarchal absorption resonates with Neumann's (1994) assessment of Western expansion: "The fundamental direction in the development of occidental humanity tends toward extending the domain of patriarchal consciousness and feeding it with whatever it can possibly incorporate" (p. 108). Setting aside the toxic hypermasculinity in the Titan mythologem alluded to at the beginning of the last chapter (*Kabeiroi*) and the similarities between monotheism and Titanism, it is important to acknowledge that the rise of Western patriarchy and monotheism is classically

---

feminine, was regarded as the coarse, sensual, tangible, material, this-worldly, and evil body that is a prison and a peril, to be associated with the lowest level of the world, with night and with hell" (Neumann, 1994).

rooted in the polytheistic Olympian order. That said, the crossings of titanic and Olympian, monotheistic and polytheistic in the rise of Western patriarchy are quite complex, especially when seen through a gendered lens. Mary Shelley's *Frankenstein* (1818/2003) presents a moment of the West that offers much related material to sort out, starting with the splitting of the Great Mother.

On splitting the Great Mother: Spiritual Themis and Monstrous Gaia

Alluding to Themis with a touch of the teratological, Jünger (1947/2006) asserts that "the further one is removed from her, more visible is the stamp of crudeness, incompleteness, and deformity" (p. 51). Updating this Greco-Roman ethos to modern monotheism, Neumann (1955/2015) underscores the same dynamic in splitting of Sophia, "a spiritual whole in which all heaviness and materiality are transcended" (p. 325) from Earth Mother. It is beyond argument that the rise of patriarchy from poly- to monotheism depended in no small measure on relegation of "good" vs. "bad" aspects of the Great Mother, and perhaps Jung contributed to this binary to an extent. Paglia (2006) argues that Neumann compensates some of Jung's short-sightedness with respect to distortions of the matriarchal feminine:

> Jung's relations with women, including his unstable mother, were blatantly conflicted, but a remarkable number of the first Jungian analysts were forceful, articulate women, who supplied what they found missing in his theories. Neumann's work belongs to that successor generation, among whom there was considerable mutual influence. (p. 6)

For Neumann, the distinctions between the earthy and spiritual aspects of the Magna Mater, the lines between Gaia and Themis (Titan and Monster), contrary to the polarized view espoused by the patriarchy, constitute more of a continuum, and certainly this resonates with the blended perspective of her son Prometheus posited earlier. Neumann (1994) describes the source of the Gaia-Themis binary: "So long as the hero could be interpreted patriarchally in the sense that he has to conquer the matriarchal world of darkness and evil, everything is in order" (p. 193). Essentially, this is the root of a split in the matriarchal feminine that progresses as a fairly consistent trope in both the polytheistic Greco-Roman and Christian monotheistic hero's journeys: one Gaia half to slay and another Themis-Sophia half to return as spiritual wisdom. Needless to say, neither pole is favorable to the feminine; it has been rendered something straight from horror cinema: either ghostly or monstrous. To this point, Neumann reminds us that "… we talk of Sophia as a heightened and spiritualized earth. But this formulation is already distorted as well. The earth has not changed at all, it is neither heightened nor spiritualized: it remains what it always was" (p. 215). What has perhaps changed is a patriarchal distillation from titanic extremes carried forward from polytheism and fashioned into monotheistic polarities.

Ghostly, Spirited Themis

This elusive Great Mother, "one person, though of various names" (Aeschylus, 1961, p. 52), is arguably the feminine Other (or Others) *por excelencia* of Western patriarchy, be it in its original polytheistic form under the Zeus Olympic order, or its heir, monotheism, from its original Judeo-Christian guises to the machinery of Western economic, political, and technological conquest[6]. Applying some of Rowland's (2002) forensic work with the Gothic feminine sublime, we discern her ghostlike presence from off-stage in *Prometheus Bound* and role as a behind-the-scenes organizer to auditor of patriarchal authority.

Accordingly, what is required in charting the cultural turn centers on the trail of various arcs, both hegemonic and overlooked, from Olympians to Titans, Mythos to Logos, polytheism to monotheism. Nicolescu (1994) refers to this as transhistory:

> Transhistory is the history of all histories. There's a book of history, just as there's a book of nature. Transhistory – movement between the lines of the book of history. A reading of the invisible rendered visible. Transhistory tells the history of the Hidden Third. (p. 68)

The Hidden Third, is a transdisciplinary notion we will explore in more depth in the last chapter, but one way to think about it in the present context is as an analogue to the ghostly or gothic feminine in Western narratives. Hillman's (1975) critique of Western history, for example, includes the assertion that the rise of philosophy in classical Greece did not eradicate the plurality of Mythos, but he failed to recognize the ghostly vestiges of Themis there. Consider Socrates, for example. Though the iconic philosopher focused on the One, his rhetorical spirals drew from the polytheistic Many, as conveyed in the connected, grounded wisdom of Diotema. One might argue that Diotema, as characterized in the *Symposium* and who prefigures the gnostic Sophia, reflects a primordial matriarchal wisdom that points to Themis.

---

[6] According to Giegerich (2007), after ingesting Pagan philosophy, Christian monotheism distilled into metaphysics, which served to break the belief system from its origins in mythos and set the roots of logical being. Metaphysics, in turn, set the stage for the Enlightenment and the rise of scientific rationalism, which gave rise to a post-Christian variety of monotheism, eventually distilling into modern technology.

To be sure, Themis's polytheistic Many, infused with the full range of Great Mother archetypes[7] was not obliterated by the rise of Western rationalism; she went underground, subverting the West's inflated *cogito* with epistemologies of planetary and social connectedness. It is ironic that as Western patriarchy shed its Greco-Roman polytheistic toga for the monotheistic cloak, it is not Zeus, the polytheistic patriarch, but his Titaness ex-wife who takes up the scepter of the polytheistic Many. In addition to overlooking the patriarchal misogyny of the Zeus Order, this omission of the titanic feminine strikes us as a rather striking oversight in archetypal psychology, and it further problematizes the tendency of Hillman and López-Pedraza to exalt the Olympian at the expense of the Titanic.

Prior to her appearance as post-Enlightenment, Industrial Age phantom, The Wise Counselor Themis has persisted in a similar, ghostly shell as Spirit Mother through the rise of Western monotheism, whether in her Sophia guise, as the Arthurian Grail Vessel, or as "the goddess of those who implore protection" (Jünger, 1947/2006, p. 51). As regards the latter, her legal authority persists as the Madonna, Christ's defense counsel for lost souls, as heralded in the *Cantigas*, leading up to her iconic presence in modern-day legal circles. Themis's iconic presence continues to exercise an influence in the court system, but within the liminal spaces of the sublime (Gothic) feminine, she continues to haunt the rise of (techno-) Logos in literary and filmic texts, though, as we will see later in this chapter, this counter-narrative centers more on her "monstrous" Gaia half.

In spite of her success as a ghostly shadow figure in the Western metanarrative's subtext, -Themis predictably was eclipsed by her son in patriarchy's progression from polytheism to monotheism. Kerényi (1997) traces the zenith of this convergence between Prometheus and Christian monotheism to nineteenth Century British literature, which ascribed to the Titan a redeemer aspect through the personage of Lucifer,[8] though, as Kerényi reminds us, Prometheus was not a redeemer but rather redeemed by Zeus. With the rise of STEM (Science, Technology, Engineering, & Math) from its foundations in the Industrial Revolution, the rise of techno-Prometheus is palpable, his kiln-hut now growing smokestacks and eventually reemerging as reactors and servers.

---

[7] In this continuum, we may add Demeter and Rhea, for example, among other, updated varieties. There are also the preceding Egyptian matriarchs, such as Isis and Mut.

[8] Shelley's (1818/2003) Frankenstein's monster, for example, identifies with Lucifer. And the chase of inventor and creative into the "everlasting ices of the north" (p. 202) reminds us of the Luciferian north of the alchymists "The North Pole was also thought of as the abode of Lucifer, the cold regions of evil, and came to symbolize a special madness" (López-Pedraza, 1996, p. 32).

Technology, for Giegerich (2007), is the crowning achievement of a logical being-in-the-world that has transcended nature, mythos, and subjectivity, all of which have been subsumed under a dialectical process of logical negation. Prometheus, in this light, emerges as decidedly post-Christian savior, the redeemer as self-creator *cum Dr. Frankenstein (The Modern Prometheus)* of Mary Shelley, arguably the forerunner of the Engineers of Ridley Scott's Prometheus cycle.

There is an alleged danger in this spiritualization of the Great Mother, as it often constellates with the patriarchal uroboros. Neumann (1994) posits, for example, that for the woman who overidentifies with Sophia as "female partner of the Spirit-Father," there is the possibility that "she has split herself off from her earthly shadow side" (p. 21).

Frankenstein, Techno-Titanism and Monstrous Gaia

Redirecting our attention to the Earth Mother side of the split feminine, we return to Rowland's (2002) explorations of the Gothic feminine, highlighting an Enlightenment-inspired masculine Logos haunted by the feminine sublime. To borrow from Austin Clarkson's (2008) discussion of Logos vs. Mythos, technical reproduction is situated in opposition to imaginal production. As the ability to imagine is likened to the feminine power to create and nurture life (Stein, 2020), the latter tends to be ascribed to a biological interpretation of gender identity. Rowland rightly reminds us that such binary reductions based on biological gender, including the assignment of Mythos and irrationality to the feminine, on one hand, and Logos and rationality to the masculine, on the other, have been contradicted and discarded in post-modern feminist critique.

In this context we turn to an iconically titanic event at the dawn of the Industrial Age: a volcanic eruption that renders the summer of 1816 cold and rainy. To pass the time, Lord Byron challenges his group of friends to see who can write the best ghost story. Mary Shelley's *Frankenstein: A Modern Prometheus* would be published two years later. In keeping with Rowland's portrayal of the gothic feminine, a potentially bold challenge to the patriarchal order is undermined in subsequent edits designed to shift the reader's sympathy from the monster to its creator (Karbiener, 2003). For our purposes, Shelley's work highlights a milestone in Titanism as it demonstrates a refashioning of the titanic from a poly- to a monotheistic mold. More importantly, *Frankenstein* demonstrates the consistency of the patriarchal arc through this shift and an underlying patriarchal preoccupation with (envy of) the feminine power to create and nurture life.

Shelley's work captures the tragic Titanism of a promethean Victor Frankenstein, holding a distorted mirror up to patriarchy that highlights a failure of the masculine to produce or nurture life, given that Victor's inflated Logos leads to failures on both counts. As he conjures his creation experiment, Dr. Frankenstein's misanthropic and titanic obsession with the creation of life[9] is evident:

> No one can conceive the variety of feelings which move me onwards, like a hurricane, in the first enthusiasm of success. Life and death appeared to me ideal bounds, which I should first break through, and port a torrent of light into our dark world. A new species would bless me as its creator and source; many happy and excellent natures would owe their being to me. No father could claim the gratitude of his child so completely as I should deserve theirs. (Shelley, 1818/2003, p. 52)

From this vantage point, a liminal space between the first order *prōtoi heûretaí* of the mythical-religious imagination and the Logos-sublated engineer-model of modern manufacturing, we discern a patriarchal preoccupation, a sort of *womb envy*[10] that drives the fabrication of facsimiles of Mother Nature's creative power by means of technological innovation.

Shelley's Industrial Age-driven, post-Enlightenment recasting of the Titan Prometheus is typical of the Romantic Era, and it echoes the classical Greek trope of Father Birth.[11] As Kerényi (1978) points out, the patriarchal Zeus order

---

[9] Noting that Shelley's mother, Mary Wollstonecraft, died after giving birth to her and that four out of five of the Shelley offspring died either before or after birth, K. Karbiener reminds us that "We are reading about Mary's deep-rooted questions regarding herself as a creator" (intro to Shelley, 1818/2003, p. xxx).

[10] According to Paul Kochmanski, a board member of Jung Center Buffalo who lectures in psychology, informed me that this expression originates in the work of Karen Horney, a neo-Freudian psychoanalyst. Though 'womb envy' is a fairly ubiquitous term and Horney does not employ the expression, per sé, her work, *Feminine Psychology* is often cited as a source for the term. The following excerpt captures her perspective on this inversion of the well-known Freudian concept (penis envy): "But from the biological point of view woman has in motherhood, or in the capacity for motherhood, a quite indisputable and by no means negligible physiological superiority. This is most clearly reflected in the unconscious of the male psyche in the boy's intense envy of motherhood. We are familiar with this envy as such, but it has hardly received due consideration as a dynamic factor. When one begins, as I did, to analyze men only after a fairly long experience of analyzing women, one receives a most surprising impression of the intensity of this envy of pregnancy, childbirth, and motherhood, as well as of the breasts and of the act of suckling" (pp. 60-61). Horney, K. (1967). *Feminine psychology*. New York: Norton.

[11] Graves (1960) suggests that the Greeks may have sketched this trope from the Babylonians by way of the Prometheus mythologem. Prometheus, he asserts, was confused "with the Babylonian god Ea, who claimed to have created a splendid man from the blood of Kingu (a sort of Cronus), while the Mother goddess Aruru created an inferior man from clay" (p. 9).

required a myth of father-birth to undermine the feminine power to procreate. According to Kerényi (1997), depending on the account, it was either Prometheus or Hephaistos whose handiwork freed Athene from Zeus's head. As depicted in the *Homeric Hymns*, this act, according to Stein, represents a great feat, worthy of Hera's envy. As Stein puts it, "Zeus has in effect rendered the marriage to Hera a mere formality, a hollow institution" (p. 70). However, Kerényi (1997) underscores limitations of production from the masculine psyche in the epic struggle Zeus experiences, both in the birthing of Athene from his head and in birthing Dionysus from his thigh.

Of course, as Creed (1993) points out, the womb is also terrifying to the patriarchy.[12] In terms of this womb-envious and monotheistic mad scientist mold introduced by Shelley, Scott's *Alien* prequels (*Prometheus*, 2012; *Covenant*, 2017) offer us the perfect modern update of this trope that pits a hyper-masculine race of Engineers, obviously cut from the Enlightenment *cogito* cloth, against a dark, creative, multi-dimensional muck that they presume to control. The Promethean figure in the series, an android named David, grotesquely eviscerates his travel companion Dr. Elizabeth Shaw in order to re-engineer his own hive of alien creatures from the aforementioned primordial goo in ways that evoke the passive, objectified role of Luna in the alchemical coniunctio. In James Cameron's (1986) sequel to Ridley Scott's *Alien* (1979), ruthless corporations attempt to co-opt a matriarchal, Gaia-like queen of the hive for their own purposes. The key distinction that pervades all of these motifs is one of masculine reproduction (fabrication) vs. creative feminine production. We also see in Dr. Frankenstein, the Engineers and in David, a decidedly patriarchal Prometheus who has been re-engineered to fit an ideologically (scientistic) and technologically updated version of Judeo-Christian monotheism.

Whether or not he is indeed an accomplice in the metanarrative of father-birth, Prometheus certainly adds to this Zeus-order-driven notion of male production as a primordial envy of feminine creative power. From the forges of Titans and Gigantes and Hephaestus's workshop to Dr. Frankenstein's laboratory, and cognizant of the volcanic (Vulcan) forces surrounding the origins of Shelley's work, let us pause to ponder the fabrication of nature, Man's incessant drive to co-opt the biological and psychic production of the feminine. For Gier (2000), this has negative consequences for both the human and divine realm: "Not only are the gods supplanted, but nature in general is denigrated in status and value. This becomes an especially serious problem when human beings

---

[12] "The womb is horrifying per se and within the patriarchal discourses it has been used to represent woman's body as marked, impure and a part of the natural/animal world" (p. 49).

develop technological means to control and to alter nature" (p. 7). Gier evokes the destruction of Gaia inherent in Prometheus´s workshop and technological Titanism:

> [S]melting and mining are intimately connected leads, at least retrospectively in some minds, to protest a major violation of the sanctity and integrity of Mother Earth. Until the industrial age smelting and mining were relatively small scale, so preindustrial peoples could not have predicted the catastrophic implications of their powerful pyrotechnology. (p. 76)

Working this fabricated *mater*ial or mater dimension further, there is obviously something of the Great Mother archetype at work. To this point, Irene Claremont de Castillejo (1997) comments:

> On the whole the menace to civilization today seems to come from man's overdeveloped thinking, and the consequent unadaptedness of his [Man's] fourth function, feeling, which thereby lets in the evil. His feeling brings with it all the dynamic forces of the unconscious, good and bad – its courage and inspiration, but also its terror – which makes us pile armament upon armament, hydrogen bomb on hydrogen bomb (p. 39).

The shadow of this "stultifying, life-destroying, anonymous machine of the civilization we have built" (p. 42), according to Claremont de Castillejo (1997), reflects the resurgence of the savage feminine through the factory of masculinist modernity, a trope that resonates with the motif of Prometheus's workshop. It is worth noting that part of Zeus's vengeance against Prometheus involves the creation of the first human woman with the help of Hephaistos and Athene. Pandora, who is sent down to bring misery to Man, is scapegoated for all "evil, tribulations and calamities" (Jünger, 1947/2006, p. 88). Pandora, the Greek 'Eve' who is betrothed to Prometheus or his brother Epimetheus, depending on the account, goes by another name: Anesidora, '*the one who sends up gifts from the earth*' (Harrison, 1912/2010, p. 281). Perhaps there is a modern resonance of this mythologem in the notion of Plutonium as a modern, empirically factual issue of the classic box we were warned not to open?

What emerges here is a compensatory sense of the monstrous matter that counters, or de*monstr*ates, *Man's* reckless drive to co-opt creation, with all the blurring of classical Greek polytheism and more modern, science- and technology-based expressions of monotheism, a particular strain of cultural anxiety that fuels the tragic madness of Dr. Frankenstein and the plot of Ridley Scott's hyper-masculine Engineers who fail to control a dark feminine substance that has as much power to devour and destroy as to create. Man is reminded by the Great Mother where He stands in the scheme of things:

techno-logic as subordinate to the eco-logic of the matriarchal feminine. There is something undeniably titanic in this counter-narrative, though it does not fit the classic casting of unbound, hubristic and hypermasculine beings; there seems to be a coherent, creative principle at work in the titanic feminine that will be explored further in the final chapter.

To be sure, in this splitting of matriarchal Titanism, Gaia fully immerses the "Moira" mode in monotheistic techno-titanism. Taking in the big picture of the matriarchal feminine's savage side, a complex web of patterns emerges, ranging from her connection with matter to a compensatory function in the patriarchy, one in which Prometheus plays a part. Giegerich (2007), echoing Claremont de Castillejo (1997), likewise portrays technologies as sublime forms of *mater* (*material*). As he points out, Psyche, like the web, has transcended the individual brain-container, dispersing across servers and social media posts. The Web is a classically feminine symbol that rewinds back to the weavings of Arachne (turned into a spider by Athene). Gaia, likewise, has been sanitized into motherboards, GPS ladies, the cooing voices that emanate from our cell phones and smart speakers. How can this not represent the power of the titanic feminine and monstrous on some level? A 'rise of the machines?' She has even transcended the techno- and ecologic binary, demonstrating that viruses may adopt both epidemiological and technological forms. It is as if the Great Mother were playing the long game, a complex collaboration with Techno-Prometheus to compensate the excesses of the Zeus Order in its progressed monotheistic casing.

The Monstrous Feminine

The monster marvels. As suggested in Pliny's commentary, that marvel has overtones of patriarchal horror in response to something perceived as supernatural and uncomfortably other. According to Neumann (1994), "Fear of the Feminine is concentrated in fear of the female body, either because the body itself is taboo, or because women, especially the female genitals, are feared as the terrible, castrating "vaginal dentata" (p. 259), and he ascribes to this phenomenon a very primitive stage of a man's anima development. Working from Neumann, but almost exclusively in the Freudian-Lacanian line of psychoanalytic critique, Barbara Creed is credited with articulating a "monstrous feminine" in horror cinema. According to Creed (1993), the monstrous feminine predominantly manifests itself in depictions of "mothering and reproductive functions" (p. 70), as well as in Freud's "monstrous fantasy" of the castrating woman, which takes the form of "femme castratrice,[13] the castrating mother, and the vagina dentata" (p. 7).

Creed's (1993) critique of the monstrous feminine is situated in Kristeva's (1982) notion of abjection, a liminal, border- and rule-defying space that disrupts the social order attributed to associations with the mother. Abjection of the mother, it is alleged, constitutes an important stage in the subject's initiation into the Symbolic, and Creed persuasively instantiates this trope in the horror film genre. Within a Freudian-Lacanian framework, the abject contrasts "the impure fertile (female) body and pure speech associated with the symbolic (male) body" (p. 25), constituted both on the subjective and social planes, including the institutions that range from the family to capitalism (citing Wood, 1986, pp. 70-94). Abjection, which arguably drives both the production and reception of the Gigantomachia as well as the hero's journey, is alleged to be fundamental to the functioning of the patriarchy, and Creed invokes Irigaray to make this point rhetorically: "...without the exploitation of the body-matter of women, what would become of the symbolic process that governs society?" (p. 166).

Abjection, according to Creed (1993), also centers on the splitting of "human from the non-human and the fully constituted subject from the partially formed subject" (p. 8). Within the social order, the abject is periodically and ritually subjected to renewal and exclusion. For the subject, engagement with the abject is necessary as it reflexively destroys and defines existence. Regarding monstrous horror, Creed offers several examples of abjected materia: perversion, sacrifice, decay, death, corpses, excretion, and in terms of the monstrous feminine, in particular, "the feminine body and incest" (p. 9).[14] For Creed, the monstrous is invoked primarily by two factors: a sense of soullessness (initiated by the corpse trope) and hypocrisy.

As the monstrous seems to center on the Earth Mother, it makes sense to revisit our critique of Ridley Scott's *Alien* (1979) in light of Creed's (1993) insights. As previously noted, an actual egg-laying Earth Mother is more directly presented in James Cameron's *Aliens* arc. In contrast, Creed captures many sublime, indirect references to the archaic mother: the alienating, engulfing shots of the *Nostromo* that recall mother "as primordial abyss" (p. 17), the antiseptic womb-like cryosleep chambers in which the crew gestates for the

---

[13] *Femme castratice* refers to murder or castration of the man during sex.

[14] It should be highlighted that the abject imbued in the monstrous feminine has a behavioral aspect. Creed (1993) points to depictions of demonic possession in horror films as "the excuse for legitimizing a display of aberrant feminine behaviour which is depicted as monstrous, abject – and perversely appealing" (p. 31).

long journey contrasted with the dank, cavernous egg hatchery of the Alien ship, a cannibalistic and castrating 'Mother' computer that colludes with a corporation to devour the crew of the Nostromo; and finally, the ejection of "smaller crafts or bodies from the mother ship" (p. 19).

According to Creed (1993), Scott's *Alien* also features the classic vampire trope, with the alien's piercing inner mouth depicted as a projected, fetishized feminine phallus that compensates for the formlessness of the archaic mother (p. 22). In addition to Dracula, Creed points to the incorporation of the Mesopotamian male deity Papuzu into the possession portrayed in the Exorcist as another example of the Archaic Mother's phallus by proxy. Ultimately, echoing Neumann, the archaic mother is totalized here in her propensity "to tear apart and reincorporate all life" (p. 22).

Creed's (1993) depiction of phallic extensions of the Great Mother resonates with similar archetypal patterns uncovered in Jungian studies. For example, Neumann (1994) sustains that "Every patriarchal world is based on banishing back into the primordial maternal womb of the underworld this titanic element, which is always regarded mythologically as the eldest son of the primeval Earth Mother" (p. 194). Likewise, and in anticipation of a full discussion of creativity and innovation in the final chapter, we find the following observation from Stein (2020) who posits that "Hephaistos represents a split off animus of the Great Mother, who mimics the creative processes in the depths of the Mother and brings to birth through this mimetic transformation his works of art" (p. 19), a "second-level creativity" (p. 10).

Arguably, Hera's children, created outside of Zeus's intervention, are monstrous extensions as well.[15] In addition to Typhon-Teras, who reflects Creed's notion of the archaic mother's phallic extension, the Olympians Hephaestus and Ares are also depicted as monstrous- Hephaestus for his physical disability and Ares for his abhorrent temperament. Creed (1993) notes a similar trope of monstrous, fatherless birth in modern horror films such as the Brood[16] and Carrie, which features blended images of menstruation and pigs' blood. Regarding the latter, Creed alludes to pig references involving the female genitals.[17]

---

[15] Interview with Davide Salvo, October 6, 2020.

[16] Creed (1993), without reference to these specific Greco-Roman sources, ascribes the monstrosity of the children depicted in The Brood to fatherless birth: "The implication is that without man, woman can only give birth to a race of mutant, murderous offspring" (p. 45).

[17] "Women and pigs are also linked in myth and language. In Greek and Latin, the female genitals are referred to as 'pig,' Even today, 'sowness' is used in German as a slang term for menstruation" (p. 80, citing Shuttle & Redgrove, 1978, p. 37).

On the trail of the monstrous feminine, we discern a global, far-seeing aspect of the matriarchal feminine that merits re-examination. Picking up where we left off in our exploration of the Titanic feminine's challenge to patriarchal engineering a la Prometheus and Dr. Frankenstein, we will now explore corresponding metanarratives in the evolution of Translation Studies and the heroic, both of which feature important hybridity de*monst*rations. In both cases, we will be crossing further from the ghost-spirit side of the Great Mother, symbolized by Themis, to the darker, Earth Mother side evinced by Monstrous Gaia.

Chapter 4

Heroes and Monstrous Hybridities

As suggested in the previous chapter, there is a curious and uniquely monstrous connection between the splitting of the feminine and hybrid truths. At the intersection of heroes and monsters, as well as between texts of origin and their translations, we find complex constellations of patriarchal projections. Just as the Gigantomachia is driven by Herakles's imposition of the patriarchal Zeus order over the monstrous feminine, the patriarchal Symbolic Order, Lacan's (2007) network of linguistic and cultural rules that bind civilization, turns to a curriculum of abjection rooted in the alleged chaotic abyss of the maternal other. When we add Jung's individuation project, it becomes clear that all of this must be whisked into the mantha-churn. So it goes analogically with heroes and monsters. What is a hero if not a monster killer?[1] Likewise, translated texts take on an abjected quality, ultimately demonstrating profound discoveries regarding the hybrid truths that emerge in the Western One, in spite of this need to both create and conquer a monstrous Other. In navigating the cultural turn, these are important considerations that further nuance the classic Greco-Roman theme of the One and the Many.

On Heroes and Monsters, Monstrous Heroes, and Heroic Monsters

From Monstrous Gaia to the Alien queen of Cameron's *Aliens*, the archaic mother is often portrayed as the beast to be slain in the hero's (or in the case of Cameron, heroine's) journey; this is a well-worn trope in the Greco-Roman origins of the classic hero trope that is arguably still *en vogue* in modern, monotheistic variants of the monstrous. So, from the standpoint of the feminine, the passage from poly- to monotheism is far from constituting a marked transition, and this split-matriarchy is perfected in Joseph Campbell's (1991) portrayal of the hero's journey: the physical deed depicted in slaying the Mater monster (my term) and the spiritual deed in attaining spiritual wisdom (Spirit Mother).[2]

---

[1] "There is a typical early culture hero who goes around slaying monsters. Now, that is a form of adventure from the period of prehistory when man was shaping his world out of a dangerous, unshaped wilderness. He goes about killing monsters" (Campbell, 1991, p. 166).

[2] "CAMPBELL: Well, there are two types of deeds. One is the physical deed, in which the hero performs a courageous act in battle or saves a life. The other kind is the spiritual

We seldom question the fact that it is exactly such classic allegories of male heroes and matriarchal monsters that drove Jung's discourse on individuation: The Great Mother and her dark, unconscious goo as the "whale-dragon" the hero must slay (Jung, 1911-12/1952/2014, para. 312), and it carries misogynistic nuances of his uneasy—if not hysterical—relationship with the collective, the dreaded nemesis of individuation:

> The problems of the inner voice are full of pitfalls and hidden snares. Treacherous, slippery ground, as dangerous and pathless as life itself once one lets go of the railings. But he who cannot lose his life, neither shall he save it. The hero's birth and the heroic life are always threatened. The serpents were sent by Hera to destroy the infant Hercules, the python that tries to strangle Apollo at birth, the massacre of the innocents, all these tell the same story. To develop the personality is a gamble, and the tragedy is that the daemon of the inner voice is at once our greatest danger and an indispensable help. It is tragic, but logical, for it is the nature of things to be so. (Jung, 1954/1991, p. 209)

Lacan's (2007) lower-case other, the unconscious oneness with the mother, is perhaps cut from the same cloth. Freud (1939/1967), in direct contrast to Jung and Lacan, sets heroic ego against the patriarchal father ("A hero is a man who stands up manfully against his father and in the end victoriously overcomes him," p. 10). Likewise, Stein (1978) affirms:

> Heroic striving and conquering can be insighted from many different mythologems: the Promethean variety as rebellion and self-assertion; the Herculean variety as escape from and defense against the persecuting mother; military stridency of the Athenean version in its distinguishing feature, and its defense against the archaic father is primary.
> (p. 78).

Whatever the case, a full appraisal of women's individuation (heroine's journey) was not within any traditional psychoanalytic purview, be it Freudian, Lacanian, or Jungian. In the classic mythological sense, we know the hero to be a white male and all of the monsters to be manifestations of the feminine. We know of its cinematic updates of Rowland's (2002) gothic feminine and Creed's (1993) monstrous feminine tropes in sci-fi and horror.

---

deed, in which the hero learns to experience the supernormal range of human spiritual life and then comes back with a message" (1991, p. 152).

What about the Heroine?

Neumann (1994) was the first depth psychologist to question the patriarchal hero trope, asking "why can there never, at any time or in any place, be anything heroic and enlightened in humanity without a battle and without a fateful immersion in this dark womb of death in the underworld?" (p. 191). Commenting on how the hero figures into feminine psychological development, Neumann argues that the hero (projected onto an actual man) enters a woman's life after she has moved from the matriarchal to patriarchal order. This passage from the patriarchy of the Great Father to the patriarchate of the husband mirrors the classic Greek hero's journey:

> In the myth only the intervention by heroic powers can break the superior power of the patriarchal uroboros manifesting in its chthonic lower form. The heroic powers appear as Theseus and as the Lapithae on the earthly level, for example, and as Zeus and the Olympians on the heavenly level, and both symbolize the patriarchal side of consciousness. (p. 60)

Nevertheless, pointing to damsels in distress who were monstrously forsaken by their heroes, Neumann (1994) also acknowledges that life in the patriarchate marriage to the hero-husband can be stunting, a move from one prison to another,[3] thus necessitating the woman's own hero's journey:

> she must come to the point in her inner development where she, as the solar hero, liberates herself from the dragon's embrace or suffers the death-marriage with the dragon [maternal uroboros] in conscious surrender and devotion so that—together with the dragon—she can emerge transformed. Here again the oft-cited tale of Amor and Psyche is paradigmatic. With her acceptance of the patriarchal uroboros and the transformation it brings, a spiritual realm of a transpersonal nature reveals itself to the woman in the second half of life, a realm belonging most profoundly to the spiritual side of her own feminine nature, a realm that makes her inwardly independent of the values and judgments of the

---

[3] "It is the mythological prototype of psychological processes, the liberation of the Feminine from the power of the patriarchal uroboros is the task of the male hero, who must redeem the captured virgin from the dragon. In contrast to the patriarchal uroboros, the archetypal Masculine now appears in individual and personal form and conducts the Feminine—as woman or as anima liberated from the powers of the patriarchal and the matriarchal uroboros—into his own domain, that of the patriarchate" (Neumann, 1994, p. 26). Once there, "The patriarchal marriage presents a not inconsiderable danger for the woman's development" (p. 30).

patriarchal, archetypally masculine spirit whose essence is foreign to her nature. (p. 61)

The invocation of Psyche's story is worth a closer analysis, especially since Psyche is perhaps the only clear heroine in Greco-Roman mythology. The science fiction writer Isaac Asimov (1961) emphasizes that this is no mere love story but rather an allegory of the soul's (*psyche* means 'Soul' in Greek) trials in pursuit of love (Eros or Cupid, depending on the Greek or Roman account, respectively). Manisha Roy (2010) offers an apt archetypal psychological synopsis of the myth:

> In the myth Psyche is married to Eros in an unconscious union, until her shadow figures make her break her promise to her husband and look at him when he is asleep. She finds out that he is the god of love himself. This disobedience costs her highly and she has to go through four painful tasks to appease her mother-in-law Aphrodite. Finally, she succeeds with the help of animals and supernatural aid and wins Eros back. Psyche and Eros are married formally, and she is accepted into Olympus as a divinity herself. Thus, Psyche (as in psychology) has to go through a heroic struggle before she can be reunited with her opposite, the god of love. (p. 77)

Though both are the only heroes welcomed into Olympus, Psyche's trials on the spirit plane eclipse those of Herakles on the physical. While Herakles struggles for his own honor, to claim his rightful place among the gods, Psyche's trials are quite literally, for love (Eros). Speaking to the importance of Psyche's example, Roy (2010) puts it, "Perhaps all psychology – including working through entrenched cultural complexes – is a heroic and arduous quest for the reunion with the archetype of love" (p. 77). Both Psyche and Herakles go to hell and back for their efforts, and eventually both are welcomed on Olympus, but if our focus here is on psychological development (individuation), Psyche's journey is infinitely more compelling, and the fact of her being overlooked by the founders of depth psychology strikes us as a galling omission and precisely where the study of cultural complexes and traumas has the most to gain.

On this matter of discerning a heroine thread in the subtext of the patriarchal metanarrative, and in light of the monstrous feminine, let us reflect further on the monster's mission to marvel and show. Is there an undiscovered heroine aspect in some of these feminine monsters? Medusa, for example, has emerged as a feminist heroine, and Ovid's account provides the context for that. For its time, *Metamorphoses* demonstrates a formidable capacity for developing complex feminine subjectivities, though Ovid's prior works edify some of the worst aspects of Roman patriarchal misogyny. In the *Metamorphoses*, Ovid (1/1995-2009) shifts the frame from antagonist to protagonist, recounting how

Medusa, known for her "marvelous hair," is raped by Poseidon in the temple of Minerva (Athene) and punished by the warrior goddess with the mane of snakes for which she is known (4.792-802). So, Medusa is double wronged: raped and blamed for the "sin," an abhorrent and all too common 'blame the victim' trope in Greco-Roman mythology. Though she is ultimately turned to stone by her reflection in Athene's shield, suggesting an internal dispute over feminine identities, I would argue that Medusa inherently constitutes a marvelous, monstrous mirror that reflects the patriarchal order's shadow. This interpretation finds support in the arguably justified vengeance of dishonored and violated feminine characters in Latin American monstrous femininities: La Llorona, La Serrana, and other feminine monsters who exact vengeance in response to men's sexual transgressions.

Are Heroes Actually Monsters?

As the *monstrum* reveals the inner workings of the patriarchal binary, the real possibility that the heroes are monsters should come as no surprise. As noted by Creed (1993), the monstrous feminine loves a good hypocrisy, and there is no shortage of that in the patriarchy, starting with the aforementioned tendency of the classic Greco-Roman hero to forsake his beloved. Even in classical Greece, Kerényi (1997), suggests there was growing skepticism regarding the Zeus Order in classical Athens. Likewise, J. A. Davison's (1949) assessment of Athens at the writing of the *Prometeia* suggests a nascent awareness of cracks in the State. The temporal context of Athens and Olympus around Aeschylus's famous trilogy writing center on the overthrow of a conservative order (their respective leaders Kronos and Cimon are both banished), and the emergence of Zeus and Pericles as paranoiac autocrats more concerned with the consolidation of their power than with the good of Humanity (see pp. 80-81). That said, Davison (1949) insists that "Prometheus is not only a thief and a double traitor, but by Athenian standards a blasphemer" (citing *Prometheus Bound,* l. 188-191). He concludes:

> Only when he has learned self-discipline will it be possible for his great intellect and indomitable courage to be put profitably to work in the service of the great community ruled by Zeus, which embraces both gods and men. (p. 73)

This is not to say that Athenians would not have been sympathetic to one man's resistance to the system, and this is consistent with a culture that engendered a sensitivity to the complex metaphysics of the One and the Many. As Davison (1949) concedes,

> the author of *Prometheus Bound,* though fully conscious of the sufferings of individuals and of the potentially good qualities displayed by Prometheus,

makes plain by the whole plan of the play his own faith in the goodness
of God and his detestation of Prometheus's pride and indiscipline. (p. 73)

More concretely, he equates Prometheus's disruption of the divine order "in
the name of humanity" (p. 73) with Protagoras, an atheistic sophist who aided
in the coup d'etat that facilitated the rise of Periclean democracy and whose
book, *On the Gods*, constituted a defiant defense of "individual human
intellect" (p. 73) as the greatest good, even greater than the Zeus Order. Like
Prometheus, Protagoras is punished for his impiety. Affirming Philostratus's
account, Davison relates how Protagoras was summarily condemned to exile,
"'island hopping' in a small boat in an attempt to escape observation by
Athenian cruisers" (p. 76). He further affirms Diogenes' account that "all copies
of the book in circulation were called in by proclamation and burned in the
agora" (p. 77) as part of Pericles's cynical ploy to capitalize on "the religious
intolerance endemic in Athens," (p. 83). All of this constitutes an important
elaboration on Themis's hallowed ground for community discourse that cannot
be overlooked, as it reveals the agora's dark, collective unconscious aspect; the
Many has its Big Brother side. Even so, Davison equates "his [Protagoras's]
belief in the importance of the individual human being and with his sense of
natural justice (perhaps symbolized in the trilogy by Gaia-Themis" (p. 79). In
matters of the One and the Many, Davison's assertion likewise nuances its
blendings: Protagoras, like Prometheus, an upstart rebel of the One[4] is infused
with the ethos of the Many. Perhaps, in this way, he is a literal brother to
Prometheus through this matriarchal connector (Themis).

If we set aside the alleged meanings ascribed to the Prometheus mythologem
and the West's debt to Zeus's Olympic roundtable for all of its psychic
differentiation and inspiration for arts and letters, could there be a more toxic,
dysfunctional rogues' gallery than the Olympians? Disney depictions aside, the
rap sheet is formidable, ranging from petty envy and jealousies to child abuse,
cannibalism, serial rape, murder, incest, manipulation, misogyny, pitiless
vengeance, and even genocide… One might argue that the Olympians are just
as guilty of the sort of psychopathic vacuity and monstrous excesses ascribed
to the Titans in archetypal psychology. For example, Hillman (1975) decries

---

[4] As regards the characterizations of Protagoras and Prometheus, Davison (1949) ascribes
reluctantly to the possibility that the author of the Prometeia received Protagoras's story
directly in Sicily, yielding a portrait cut from Protagoras's cloth:

Uncontrolled in thought and speech and action, conceited, blasphemous, revengeful,
long-winded, inconsistent, and hideously muddled in his lectures on geography, Prometheus
is surely drawn from the life by someone who had had an opportunity of studying
Protagoras's reactions to his ignominious expulsion from Athens, and who knew his style
as a lecturer. (p. 85)

Apollonian inflations in the academy. Likewise, López-Pedraza (2005) describes extremes of Artemisal (virginal) purity in monotheism, starting with the origins of the Christian Church or ideological forms such as National Socialism (2000a). In a sense, the monstrous demonstrates the shadow of patriarchy, from Zeus to present-day strongmen, problematizing polarities of Self and Other, Hero and Monster, Olympian and Titan. One may rightly point out that Olympic misbehavior is not limited to the male deities, which is certainly true, but just as modern misogyny is committed in the name of patriarchy regardless of gender, the same could be said of Aphrodite's, Artemis's, Hera's or Athene's apparent conformity to patriarchal reductions of the feminine.

Accordingly, the hero-monster binary merits a mantha. Hillman and López-Pedraza, perhaps aided by Neumann, were the first psychoanalysts to mount the first serious challenges to the hero trope. Hillman (1989), for example, equates the hero archetype with ego-based psychology, the nemesis of his own archetypal psychology:

> The hero myth tells the tale of conquest and destruction, the tale of psychology's "strong ego," its fire and sword, as well as the career of its civilization, but it tells little of the culture of its consciousness. Strange that we could still, in a psychology as subtle as Jung's, believe that this king-hero, and his ego, is the equivalent of consciousness. Images of this psychological equivalence were projected from television screens straight and live from the heroic-ego's great contemporary epic in Vietnam. Is this consciousness? (pp. 32-33)

At the core of López-Pedraza's (2002) challenge to the hero myth, his hero *complex*, is the assertion that the worship of heroes and heroism is an alleged epidemic of identification, a pathology of the collective alleged to undermine individuation. There are essentially two facets of heroic "madness," the first being an overidentification with the Homeric notion of heroic deeds. López-Pedraza contrasts this stance with the warning Krishna gives to the Hindu hero, Arjuna, which is essentially a warning not to do just that, to avoid getting overly obsessed with his deeds. On the Homeric origins of the Hero Complex, the author comments:

> The Iliad tells us how the lives of the heroes who fought in Troy centered on a strong identification with their war stories and how their life's goal was that posterity record their heroism and the fortitude of their character. Posthumous fame was the core ambition of living. People would sing of their lives of warrior deeds and in the ethos and valor that accompanied them. (p. 43)

Aside from an unhealthy obsession with heroic deeds, the hero complex, for López-Pedraza has some help from the Terrible Mother, who purportedly plays an important role in the hero complex, finding access through the animus of mothers. In an analogous way, Marie Louise Von Franz (1970/2000) discusses *death mothers* who would have elaborate black dresses at the ready in anticipation of their son's mortal sacrifice in battle (pp. 23-24). This death association is classic Monstrous Gaia, of course. As Neumann (1955/2015) reminds us, the Great Mother both creates and destroys.

López-Pedraza (2002) also sees the hero complex as a sort of death cult associated with Hecate, goddess of restless spirits, who, he alleges, gives the hero his "fatal attraction" (p. 30), as well as the "hecaterian charisma" (p. 31) alluded to earlier, and this characterization also complements Jünger's trimorphic characterization of Hecate as ruler of "the night, the tomb, and the blood of assassins" (Jünger, 1947/2006, p. 47). For López-Pedraza, the hero is psychopathic, barren, incapable of individuation, which is why he deigns to even recognize the hero as an archetype but rather a mere "figure." Rather than being cultured, he alleges that culture can only be sacked as 'booty.' This conclusion also finds support in Jünger's trimorphic characterization of Hecate- as the goddess who supports the pursuit of "victory, booty, and glory" (p. 45) in heroic journeys.

In a literal sense, the hero and the heroine are indeed monstrous, de*monstra*ting a nuance of the laws of necessity, and as Neumann (1994) points out, it is perhaps the gods, not just the monsters, who play a corresponding role in staging the heroic curriculum:

> Just as the hostile goddess Hera in the development of Hercules and the goddess Aphrodite in the corresponding path of Psyche embody the terrible aspect of necessity without which no development is possible, so there is no night sea journey of the hero without night, no sunrise without darkness. (p. 158)

Such blended constellations of heroic and monstrous are arguably part and parcel of all of our narratives. Would psychological growth be possible without this law of necessity to which they are bound? As purported in Dynamic Systems Theory and the evolutionary theory of Teilhard de Chardin, one might argue that all radius and no tangents, or in the language of Dynamic Systems Theory (DST),)a predominance of basins of attraction over strange attractors in a system, risks psychological and or social fossilization, depending on the context. The Titan's tendency to get stuck in its own circle noted by Jünger (1947/2006) and his related analysis of Atlas's petrification in the Gigantomachia suggests an ancient Greek expression of this phenomenon. By corollary, one could argue that Hercules, Psyche, and Prometheus act as strange attractors in their tangential orbit beyond the system. In this sense, their existential heroism stands apart from the pathological portraits proffered in archetypal psychology. Likewise, the mantha of the heroic and the monstrous is crucial to systemic vitality, their bold moves and charged interactions resembling what in Dynamic Systems Theory is referred to as a birfurcation cascade, a critical, enantiodromia-like tipping point at which the system starts to move over to the 'new way' (Rogers et al., 2005). We will revisit this point in the final chapter on creativity and innovation.

Translation's Monstrous Body

From Cicero to Steiner, there has always been a sense of something monstrous in translation. Be it a quality of violent sacking of the treasures of a 'target culture' or its subsequent zombiesque consumption or dissection by a sort of mad scientist-rhetorician, something always seems violated in translation, rendering it —in the double sense of rendering, both as a new creation or a sort of tearing to pieces[5]— something undeniably monstrous.

Given the de*monstr*ative nature of the Latin root *monstr-*, -there is something both in the process and products of the translational act that have something to show. The translation may present itself phantasmagorically as a sort of "spirit" (Nabokov, 1955/2012; Pound, 1929/2012) inherent in the text of origin, or even as a transcendent "golden vessel" (Benjamin, 1923/2012), or in Umberto Eco's (2001) alchemical resonance of a mystical, *Mercurius*-third man that reminds us of the ominous 'mothman' or 'thin man' of contemporary urban legends and sci-fi lore.

Considering Nicolas D'Ablancourt's (2012) "unlovely in between realm" (p. 48), a sort of ghostly purgatory traipsed by the translator, the location of translation does not stray far from sci-fi and horror; however, it is probably the monstrous body of the translation product where the true horror is manifested. The formidable corpus of body horror films resonates with the distorted funhouse mirror quality[6] of translated works and the discourse of Translation Studies; both paths lead us to that familiar misogynistic point of origin: the monstrous feminine, and ultimately the "fetid" realm of the Great Mother. Likewise, David Robinson (1991) has underscored the somatic nature of translation corpora; translation is not reducible to abstract operations but rather grounded, embodied.[7]

---

[5] To this point, Spivak (2012) characterizes translations as *frayings*.

[6] Commenting on this aspect of distortion, Lefevere (2012) invokes the less pejorative resonance of *refractions*. Source: Lefevere, A. (2012). Mother Courage's cucumbers: text, system, and refraction in a theory of literature. In L. Venuti (Ed.), *The translation studies reader* (3rd. ed., pp. 43-63). Routledge.

[7] Thanks to Marko Miletich for pointing out this pertinent contribution to the present discourse on translation's monstrous body: Robinson, P. (1991). *The translator's turn*. Baltimore, MD: Johns Hopkins University Press.

The Stinky and Foul Literal and Fidelity

In Translation Studies, a monstrous point of origin lies in the literal. Lawrence Venuti (2012) highlights St Jerome's descriptions of excessively literal translations as "foul" and "stinky" (p. 491). Centuries of sacking the arts and letters of conquered and bygone cultures recast literalism as a praiseworthy move toward the translated Other, establishing foreignization as an accepted translation strategy, though this approach was not (and arguably still is not) without critics. Walter Benjamin (1923/2012), for example, chides Friederich Hölderlin, a famous German philosopher-translator, alleging: "Hölderlin's translations of Sophocles were seen as a monstrous example of this kind of literalness" (p. 81). If monstrous, foul, and stinky are descriptions that constellate with patriarchal casting of the Great Mother, there are many more direct examples of her presence in the translation of Western letters.

Though it constitutes a translation quality that has waxed and waned in importance over the evolution of Translation Studies, "fidelity" to the text of origin has always been a principal preoccupation of the translator, and it is inextricably connected to literalness. Curiously, that text of origin has been cast as both a lover and a mother, adding a classic touch of Mother Complex to the virtue of being faithful, extending notions of "mother tongue." As Littau (2000) has established, the mother tongue is inherently multivocal despite attempts to render her monotheistic (yet another shade of the One and the Many). In matters of the monstrous feminine, this tendency merits closer examination.

On matters of fidelity in translation, Lori Chamberlain (2012) takes aim at the cliché misogynistic expression: *les belles infideles* (the beautiful unfaithful), which claims that the translated work, like a woman, cannot be both beautiful and faithful. In this frame, the translator is cast as a portrait painter charged with preserving the virtues of the original, likened to a model, and he must take great care in managing this paradox. Chamberlain describes the consequences of favoring the translated product: "to follow the text yet further, make[s] her monstrous" (p. 256, citing Cowper. 1891/1975). This ethos has matriarchal inflections as well: "Because the mother tongue is conceived of as natural, any tampering with it – any infidelity – is seen as unnatural, impure, monstrous, and immoral" (p. 257). Similarly, Robert Cawdrey (2007) comments: "Some men seek so far for outlandish English, that they forget altogether their mother's language, so that if some of their mothers were alive, they were not able to tell, or understand what they say" (p. 45, cited by Cronin, 2012, p. 473). Adding to this sense of monstrous betrayal of the mother tongue, the theologian Friederich Schleiermacher (1813/2012) comments:

Who would gladly consent to be considered ungainly for striving to adhere so closely to the foreign tongue as his own Language allows, and to being criticized, like parents who entrust their children to tumblers for their education, for having failed to exercise his mother tongue in the sorts of gymnastics native to it, instead accustoming it to alien, unnatural contorsions? (p. 53)

There emerges here another paradox: the more a translation is "domesticated," a term that references a bias toward the language and culture for which the text is translated, the more it is estranged from the "mother (tongue)." As Western arts and letters are conveyed across the Atlantic, the family dynamic grows even more monstrously distorted, adding yet another constellation around the family dysfunction explored earlier in the context of cultural trauma in Totalitarian states.

Fidelity in (post-) Colonial Contexts and Monstrous Rebellions

Eventually, fidelity, like its close cousin in literality, is discarded in favor of freer, more *natural* translations.[8] Though the core objectification of Mother Nature as matter (mater) to be curated through patriarchal craft, it is worth noting the displacement of the monstrous from Monstrous Gaia to the depiction of transgressions against the Great Mother, not that this, in itself, undermines the patriarchal arc from poly- to monotheism. We also note the displacement of the feminine Other to that of the cultural variant, which is denoted by *foreignized* translation.

From a post-colonial perspective, and as Gayatri Spivak (2012) suggests, foreignization of the colonizer's letters constitutes a necessary, perhaps monstrous betrayal. In efforts to create new literatures, the Terrible Mother Tongue threatens to use all the tools of linguistic imperialism at her disposal to prevent her children from finding their own voices, resulting in some peculiar inter-generational disputes around the language family dinner table, an all-too-common trope in horror movies centered on adolescent rebellion, with an emphasis on hybrid monsters: the kids are warned not to allow themselves to be contaminated by outside influences, and yet the suffocating insularity of the Mother Tongue[9] demands exactly this sort of adolescent rebellion in the

---

[8] At the suggestion of my colleague, Marko Miletich, an elaboration may be helpful here: natural=more idiomatic.

[9] Brisset alludes to Lalonde's monstrous [my word] translations in Quebec: "the language of our 'vulgar' is a barbarous and impure way of speaking that should be punished mercilessly for being an inept way of speaking French" (p. 292). Source: Lalonde, M. (1979): Défense et illustration de la langue québécoise, Paris, Seghers- Laffront.

language family. Annie Brisset (2012), for example, comments on Quebecois rebellion from continental French with teratological (monstrous) overtones: "Creating a distinction between a native language and a mother tongue entails more than the reappropriation of the native language, a language deformed and alienated by interference from English" (p. 291).

Issues of English linguistic imperialism aside, in the Age of Globalization we understand the inherent fluidity of form in all languages and cultures. Consider Gaia's ultimate offspring: like Typhon-Teras's many heads, growing out of their Greco-Roman body, each new variant of language and culture across time and space nuances capital T truth. As Ong asserts, the literate variants are prone to stray from the Great Mother. To this point, the reader may recall the footnote on the first quote from Jünger (1947/2006). Absent an English translation of the original text, written in German, I was obligated to resort to the Spanish translation. Consequently, the potential for monstrous mistranslation is significant. Likewise, multiple monstrous mistranslations characterize Freud and Jung's translation of classical texts and the transference of the patriarchs' psychological theories outside of their original German-language context.[10] As with the work of the iconic mad scientist of sci-fi horror, Translation Studies and depth psychology arguably share a common mission of *re*capitating Typhon-Teras. Or, returning to the case of Quebecois French literatures, perhaps this process is more rightly construed as a re-dismembering, as the adolescent-colonists struggle to render the monstrous body of continental French something befitting a cultural individuation, an initiation reminiscent of the struggle of Persephone to free herself from Demeter's Devouring Mother aspect. Again, we see this paradox of "domestication" that ironically pulls away from the mother (tongue), resulting in a monstrous hybrid of foreignization and domestication in the colonial and colonized world. Arguing that the Quebecois bond to the Mother Tongue was "a tie that, in any case, was never nourishing" (p. 292), Brisset, again with teratological overtones, argues that the "deformed spelling" (p. 300) of Quebecois translations, far from constituting monstrous transgressions of the mother tongue, instead connote "differentiation" (p. 300), and encourages the same treatment of translations of English works, applauding "the gift of disfiguring' American theatre" (Brisset, 2012, citing Tremblay, 1969).

A similar adolescent rebellion was likewise experienced in the early years of the post-British United States. Vicente Rafael (2012) recounts Webster's linguistic declaration of independence: "Great Britain, whose children we are, and whose language we speak, should no longer be our standard, for the taste

---

[10] For a full review of the related literature in translation studies, see Warford (2019).

of her writers is already corrupted and her language on the decline" (p. 456). Rafael invokes what reminds us of the classic hero's journey trope used by Jung: the victory over the Mother Complex: "while 'we' have abandoned the mother, we can retain the mother tongue only if it can be reformed and turned into 'our' National language" (Webster, 1789: 21, in Rafael, 2012, p. 456).

Situated in post-colonial hybridities, deformations, dis-(re)membering, and other forms of rendering translation bring us back to Frankenstein's monster. The Monster must rebel against the creator, as his very existence means he has something to show (de*monstr*ate), something about the limitations and strictures of the creator. Much to the embarrassment of the parent, there will be some outlandish rebellions to suffer on the plane of culture and language.[11] These new, hybrid discourses, however, are a threat to the patriarchy; as post-modern feminist critics suggest, the long arc of the feminine understands the rhizomic interdependence of diachrony and synchrony in the growth of languages. Concretely, diachrony denotes the fairly steady recycling of language rules from age to age; synchrony, in the form of dialects and other phenomena that emerge in the present, serves an adaptive function to make sure that the rules will be revitalized from generation; the linguist Carmen Silva-Corvalán (2001) describes the point at which these linguistic forces intersect as panchrony. In Jungian terms, panchrony resonates with the coniunctio and the mantha. Adolescents 'hang ten' on this panchronic wave. While much of their innovative, mutant patois quickly becomes dated (*ginchy, groovy, gnarly...*), other expressions have a *cool*ness that anchors into the diachronic undertow. So, in the translatological family drama, let us focus further on this hybrid, adolescent rebellion aspect of language's monstrous body in archetypal perspective. According to López-Pedraza (1991), adolescence is very rooted in the Freak archetype, represented iconically by Aphrodite and Hermes' monstrous children: Priapus, with his enormous phallus, and Hermaphroditus, who is fused to Salmacis, thus constituting a truth of nonbinary gender identity. For the author, such figures inspire psychic movement and are always generative presences in the consulting room. Similarly, Nicolescu (1994) unequivocally embraces trisexuality as a human right basic to a transdisciplinary approach.[12]

The Freak in translation is not a new kid on the block. Certainly, St. Jerome's (2012) swapping of *letter-for-letter* literalness for sense-for-sense was a bold move for his time. Likewise, Luther's domestication of the Canon for common

---

[11] We may also include here, as pointed out by my colleague Marko Miletich, the exuberant, exoticized pseudo-translations highlighted by Borges (1936/2012).

[12] From Nicolescu (1994): "Trisexuality is the basis for human rights...All human beings are trisexual. Neither man, woman, nor androgyne – trisexual" (p. 140).

volk of Germany resonates with the very natural drive to establish one's own individual –or in this case cultural—identity (Robinson, 1991). Still, myth teaches us that one can fly too close to the sun in adolescence, and in translations, such misadventures often yield monstrous results. The writer and Translation Studies scholar Vladimir Nabokov (1955/2012), for example, ridicules Lord Byron's "monstrosities" of free translation (p. 125). Likewise, Antoine Berman (2012) likens too-free translations as a sort of "textual deformation" (p. 242) that recalls the tower of Babel. In other cases, such free translations are praised. In the case of the Quebecois movement, Sherry Simon (2012), for example, praises the "misuse and perversion of other languages and cultural references" (p. 446). Echoing the linguistic *mantha* of diachrony, synchrony, and panchrony, Gideon Toury (1995/2012) suggests that the final judgment of monstrous vs. standard is ultimately arbitrary. In other words, freer translations may contribute to enduring new linguistic and translatological directions; likewise, they may also be discarded as "idiosyncrasy which never evolved into something more general can only be described as a norm by extension" (p. 176).

It is said that all teenagers eventually become their parents, and the colonist-rebels are no exception. Bearing in mind that we have limited most of our discussion to settler colonization, it is important to consider the more un*settling* reality of colonized languages and cultures, especially in the context of forced colonization and enslavement. Demonstrating a monstrous lack of reflection and empathy in light of his own struggle to create an independent, United-States English, Webster, according to Rafael (2012), eventually derided non-Anglo-American dialects as "shameful mutilations" (Webster, 1789, p. 103, cited on p. 458).

What the monstrous wants to show (de*monstr*ate)

So, what does the monstrous have to de*monstr*ate to us? The examples we have explored in Translation Studies suggest a more expansive, multivocal, and perhaps even post-human perspective of the subject: we are each of us constituted by a dynamic, rhizomic body of words, a complex and diverse family tree. Like the Borg, the body snatchers, the alien hives, the zombie pandemics, and all-consuming blobs, we are all mere members of this monstrously translated body called language. With every conquest and commercial expansion, Typhon-Teras stretches forth a new head. Bearing in mind the monstrous nature of language and letters, I will attempt to pronounce some specific lessons inherent in the monstrum.

It is said that Frankenstein's monster was used to caricature Irish Nationalists (Karbiener, 2003, p. xv). Indeed, Shelley's narrative's monstrous perspective has a lot to show us about cultural complexes and trauma, and it is certainly a message that juxtaposes Self and Other, the One and the Many. Speaking from centuries of the Western patriarchal One, Dr. Frankenstein captures the consequences for its marginalized (monstracized) Many:

> If the study to which you apply yourself has a tendency to weaken your affections, and to destroy your taste for those simple pleasures in which no alloy can possibly mix, then that study is certainly unlawful, that is to say, not befitting the human mind. If this rule were always observed, if no man allowed any pursuit whatsoever to interfere with the tranquility of his domestic affections, Greece had not been enslaved; Caesar would have spared his country; America would have been discovered more gradually; and the empires of Mexico and Peru had not been destroyed. (Shelley, 1818/2003, pp. 53-54)

Meanwhile, his monster, to whom he refers as "my vampire, my own spirit let loose from the grave" (Shelley, 1818/2003, p. 75), wanders the margin, ostracized, seeking out the communion of the Many, with exactly the sort of global empathy his creator lacks as he learns of the trail of tears of Western conquest recounting how he "heard of the American hemisphere, and wept with Safie over the fate of its original inhabitants" (p. 118). Ultimately, he draws the Western shadow his master can only faintly perceive into the light, calling the question: "Was man, indeed, at once so powerful, so virtuous, and magnificent, yet so vicious and base? He appeared at one time a mere scion of the evil principle, and at another as all that can be conceived of noble and godlike" (p. 118).

The monster begins to contemplate his own wretched existence as a shadow projection of the Western hegemony: "When I looked around, I saw and heard of none like me. Was I then a monster, a blot upon the earth, from which all men fled, and whom all men disowned?" (Shelley, 1818/2003, p. 119). His exile and isolation unbearable, the monster fantasizes about taking a created companion off to South America. Dr. Frankenstein grows incensed by this proposition, terrified of the possibility of a "race of devils" (p. 164), and he ultimately dismembers the she-monster that he has reluctantly begun constructing. The parallels to the Titans' dismembering of Dionysus are unmistakable. What it is also being demonstrated here is the titanic inability to transform, as it is clear toward the end that Victor is unrepentant where his creation is concerned. As with cultural complexes and trauma, which are purported to be extremely difficult if not impossible to educate and heal, the tragedy of Frankenstein is felt in the inability of Frankenstein and his Monster to attain the fellowship of the Many. For Frankenstein, this stems from an inability to see beyond the family bonds, which are arguably limited to the small sphere of the Self-Same of the One. To this point, Jung Eun Seo (2018) suggests that Shelley's vision was a cross-cultural, expanded sense of fellowship that resonates with Lehr-Rottman's (2014) *Opus Contra Naturam* of transcending one's cultural comfort zones: "Frankenstein is a literary project attempting to disassociate sympathy from the natural bond that one is born into, and instead, re-associate it with fellowship as a second nature to be cultivated and practiced" (p. 215).

Perhaps a better description of this existential challenge is an *Opus Contra Prima Cultura*, in which case, the monster has not even been bestowed an education in a first culture. In any case, were it not for the scars of the fatal trauma of rejection by his creator, the monster proves himself quite apt and expansive in cultural learning. In observing the inhabitants of a cottage where he is secretly squatting, for example, he learns the ways of community and demonstrates his at least partial integration of the lesson:

> This trait of kindness moved me sensibly. I had been accustomed, during the night, to steal a part of their store for my own consumption; but when I found that in doing this I inflicted pain on the cottagers, I abstained, and satisfied myself with berries, nuts, and roots, which I gathered from a neighboring wood. (Shelley, 1818/2003, p. 110)

As the monster, his duty is to press this *contra naturam* lesson regarding fellowship, one that his creator is ultimately incapable of processing: "Do your duty towards me, and I will do mine towards you and the rest of mankind" (Shelley, 1818/2003, p. 97).

Of course, this sort of cross-cultural curriculum is not without its own hazards of fetishizing and exoticizing the cultural Other, the proverbial "Western gaze" (Lehti et al., 2010) and its corresponding orientalisms (Said, 1979).[13] Consider Dr. Frankenstein's best friend Clerval: "Resolved to pursue no inglorious career, he turned his eyes toward the East, as affording scope for his spirit of enterprise. The Persian, Arabic, and Sanskrit languages engaged his attention..." (p. 67). Clerval also declares his intention to advance colonization and commerce in India (Shelley, 1818/2003, p. 157). As we have learned from the trajectory of Translation Studies, there are forms of conquest that demonstrate semiotic, not just physical varieties of pillage. Whether or not Shelley wrote with such intention is a moot point; the warnings about the West's Eastern gaze are well-established in critical theory, as well as in classic Jungian and archetypal psychology.[14] Restated from a cultural complex and trauma perspective,

---

[13] Thanks to Marko Miletich for suggesting this apt connection.

[14] Again, the Western Gaze is a construct proposed by Lehti et al. (2010). Edward Said's *Orientalism* (1978: Pantheon Books) is a seminal work in studies of the Eastern Other. Jung (CW11: 759-800) had the sense to caution Westerners eager to consume Eastern wisdom. Hillman (1975) likewise, advises: "To flee to the East, or up in transcendence, or

working through these psychic disturbances by embracing the cultural Other may present a transgression of nature, a sort of experiment in cultural technology.

This move toward the cultural —and even the global— Other is what is constituted in an expanded sense of the Many: one planetary family. In approaching such ecocritical stances, we must first confront the centuries of degradation of Mother Earth and abjection of the non-human. To this point, Neumann (1994) sustains that "mankind has animated the earth everywhere with the deadly monstrosities of its fear and its terror" (p. 190), thus rendering our planet "wholly other" (p. 193).[15] A cursory review of post-human themes in Latin American literature demonstrates a path toward a more elemental (Titanic) un-Othering beyond the Olympian, cultural sphere. Short stories like Cortázar's *Axolotl*, in which a jaded zoo patron changes places with a primordial lung-breathing fish on display, Rulfo's *Luvina*, in which an austere, remote area of Mexico takes on the form of a sort of Death Mother, and Bolaños *El Gusano,* in which an inscrutable campesino is reduced to an appendage of an equally hostile and humbling land, all portray[16] the possibility of both interspecies and elemental (topos)-based subjectivities abjected under the monotheistic and patriarchal One.

Ultimately, as underlined in arts and letters from Hesiod to Creed, the through line of the monstrous focuses on a gender-based message. As we have established, the elemental (Earth-based) Other is inextricably tethered to the Great Mother. We can add to Monstrous Gaia the timeless worship of Pacha Mama in the Andes, who currently serves as a beacon for ecological movements in the American hemisphere. The cultural Other also has something of the feminine as it is subject to the Western male gaze (Lehti et al., 2010). As Mogenson (2005) notes, Jung's anima often took the form of a foreign woman (citing Jung CW 9, I, para. 518.; CW 10, para. 714; CW 12, para. 112).

A hybrid sense of the monstrous feminine merits closer analysis. As Asimov (1961) points out, though most of the half-animal, half-human monsters in Greek mythology are depicted as half-woman, often with misogynistic

---

out into futurology leaves the land in dismay, no ground for homecoming, no nourishing soil" (p. 224).

[15] To some degree, Neumann (1955/2015) regards such phenomena as pre-Western conceptions of the Terrible Mother as, for example, the "devouring maw of darkness "the flesh-devouring sarcophagus" who "must be satiated with offerings of living blood" (p. 189).

[16] Cortázar, J. (1967). *End of the game and other stories* (P. Blackburn, Trans.). New York: Pantheon; Rulfo, J. (2019). The burning plain and other stories (G. D. Schade, Trans.). Austin, TX: University of Texas Press; Bolaño, R. (2006). Last evenings on earth (C. Andrews, Trans.). Toronto, CA: Random House Canada.

ascriptions that passed into everyday pejoratives: harpies as "greedy women" or a gorgon as a terrible or "terrifying woman" (p. 114), a siren has been passed down as "a flirtatious woman" (p. 120). Let us also consider the minotaur. Though male, he is the cast-off offspring of the Cretan queen, Pasiphae, the product of an adulterous affair with a bull and depicted by Ovid (through Scylla) as a "a hybrid monster" (8.133). Aldo Carotenuto (1985), working within the classic Jungian frame of the hero's journey, reminds us that the minotaur ultimately reflects a monstrous (devouring) mother who must be conquered in the quest for individuation. In his words, Theseus's rival (the minotaur) in the labyrinth parallels "the maternal monster the hero must destroy if he is not then to be destroyed by it" (p. 49).

Of all the hybrid feminine monsters, the Sphinx is perhaps the wisest teacher. Campbell (1991) sets the scene of her encounter with Oedipus as follows:

> The Sphinx in the Oedipus story is not the Egyptian Sphinx, but a female form with wings of a bird, the body of an animal, and the breast, neck, and face of a woman. What she represents is the destiny of all life. She has sent a plague over the land, and to lift the plague, the hero has to answer the riddle that she presents: "What is it that walks on four legs, then on two legs, and then on three?" The answer is "Man." The child creeps about on four legs, the adult walks on two, and the aged walk with a cane.
>
> The riddle of the Sphinx is the image of life itself through time—childhood, maturity, age, and death. When without fear you have faced and accepted the riddle of the Sphinx, death has no further hold on you, and the curse of the Sphinx disappears. The conquest of the fear of death is the recovery of life's joy. One can experience an unconditional affirmation of life only when one has accepted death, not as contrary to life but as an aspect of life. Life in its becoming is always shedding death, and on the point of death. The conquest of fear yields the courage of life. That is the cardinal initiation of every heroic adventure—fearlessness and achievement. (pp. 187-188)

Without contradicting Campbell's (1991) interpretation, I would like to posit a supplemental reading. First of all, the Sphinx embodies the Many of the Great Mother, including her elemental, natural forms and also in her capacity as a spiritual counselor, uttering the ordinance of human existence. Her hybridity as monster and woman, Earth Mother and Spiritual Mother, conveys a holistic trope that a hero's journey conveniently divides in order to outline the patriarchy's preferred and abhorred aspects of the feminine, as evidenced in this split.

Of course, this strange fusion of feminine and monstrous in the Zeus Order was transferred (translated) through time and space, from Greco-Roman exploration and conquests of the New World, across languages, arts and letters, appearing from time to time in the exoticized Greco-Roman projections in the logs of the early explorers,[17] myths that fueled the Renaissance imagination and inspired works like Shakespeare's *The Tempest.* To the latter point (arts and letters), the monstrous holds up a mirror to Western, patriarchal culture. Edward Edinger (1984) comments on this phenomenon, though, as I will point out, there are some particularly important oversights, from a feminist perspective:

> The classical mythical example of the value of separating subject from object by the power of reflection is found in the myth of Perseus and Medusa: to look upon Medusa directly is to be turned to stone, i.e., she represents a psychic content that destroys the ego; she can be overcome only by viewing her through reflection in the mirror-shield which Athena provides for Perseus. I consider Athena's mirror-shield ultimately to symbolize the process of human culture itself, which redeems man from the destructive Medusan horror of raw being. Language, art, drama, and learning provide the Athena mirror for humanity, allowing the psyche to emerge and develop. What Shakespeare says about drama is true for all culture-forms, they hold the mirror up to nature. (pp. 39-40)

Such commentary evokes Harrison's notion of the Great Mother mythologem, Moira, the continuum from primordial nature to refined, civil culture: the opposition of Medusa-Athene more or less reflects this, and in light of Ovid's account, this is reflected in Medusa's shadow mirror.

Hybridities in the monstrous feminine are endemic of the patriarchal binary, in which "all those components of the individual's 'bisexual' nature not corresponding to the requisite ideal type are repressed or suppressed" (Neumann, 1994, p. 33). Though Neumann affirms the essential nonbinary nature of the psyche, he asserts that men are somewhat disadvantaged to the extent that, while women are expected to develop both feminine and masculine traits in the patriarchal system, men are not required to develop their feminine side (p. 55). Perhaps this is why it has to be shown to him through monstrous feminine abjection in all its hybrid glory. Though ultimately considered monstrous in ancient Roman culture, the many "transgressions" of

---

[17] Columbus, for example, described inhabitants of the New World with Greco-Roman monstrous feminine flourishes, describing Amazon-like women and "gentes sin pelo" [hairless people]. See p. 96 of Pereira-Muro, C. (2015). *Culturas de España* (2nd ed.). New York: CENGAGE.

gender and sexuality norms depicted in Ovid's *Metamorphoses* (1/1995-2009), from Salmacis's seizure and envelopment of Hermaphroditus to the gender-bending affair of Iphis and Ianthe, open spaces for blending binaries of gender and sexuality. This is a classically Jungian individuation concept of the Quaternity, the notion that between a man and a woman there is a cross-sexual doubling, such that Man, Woman, Man's Anima and Woman's Animus are the prima materia in need of integration. Neumann (1994) addresses the Quaternity in patriarchal context: "Only when this 'pure masculinity' of the patriarchy has been overcome through this process of transformation does a man overcome the fear in which his 'pure masculinity' screened itself from the otherness that appeared symbolically as feminine" (p. 279). He advocates a similar, reverse process for women.

On the mythological origins of post-modern hybridity, Claire Sommers (2017, March; 2020, September 17), in her analysis of Plato's *Phaedrus*, reminds us that the term "monster" picks up the root Teras, from the Greek, as in Typhon-Teras, the many-headed creature Gaia spawned to defeat the Olympians during the Gigantomachia, once again reminding us of the close connection between the monstrous and the maternal feminine order. In *Phaedrus*, the famous philosopher recounts the last days of Socrates, who is about to be tried and executed for his incessant questioning, and generally being a nuisance in Athenian society. In short order, he will willingly take the hemlock that will ensure that the death sentence is carried out, though generally it is believed he could have argued his way out of this fate. Such was Socrates. Following is an excerpt from his final statement:

> SOCRATES: The wise are doubtful, and I should not be singular if, like them, I too doubted... Gorgons and winged steeds flow in apace, and numberless other inconceivable and portentous natures. And if he is skeptical about them and would fain reduce them one after another to the rules of probability, this sort of crude philosophy will take up a great deal of time. Now I have no leisure for such enquiries; shall I tell you why? I must first know myself, as the Delphian inscription says; to be curious about that which is not my concern, while I am still in ignorance of my own self, would be ridiculous. And therefore, I bid farewell to all this; the common opinion is enough for me. For, as I was saying, I want to know not about this, but about myself: am I a monster more complicated and swollen with passion than the serpent Typho, or a creature of a gentler and simpler sort, to whom Nature has given a diviner and lowlier destiny? (Plato, 1994-2009, l. 229)

The highlighted excerpt, for Summers, de*monstr*ates (my word) the true nature of the monstrous: like the parade of gorgons and pegasi (Pegasus was the son of the Gorgon Medusa) and the many-headed Typhon-Teras, ultimate truth has a hybrid aspect; for every question Socrates asks, another head pops up: apparently this perhaps too annoying for Athens in the Zeus Order, but now it strikes us as the beating heart of post-modern, global approaches to the Humanities, an inheritance of Typhon's translated trail of languages, arts and letters.

Concluding thoughts

Subjecting patriarchy's hero and spiritual mythologems to the "monstrous" mantha, we have established here the core subtext of resistance to the patriarchal binary rooted in both the Titanic and Monstrous Feminine. Thankfully, our daughters now have a growing array of empowering narratives in which the monstrous feminine is recast as the heroine-protagonist. Consider Nory, the main character in the young adult *Upside-Down Magic* series (Mlynowski, Myracle, & Jenkins, 2015). Nory is a "fluxer" who struggles to hold the form of the animal into which she wishes to morph. Eventually, she learns to embrace her wonky magic, helping her classmates to do the same. Likewise, Madeline Miller (2018) has deftly recast the incidental drive-by *femme castrice* Circe of Homer's *Odyssey* as compelling, complex protagonist in her own right.

In concluding this discussion of the monstrous and its close ties to the Western cultural complex, it is important not to allow ourselves to be lulled by a simplistic reduction that exalts the Many over the One, with all the attending gender-based associations. Arguably, the monstrous is just s at home in the too-essentialist perspective of the One as it is in the too-pluralistic sense of the Many. As Marlan (2021) reminds us, "Unity becomes a Cyclops, and multiplicity, a hundred-eyed Argus. Both are monsters" (p. 239). Concretely, then, the monstrous serves as a counterweight to one-sided binaries, an important tool for the mantha.

One way to view this counterweight recalls discussions of the *Opus Contra Prima Cultura*, introduced in the preceding exploration of cultural complexes and traumas that characterize the cultural turn in psychoanalytic studies. In order to steer through the turn (or churn?), we will have to mantha Jung's legacy a bit further, subjecting it to a very Jungian oppositorum; this includes much of the Marxism and "rank materialism" (CW17, para. 128) that so irritated the Swiss philosopher. In the next two chapters, this work will be carried out under the framework of "integration."

Chapter 5

Integration of *Cogito* and *Cultura*

"Why do they say that the sleep of reason engenders monsters? What reason are they talking about? The delirious logic of reasoning reason engenders just as many monsters. (Nicolescu, 1994, p. 25)

"The forgetting of oneself by oneself gives rise to monsters" (Nicolescu, 1994, p. 170)

The Prima Materia: Cogito and Culture

Alchemically speaking, the *prima materia* that needs to be worked through in the cultural turn centers on integration, a mantha of mounting schisms between the One and the Many in the Western psyche. To that end, this chapter and the next center on a blend of some relevant pedagogical and psychological concepts, as well as the integration of innatist and social epistemologies of the subject. Having blurred notions of what is monstrous in the previous chapters, I begin this one with Nicolescu's challenge- that an excessively involuted or innatist approach to psychological development based on the fantasy of pure reason, in itself, is arguably monstrous. In the frame of mantha, this chapter envisions a quality of learning and psychological development that alchemically maximizes both breadth and depth of integration, a sense of relatedness to outer as well as to inner experiences, and all of this certainly spirals back to the One and the Many. To resurrect alchemy in modern academic discourse constitutes an inherently audacious act, and yet Nicolescu's (1994) vision for transdisciplinary academic inquiry unabashedly embraces the term as a way to counter the atomistic "anti-alchemy" that constricts contemporary scholarly endeavors. As he puts it, "Modernity is the triumph of anti-alchemy: the transformation of gold into filth" (p. 88).

In the present context, and in matters of the One and the Many, what I call the One loosely references the Western tendency to proffer a universal mind in psychology and pedagogy at the cost of cultural influences on cognition. This approach, which to an extent reflects Jung's analytical psychology, reflects the legacy of the Cartesian Cogito ("I think, therefore I am") of Enlightenment Rationalism. Dating back to Plato, the capacity for the individual subject, the "One," to access "capital T" truth has been questioned. Echoing both Plato and Panikkar, Coward (1996) reminds us that "*Logos* passes by way of the Man, and

Man is not its sovereign" (p. 88). Similarly, Panikkar (1995), himself, is quite clear about the violent and deleterious implications of unchecked rationalism:

> Our cultures are customarily belligerent, and treat others as enemies, barbarians, goi, mleccha, khafir, pagans, infidels, and the like. Let us add, further, that more than one culture makes use of reason itself as a weapon: reason is used to deceive and convince. (p. 19)

Though he does not make the association explicitly, we may infer from this assertion that reason is no less a weapon of conquest than the musket or the mauser, and further, that its uncritical employment runs counter to his proposal for cultural disarmament. As he describes it, "'cultural disarmament' refers in a unique way to the predominant culture, which has a scientific and technological character and is of European origin" (p. 34). Concretely, what Panikkar (1995) seeks to disarm is an uncritical acceptance of "progress, technology, science, democracy, and the world economic market, not to mention governmental organizations" (p. 34). All of these cultural manifestations, according to Panikkar, constellate around the human race in its current evolutionary status as homo technologicus.

Integration also calls for post-gendered perspectives of the One and the Many, beginning with a mantha of the patriarchal and matriarchal realms. To this point, Neumann (1994) evokes a binary of the One and the Many, respectively, in discerning matriarchal vs. patriarchal strata of the psyche. While the matriarchal allegedly represents "the culture-building level operative at the dawn of human history" (p. 66), the patriarchal points to "objective consciousness" based on the symbolic "separation of the Masculine and Feminine" (p. 6). In post-gendered perspective, and with Themis and Prometheus ever-present, these forces reflect more sublime, basic tendencies of consciousness: the need to connect, on one hand, and on the other, the need to split off. Balancing and fully engaging these forces is arguably the central aim of an education; it is likewise even more likely to be the core work of being human. Consequently, the reader will forgive me if this chapter floats freely between the pedagogical and psychological.

In both pedagogy and psychology, the work of integration confronts conflicting yet not irreconcilable epistemologies, one rooted in rationalist (cognitivist) assumptions that resonate with the One, and empiricist stances that focus on concrete material and social influences on the subject (the milieu of the Many). The Chomsky-Skinner debate over the nature of language and language development serves to contextualize these explorations. Operating from an empiricist stance, B. F. Skinner dismissed rationalist (mentalist) epistemologies of psychology and learning as *explanatory fictions* (Graziano & Raulin, 2020). Ultimately, however, he would lose decisively in an age-old

Enlightenment debate between Descartes' Rationalism and Locke's Empiricism. While Skinner opted out of fumbling through the 'black box,' choosing to stick to what was scientifically measurable and verifiable (Skinner, 1977), Chomsky (1959), in his review of Skinner's iconic work, *Verbal Behavior*, rightfully argued that the social context cannot account for the full measure of language development, pointing to children's novel utterances and their obvious creative capacity. That said, Chomsky's (1965) notion of Universal Grammar, which asserts that we are innately endowed with the capacity to *acquire* language rules, has failed to convince many that one can develop grammatical competence without conscious learning.[1]

In Jungian circles the Rationalism vs. Empiricism debate is somewhat more complex. Though Jung was cut from the rationalist cloth, he rejected the dismissal of what he saw as the empirically factual evidence of spiritual forces at work in the psyche. Jung, an admirer of Kant, shared the philosopher's skepticism with regard to the workability of a purely rationalist epistemology. As we bring Jung into the conversation, we find that his legacy falls somewhere in the middle with regard to the rationalism-empiricism debate. He was recognized and considered himself to be an empirical scientist, and yet his innatist emphasis on the archetypes and individuation hint at a discernable rationalist foundation, in spite of his Kantian formation. In many ways, Jung was satisfied with neither epistemology. The rationalist need to encapsulate the psyche in theories and conceptual categories was, for him, as it was for Skinner, so much nonsense.[2]

---

[1] The engine of grammar acquisition centers on an allegedly innate "Language Acquisition Device" or LAD, which connects input to Universal Grammar rules through passive cognitive processes, as suggested by the notion of "acquiring" vs. "learning." To the contrary Wilson (2017) argues that "Grammatical rules, on the other hand, are mostly learned. The theory of a universal grammar, famously advanced by Noam Chomsky in the mid-twentieth century, was so complex and jargonized as to escape the indignity of being understood and has in recent years been largely abandoned for lack of evidence by researchers on linguistic psychology" (p. 27). Likewise, in second language acquisition research and methodology, there is a long trail of studies and commentary demonstrating that mere "input"-based approaches are insufficient for attaining high levels of grammatical competence. Generally, as suggested in the World Readiness Standards framework for Communication, one needs to progress from input (interpretive mode) and interaction (interactional mode), to output (presentational mode). Source: The National Standards Collaborative Board. (2015). World-Readiness Standards for Learning Languages (4th ed.). Alexandria, VA: Author.

[2] "Theories in psychology are the very devil...they should always be regarded as mere auxiliary concepts that can be laid aside at any time...No doubt theory is the best cloak

In distinguishing Giegerich's rationalistic approach to psychology from that of Jung's, Mogenson (2005) refers to Jung as the Jung as a self-styled "empiricist of the psyche" (p. 70). At the same time, we must acknowledge that, perhaps partially in reaction to Freud, Jung found empirical science overly materialistic and lacking in depth, though he at least tacitly understood the difficulties of subjecting the richness of psyche to empirical analysis.[3] Jung considered himself to be an empiricist of the inner world, which was just as real to him as any variables manipulated in a controlled lab experiment. Consequently, he abhorred what he perceived as purely objective, laboratory-based psychological inquiry. The following quote puts this stance in perspective:

> Thus, modern empirical psychology was cradled in an atmosphere of rank materialism. It was first and foremost a physiological psychology, thoroughly empirical in its experimental basis, viewing psychic processes exclusively from outside and mainly with an eye to its physiological manifestations. Such a state of affairs was fairly satisfactory so long as psychology was a department of philosophy or of the natural sciences. So long as it was restricted to the laboratory, psychology could remain purely experimental and could regard the psychic process entirely from outside. Instead of the old dogmatic psychology, we now had a philosophical psychology no less academic in its origins. (Jung, CW17, para. 128)

Though his psychology was guided by disenchantment with the West's allegedly one-sided rationalism, this quote suggests a bias toward a rational, innatist epistemology of psyche, with its corresponding focus on individuation. Perhaps it explains Jung's failure to transcend his aversion to the social (collective) plane. Rowland (2002) points to Jung's "moments of crisis in which the cultural, the theoretical and the personal intersect" (p. 2). From a feminist perspective, she argues that "Jung takes directly from Enlightenment grand narratives the prejudice that desirable qualities of reason and logical thinking are to be gendered as masculine leverage against an 'outside' of feminine irrationality" (p. 130). However, she recognizes in Jung's alchemical investigations a measure of rebellion against Enlightenment essentialism, a refusal to split mind and matter; mind and body, for Jung, are at once separate and connected;

---

for lack of experience and ignorance, but the consequences are depressing: bigotedness, superficiality, and scientific sectarianism" (Jung, 1954/1974b, p. 7).

[3] "[M]odern empirical psychology was cradled in an atmosphere of rank materialism" (Jung, 1954/1974b, p. 56).

"In science, I missed the factor of meaning; and in religion, that of empiricism" (Jung, 1963a/1955, p. 72).

particle and wave; "vitally interrelated" (p. 134). In a similar way, Jung finds a way out of the empirical vs. innatist-rationalist binary by privileging 'psychic facts' over 'theories about facts' (p. 42).

Ultimately, it is the rationalist (innatist) Jung that has been carried forward. Neumann (1994), for example, appears to have been influenced by Jung's innatist rationalism when he asserts that:

> The radical turning of consciousness towards the so-called objective external world has led to a progressive splitting off of the conscious mind from the world of the subject, the "Inner World," which has culminated in the isolation of the individual, and the individual and collective neuroticization of modern man. (p. 187)

Giegerich (2012), who has challenged Jung's alleged lack of logico-deductive rigor, has likewise affirmed the value of Enlightenment Rationalism's deliverance from the feeling-tinged tyranny of the feudal state. Even Rowland (2002), a staunch critic of Enlightenment essentialism, concedes that the Age of Reason edified the important values of "autonomy and freedom" (p. 136).

In introducing Jungian thought to socially situated ways of looking at integration required for the cultural turn, I neither seek to restore empiricism or rationalism, per se, particularly since the former does not necessarily gravitate from the laboratory to the social milieu in its orientation toward objectivity. If anything, just as in psyche and culture, the empirical and the rational need to be 'subjected' to deeper inquiry, starting with the premise that a lot of the research we will explore here does not fall completely on one paradigmatic side or the other. In fact, most research in educational and social psychology incorporates both empirical and rational approaches. In the interest of deepening the concept of integration, and following Rowland's lead, I hope to open an epistemological space in which modernist grand theory submits to the complexities of post-modern personal myths, and this certainly is the core work of reconciling the One vs. the Many. Likewise, this is the work Jung has passed forward, and studies in cultural complexes and trauma have opened the portal. Though self and society, mind and milieu seem at odds at times in Jung's psychology, I concur with Rowland's (2002) assessment that the central focus of Jung's work was "a systematic account of psyche and culture" (p. 102); it just needs a good mantha.

Revisioning Jung for the cultural turn: Toward an *Opus Contra Prima Cultura*

As noted in the first chapter, Jung made it his life's mission to push himself past his unilateralist western roots, and he was apparently 'globally engaged,' as they say these days, committed to the *Opus Oppositorum*. Ultimately, however, he failed to integrate the individual-collective polarity: identification with the latter was often positioned in opposition to individuation, "the process by which archetypes intervene in and educate the ego" (Rowland, 2002, p. 30).

Hillman (1975) was more direct in confronting Cartesian Rationalism's all-seeing *Cogito*, which he criticized as an impossibly unified, disconnected self. His archetypal psychology indeed opened the cultural focus around psyche's alleged diversity, a *polytheistic* psychology. More recently depth psychology has truly 'engaged' with the current discourse on the influence of culture through the investigation of cultural complexes and trauma. It is the emergence of a cultural critical perspective that has made possible the current proposal of an *Opus Contra Prima Cultura*.

If we accept, as Rowland (2002) posits, that Jung's emergent interest in alchemy did not connote indifference toward the cultural and historical dimensions of his research, that his notion of individuation was tethered to one's "own history and culture" (p. 135), then this fusion of inner alchemical work and the cultural frame is an essential next step in Jungian thought. Still, coaxing depth psychology out of the head and into Jung's dreaded collective is a tall order. What is needed is a model that *integrates* the deep and dynamic interconnectedness of mind and milieu, a way of truly folding into one another in an education of psyche and culture, and ultimately a way out of the Enlightenment-rooted "fixed opposition between essentialism and social constructivism" (p. 108). Likewise, the field of education must see through a vicious circle within the post-Enlightenment predicament just depicted: mind over society to society over mind and back again. *Ad nauseam.* A less binary and more blended view of teaching and learning seems always just out of reach.

What I will attempt here is a fusion of Jungian and archetypal psychology with emergent sociocognitive perspectives of development, including Dynamic Systems Theory (DST), Sociocultural Theory (SCT), and Ecological-Semiotic Linguistics (E-SL) (van Lier, 2004), which factor in a range of social contextual factors that influence learning and psychological growth. These approaches are not irreconcilable with mainstream cognitive psychology in individual differences, nor are they anathema to scholarship in Jungian and archetypal psychology. All combine, 'integrate,' to demonstrate that the true measure of transformative psychological change and deep learning is ultimately situated in intersections of interaction, contexts, competencies, and what Vygotsky (1932/1994), the founder of sociocultural theory, categorized as learners' affective-volitional dispositions.

There are, certainly, aspects of these approaches that do not initially find fit with the Jungian tradition, in particular the Swiss psychologist's abhorrence of Marxist materialism, which guides Vygotsky's sociocultural theory of mind; however, I would argue that these ways of thinking fit together surprisingly well, provided we do not lose ourselves in dogmatic adherence to this or that paradigm. In any case, as Jung taught, that which irritates us opens the door to deeper learning through the tension of opposites.[4] In establishing a dialogue between emergent sociocognitive research and (Post-) Jungian Studies, we find a useful 'third,' much in the same way opening oneself up to a different language and culture offers new tools that are much more than the sum of the native and target cultural perspective. This third is not a simple linear layering of experiences and interventions but rather an organismic, rhizomic process of continuous (co-) creation and reshaping. There is a constant, dynamic unfolding, with no point of termination; consequently, traditional product-oriented (data-driven) measures of learning and treatment typical of transmission models are not acceptable within this framework. The way we learn and grow psychologically is emergent, holistic, and transformative; we will see it in a qualitatively more nuanced, differentiated way of engaging with the world, full of leaps and setbacks in the mantha.

Introduction to the Integration Model

Innatist and social views of cognition have danced superficially around one another long enough. An integrative approach is needed to fully engage breadth and depth of learning and psychological development. The transcendent function serves to remind us that the Truth is somewhere between Cogito and Culture, one blending into the other, as connoted in the mantha: no sublation, no clear victor, but rather a dynamic churning. The Integration Model I introduce here is at ease with the aforementioned theoretical foundation, and it connects with the diverse and dynamic empirical realities of psychology and pedagogy. That said, it is important to clarify upfront that there is a polarity that must and will be reconciled in ways that do not detract from the integrity of the positions represented. The roots of this polarity center on innatist vs. (social) empiricist epistemologies of cognition. Other challenges center on the contrast between unified or fixed, as in the notion of a human 'subject,' vs. dynamic conceptions of the Self, a more fluid, Heideggerian sense of human 'being;' the related question of conscious vs. unconscious conceptions of the Symbol, and the longstanding polarity between individuation and identification in analytical psychology. If we can appreciate that learning must be as deep (innatist) as it is extensive in its reach (empiricist), these polarities are not irreconcilable. With that target in mind, a path opens to this emergent global, holistic logic of being-in-the-world worthy of the cultural turn.

---

[4] "Everything that irritates us about others can lead us to an understanding of ourselves" (MDR, p. 246).

Confronting the complexities of "integration" and "culture"

Before introducing the major dimensions of the proposed model (next chapter), it makes sense to start with the meaning of the term *integration*. Webster's New Collegiate Dictionary (Editors, 2008) defines integration as "a: incorporation as equals into society or an organization of individuals of different groups (as races)" and "b: coordination of mental processes into a normal effective personality or with the individual's environment" (Editors, 2008). Applied to the cultivation of new knowledge, skills and discourses in ways that complement each individual's unique unfolding, the integration metaphor conveys two central and more or less simultaneous movements: a 'reaching out' and 'a taking in' that matches breadth of exploration with depth of introspection.

It is impossible to understate the barriers to such a proposal. Beyond the rationalist-empiricist dichotomy, there are a number of misunderstandings in need of clarification, and these gray areas center on notions of self and culture. The best illustration I can think of for this predicament is the emergent notion of 'deep learning,' as promoted by The Hewitt foundation. This is not the deep of depth psychology, which has long been eclipsed by the dominant view in psychology of a unified Self, a mainly biological entity that is somewhat shaped by its environment; it comes as no surprise, of course, that there is no room here for the unconscious, for imagination, for, dare we even use that fringy term, a 'soul.' Like many modern Western enterprises, the foundation sees depth from the point of view of its corporate benefactors, a corresponding Titanism-infused shadow of global engagement. Consequently, depth is cast out into the culture, denoting a depth of problem-solving skill sets that can be set off across the world for profit-generating endeavors. This has more of the feel of 'breadth,' the cultural component in an integrative education, but with none of the genuine interest in expanding both cognitive and personal horizons. The only depth measure that reflects a 'taking in' centered on inner development rather myopically targeted to a sort of pragmatic, productive set of capabilities typical of ego-based psychology, as already established. Consequently, "creative thinking skills, perseverance, locus of control, or self-management" (Zeiser et al., 2014, September, p. vi) ring somewhat hollow. On the contrary, authentic engagement in different cultural contexts should deepen notions of self beyond what Hillman (1975) referred to pejoratively as the unified *heroic ego* of the West.

This is not to say that the aforementioned outcomes-driven pragmatism should be discarded, but it neglects the one thing essential to true integration: an authentic, expanded notion of oneself beyond the ego. Without tethering ourselves to religious or mythological, or for that matter, even purely logical senses of soul, as posited by Giegerich, let us allow soul to represent the diversity of one's inner world beyond the ego. As Hillman (1975) put it, a *stewardship* to this psychic diversity, the evidence of whose immanence within and without is plainly obvious to all, yet somehow serially written off in Modern thought, both within rationalist and empiricist epistemologies. An integrative education is —dare we say it?— an education of the soul.

While an integrative education of the soul does not require the spiritual associations of the latter, it must be matched by an education of culture. Here, in addition to barriers related to the conventional wisdom on the 'black box,' this mysterious engine known as the brain, we also confront the problem of how to conceptualize culture. Culture, though ubiquitous and empirically verifiable, is not just a race, a nation-state, or a geographical cluster of behaviors. As Clifford Geertz (1973) and Lev Vygotsky (1932/1994) paradoxically assert, the essential 'nature' of culture is that it is not natural. Though most species possess at least some rudimentary ability to fashion physical tools to make their way in nature, we are unique in fully possessing and wielding this cultural tool called language. Unlike our closest hominid competitors in the animal kingdom, we have the unique capacity to signify, to *mean*. This symbolic capability is not possible for the animal, who may possess some modicum of language ability by way of signaling (screeching, roaring, etc.), but these utterances do not necessarily encode a specific meaning. Not only can we transform nature literally and empirically through physical tools, but we can also name, categorize and reshape her away from direct contact.

To summarize, culture *is* meaning, and no *inner* meaning could ever have been possible without it. It is neither likely that the archetypes, the meanings that seem to transcend the grasp of consciousness and language, would have attained their symbolic potential were it not for the language endowment, which was necessary for us to encode the universal patterns of existence, beginning with the positive factual, natural world. As Vygotsky (1932/1986/1994) pointed out, thought *is* language. Though sublated into what Jung presumed to possibly be a 'psychic gene' in our ancestral inheritance, the archetypes are cultural at the core. Consequently, his trepidation about the 'collective' and its potential threat to the individual was misplaced, though he raised a critical point for purposes of developing an educational model for integration: the individual must undertake a critical examination of 'mass thinking.' Nevertheless, the 'collective' framework is problematic for two reasons: 1) it undermines the tremendous engine for individuation represented in engaging with a culture different from one's own and 2) the individual is not a pawn of a unitary collective, but rather an active participant in a diverse array of interconnected cultural systems within said collective, from conventional nationalistic or ethnic conceptions to participation in clubs and groups, teams, social networking or gaming communities. This expanded notion of culture is critical to our discussion.

According to Semetsky and Ramey (2013), the goal of Jungian psychology is the *Unus Mundus*, the holistic union of physis and psyche that occurs at the deepest, psychoid level of consciousness. They liken this alchemical principle to Gilles Deleuze's idea of enfolded consciousness: *the inside of the outside* (citing Deleuze, 1988, p. 97). In individuation, they argue, "the fractured pieces of a dissolved Cogito will be put together in analysis or integrated into consciousness in the process of becoming-other and achieving, for Jung, a 'greater personality'" (citing Jung, 1953/1972, p. 136). Echoing Vygotsky, the authors state: "experience is not confined to the individual Cogito of a Cartesian subject but is socio-cultural and always involves the other, the integration of such a generic 'other' is paramount for understanding and re-valuation of such an expanded experience" (p. 71). Seen through a more classical Jungian lens, psyche is an integrated totality and plurality that extends infinitely inward and outward. That said, psyche's Many inner and outward manifestations cannot be reduced to the One; the engine of the mantha is generated by the rhizomic synergy of both.

Integration, as we are fashioning it for the cultural turn, is inextricably tied to motivation. In addition to Vygotsky's sociocultural theory of mind, two motivational theories from individual differences research help to define the quality of this 'expanded experience' in the context of the dynamic, emergent nature of cross-cultural integration. In the field of second language acquisition, Gardner and Lambert (1972) advanced two constructs relevant to foreign language (FL) learning motivation: integrative and instrumental motivational orientations. Integrative motivation refers to a genuine commitment to studying another language and culture out of a desire to *integrate* with its speakers. Instrumental motivation refers to more practical reasons for committing to such work- for a requirement, for example, or for professional reasons. Originally thought to be contrasting constructs, the relationship between instrumental and integrative motivation is now judged to be much more nuanced, and in some ways, even complementary (Cziser & Dörnyei, 2005; Dörnyei, 2003).

In some ways, integrative motivation is similar to "integrated" regulation, a construct advanced in Self-Determination Theory (SDT) (Deci & Ryan, 2000). Deemed to be the most self-regulated form of extrinsic motivation, Deci et al. (1994) describe integrated regulation as "the process of transforming external regulations into internal regulations and, when the process functions optimally, integrating those regulations into one's sense of self" (p. 120). What is curious in applications of SDT to second language study led by social psychologist Kimberly Noels and colleagues, is that the next- most-self-determined form of regulation, "identified" regulation, is just as, if not more, predictive of sustained, successful language study as intrinsic motivation (Noels, Clement, & Pelletier, 2001a; Noels, Pelletier, & Vallerand, 2000). Stated psychologically, those learners with the capacity to value the Other fare better in language study. Indicative of its origins in Rationalism, SDT posits that there is such a thing as a purely self-oriented form of motivation that is rooted within the individual, as if that were, in itself, a virtue. The originator of Ecological-Semiotic Linguistics Leo Van Lier (1996) asserted that intrinsic motivation is not necessarily a good unto itself, pointing out video games, for example as less-than-wholesome fruits that enjoy the sanction of the self. The epistemology is not all that far from Jungian assumptions about the psyche. The lesson here is that virtues, or at least those that we hold most dear, are *social*, not solely products of the Cogito. Perhaps in response to such data, Ryan, Huta, and Deci (2008) unearthed the Aristotelian distinction of *hedonia* vs. *eudaimonia* to distinguish the latter, which centers on virtues associated with social engagement as closer to an *intrinsic* core than the former, which they associate with basic (and not necessarily healthy) affective needs. The implication is that any human activity that is construed as ultimately destructive to the self cannot be truly intrinsic. This invocation of a priori logico-deductively generated categories is a classic relic of the rationalist Cogito. Of course, like any statistics, such categories may be 'verified' as statistical truths, but as Hillman (1975) pointed out, they remain empty nominalisms.

A Marxist-empiricist perspective reveals some of the weaknesses in Self-Determination Theory. It is astounding, for example, that integrated regulation, alleged to be the most self-regulated form of extrinsic motivation, is overlooked in SDT's arsenal of research tools; measures of integrated motivational variables were not employed in the aforementioned studies. Why? The conventional wisdom is that integrated motivation because it is so authentically woven into the self-concept, is virtually indistinguishable from intrinsic motivation, though it is asserted to be fundamentally distinct from IM because it connotes a movement from the outside-in (Deci & Ryan, 2000; Noels et al., 2001b). As van Lier (1996) and Noels (2001) suggest, it is highly unlikely that learners engage in second language learning out of sheer curiosity or the competency-building 'thrill' of working out the logarithms of L2 grammar transformations.

Furthermore, is anything truly intrinsic? From a Vygotskyan (1932/1986/1994) standpoint, a 'pure' (eudaimonic) form of intrinsic motivation could only be autistic; Vygotsky posits that all higher-level functioning rests on social engagement, the dynamic dialogue between self and society. As previously noted, this conversation starts on the social plane and is internalized into the psychological plane and back out again ad infinitum. As van Lier (1996) puts it, "inter and intra-psychological forces merge dialogically to the point that it become[s] impossible to tell one from the other" (p. 111). Generally, this fusion of innate, biological, and social forces, for Vygotsky, was understood as phylogenesis and ontogenesis, respectively. Fundamentally, however, the Russian psychologist believed that cognitive development begins on the social plane.[5]

Furthermore, is anything truly intrinsic? From a Vygotskyan (1932/1986/1994) standpoint, a 'pure' (eudaimonic) form of intrinsic motivation could only be autistic; he posits that all higher-level functioning rests on social engagement, the dynamic dialogue between self and society. As previously noted, this conversation starts on the social plane and is internalized into the psychological plane and back out again ad infinitum. As van Lier (1996) puts it, "inter and intra-psychological forces merge dialogically to the point that it become[s] impossible to tell one from the other" (p. 111). Generally, this fusion of innate, biological, and social forces, for Vygotsky, was understood as phylogenesis and ontogenesis, respectively. Fundamentally, however, the Russian psychologist believed that cognitive development begins on the social plane.[6] Take away the cultural signs and tools that the individual has appropriated from and negotiated with his or her social milieu; apparently, what remains would be some sort of raw container of biological endowments and instincts. Development without culture would connote pure phylogenesis (hedonia), a condition Vygotsky (1932/1994) expressly attributed to autism, within the limited knowledge of that psychological factor of his time; eudaemonia, rather than representing an innate phylogenetic endowment, would represent culturally mediated behavior (ontogenesis) rather than some sort of intrinsic endowment. It seems fair to call the question; is it impossible, as Vygotsky and his followers have asserted, to divorce motivational variables from their particular culturally embedded meetings? The aforementioned frameworks for human motivation offer case studies of unexpected intrusions of a socially situated view of cognition into individual differences research in cognitive psychology. In the face of empirical realities, the rationalist cogito collapses.

Dynamic Systems Theory finds favor both in the classic Vygotskyan framework and in progressed iterations of his theories. Vygotsky (1932/1994) proposed a similarly non-linear view of development, one that viewed cognition as dynamic and dialogic, highly subject to the learner's affective-volitional disposition. As his translator Alexander Kozulin (Vygotsky, 1932/1986) put it,

---

[5] "Individual consciousness is built from outside through relations with others" (Vygotsky, 1932/1986, p xxiv).

[6] "Individual consciousness is built from outside through relations with others" (Vygotsky, 1932/1986, p xxiv).

"Vygotsky perceived development as full of upheavals, sudden changes and reversals" (p. 106). Activity Theory, considered to be a later generation of Sociocultural Theory, applied Vygotsky's macro-theory of development to the microgenetic study of shifting interconnections of individual and collective roles, goals, and motives.

A movement that has paralleled the rise of Activity Theory is that of van Lier's (2004) Ecological-Semiotic Linguistics (E-SL). At home in post-structuralism's emphasis on grounded, local truth, E-SL is an embodied, holistic educational theory that takes the biological science of ecology and applies it to the development of sign systems. The result is a democratized, connected, and social critical pedagogy in which the development of symbolic capacities is viewed as a highly organic, ideological process. The key unit of development in E-SL is the "affordance." Affordances denote the multiplicity of changing events, as well as physical and psychological artifacts, which engage learners' perceptions within educational ecologies. In addition to upending the traditional focus on the acquisition of morpho-syntax within linguistic research, E-SL respects the fullest measure of sign mediation in today's classrooms, beyond teacher-learner interactions; that is, if we accept the affordance as the essential unit of learning, then we have to consider the totality of the classroom environment, including all of the traditional and multimedia artifacts associated with participation in instructed learning contexts.

All of the aforementioned theories fall somewhere along a continuum from fixed, innatist rationalism and socially situated empiricism. Ultimately, for purposes of generating a rigorous model of learning-as-integration, none offers an ontologically satisfying explanation of the mind vs. milieu question. The inherent Marxist materialism that drives sociocultural theory and its paradigmatic offspring, in particular, leaves the impression of the learner as one who horse trades among a given set of symbolic capabilities. On the rationalist side, we are left with the dubious and empirically refuted portrayal of a 'unified self.' Is that all there is? Or is there a parallel richness of depth to match the diversity of cultural manifestations that influence development? A true model of integration needs depth as well as breadth.

Generally, there is support for deep learning within a cognitive framework. Deep thinking, for example, is reflected in higher levels of Bloom's Taxonomy, a framework commonly used in the elucidation of student learning outcomes (Students will be able to synthesize, evaluate, etc.). The hegemonic notion of a unified self, devoid of any sort of unconscious or subconscious aspect, fails to really integrate on a level that produces transformative change. We could stop with Vygotsky's notion of internalization as essentially a concept-building process constructed on appropriation of symbolic operations experienced on the social plane. We could even accept that the learner plays an 'active' role in this process, but are learning experiences really *integrated* into the learner's ongoing self-narrative? Integrative learning should be equal parts mythos (narrative) and logos (logic), feeling and thinking, or to borrow from Vygotsky, experiential (spontaneous) and scientific (schooled) concepts. By dint of the mantha, one needs churning into the other. As Nicolescu (1994) reminds us: "Understanding is engendered through experience. Any explanation or theoretical generalization is merely an approximation of this understanding" (p. 28), and he situates his elusive Hidden Third somewhere in the dynamic interaction of scientific and experiential knowledge (p. 136). Vygotsky would likely recast this model less mystically, focusing instead on the practical crafting of concepts through dialogic mediation.

In churning Vygotsky into Jung, it is important to point out their very distinct notions of what constitutes a symbol: Vygotsky's is the symbol of conscious concept development; it does not necessarily encompass the Jungian notion of the symbol, which is inherently imaginal, pre-conceptual, an artifact of archetype; in essence, it is more experienced than conceptualized. Marlan (2021) presents a mantha of symbolic image and concept that thoughtfully blends this scholarly binary rooted in Jung's anticonceptual stance: "For Jung, the prospect of rising above images and symbols in to the conceptual abstractions of science, philosophy, and religion was questionable" (p. 142). Differentiating his own stands, Marlan mantains: "From my perspective, it is important to continue to struggle with the relationship of concept and image without subjugating one to the other, without letting one or the other fall into the shadow" (p. 144). Likewise, Nicolescu (1994) presents a related alchemy of experience and concept in which their interaction with the Hidden Third "gives rise to different levels of knowledge" (p. 136).

Jungian educationists Semetsky and Ramey (2013) point to a way out of the conscious vs. the unconscious symbol binary. Both Deleuze and Jung, according to the authors espoused symbolic mediation as a tool for uniting the unconscious with the conscious. This is a vastly different sort of symbolic mediation from Vygotsky's that privileges affect as a mediational tool. Though Vygotsky (1986) conceded a role for an 'affective-volitional' aspect of development, his ultimate goal was logos-centered, directed to concept development. Affect, as the authors see it, centers on the capacity of being Other-centered, 'to affect and be affected' (citing Deleuze & Guattari, 1987, p. xvi). In other words, outside consciousness reflects the inside, in thought that integrates sensing, feeling, and intuiting. This, according to the authors, is a way of mending fractured, divided consciousness that is the inheritance of the Cartesian cogito that separates mind from body.

Concluding thoughts

This survey of the theoretical foundations of psychological and pedagogical integration suggests a pervasive sense of shallowness. All too often, the learner does not meet the taking-in process with the requisite level of introspection, with consequences for both well-being and deeper, more transformative learning experiences. Furthermore, what *is* taken in can be quite toxic. Deci and Ryan (1985) portray an insidious level of regulation that sits between purely extrinsic rewards or punishments and more identified forms of regulation: introjection. We underestimate just how much of what we learn wastes away in this purgatory, propelled by external pressures even when they are not present in the social context. As Ed Deci and Richard Ryan of the Human Motivation program at the University of Rochester describe it, introjection is "the process whereby a regulation is internalized in essentially its original form; children regulate themselves by carrying on a relationship with an internal representation of the previously external contingencies" (p. 135). Introjection, which acts as a kind of cancer or intruder within the self-concept, should not be confused with integration; introjection, which echoes Jung's corrosive sense of the Collective, is anathema to the kind of integration espoused in this model. However, it fails to capture the depth of introspection that is only possible within a Jungian framework, which embraces the contradictions of ongoing self-transformation within the individuation process. Consequently, we will gather the threads explored in this chapter, add a few more stands, and attempt to braid them into a depth psychological approach to integration.

Chapter 6
Elements of an Integration Model

The integration metaphor is infused with both centrifugal and centripetal forces: integration from without and integration from within, and these forces should not be seen as contrasting poles but rather as complementary processes that are mutually reinforcing. Reflecting an overdue need for match of breadth and depth in learning experiences, the Integration Model presented in this chapter considers both vertical (inward) and horizontal (outward) dimensions of the same. In a sense, Shelley's *Frankenstein: A Modern Prometheus* (1818/2003) is an allegory of these disparate curricular paths. Dr. Frankenstein's vertical journey flows down and into ancient texts, "the search of the philosopher's stone" (p. 37) and into "the dreams of forgotten alchymists" (p. 44). Meanwhile, his creation studies the ways of fellowship: "these people possessed a method of communicating their experiences and feelings to one another by articulate sounds" (pp. 110-111). The sense of incompleteness in both characters is poignant: put them together and you have one exquisite and whole human being in the best possible sense.

Clearly the role of social context as an influence on the quality of learner engagement and psychological growth is essential. Likewise, there must be a commensurate level of intrasubjectivity to match this intersubjectivity. In either direction, the motivational quality and dynamic nature of engaging these processes, as discussed in the last chapter, needs to be recognized, though we are arguably ensconced in a pedagogy of the One: One-size fits all, "data-driven" models to meet the demands of aggregation economics: the less differentiation, less expenditure. What is acquired is an extraordinary mantha of Jung that targets integration of the One and the Many at deeper levels of psychological and cultural transformation.

The *Opus Contra Prima Cultura* and Communities of Practice (outward integration)

The *Opus Contra Prima Cultura* we have introduced addresses cultural complexes and traumas as well as the need for deeper levels of psychological growth and learning. Additionally, it challenges us to think more broadly about what it means to expand one's horizon, imagining the broadest sense of cross-cultural capability and deepest levels of individuation. Lave and Wenger's (1991) notion of learning as situated in what they have referred to as apprenticeship in a 'community of practice' (hereafter referred to as CofP in the singular and CsofP in the plural), a phenomenon that was universally noted in an expansive study of learning practices that spanned a variety of social contexts, serves as a critical bonding construct for this Integration Model. The authors' social learning view of development recognizes the learner's agency in choosing from opportunities to participate in a vast array of communities of practice. Academic fields, clubs, social media, listservs, gangs, professions, religious groups, gaming clans are just a few examples of CsofP, and as the reader will note from the list, the digital age has clearly expanded both the categories and nature of competent, authentic, and socially integrated membership in such groups. Given the diversity and uniqueness of each learner's milieu, Lave and Wenger use the construct 'legitimate peripheral participation' to emphasize that we all stand at the periphery of a number of social and formal spheres that may or may not invite us in. Furthermore, the CofP is often quite insular, demonstrating, at best, little awareness of its own unwritten and written rules of full membership, and at best, a petty distrust of any dissent; in other words, a fossilized Many that is impermeable to the One. To this point, the 'Visions' seminar collection features the following related quote from Jung (1997/1930-1934): "So, a dim consciousness is always inclined to form something like a sect, a small group, within which there is complete identity; as soon as somebody has one thought that differs from the feelings and thoughts of others, there is trouble, then there is an explosion" (p. 942). It is easy to imagine the loosely constellated circles in the Pollina (2009/2013) drawing as peripheries of CsofP, but the prospects need not be quite so insular. To the contrary, Pollina discerns in his Omega Point project a gradual emergence from divergence and separation to relational convergence that might likewise be construed as a trendline from the One to the Many. In his own words,

> I think that as false structures fall (when given enough rope, greed undoes itself) man will find his way to a cohesive and functioning organization of smaller-unit local systems. These smaller systems seen in part or as a whole will reflect the same resonating structure of love and common sense and will increase in these qualities as we are drawn and approach the Source of our Identity.

This prediction notwithstanding, and given the plurality and vicissitudes of membership, each of us confronts, as Lave and Wenger posit, a legitimate choice regarding the depth with which we participate (if we even have choice in the matter) in various CsofP within our social context. The corresponding apprenticeship required for membership involves the appropriation of new ways of communicating and being, and language learning perhaps presents the greatest challenges in matters of membership in a CofP. For example, in instructed second language learning settings that involve the teaching of a non-dominant language and culture to students of a dominant language and culture, one might need binoculars to even catch a glimpse of the periphery of communities for whom that language is dominant, let alone achieve a core sense of integration. Furthermore, it is not a given that teachers of world languages themselves possess significant experience and competencies in the language and its cultures. In contrast, those learning the dominant language are surrounded by opportunities to engage but undermined by a different set of barriers, not the least of which may center on discrimination or the risk of being detained and or deported for not possessing legal citizenship status.

As sociolinguist John Schumann (1978) noted in his Acculturation Model, distance between languages and cultures is not just social or geographic; it is also psychological, and language teachers readily relate to the daunting nature of this proposition. In combining Lave and Wenger's sense of integration as participation in communities of practice with Gardner and Lambert's (1972) integrative motivation construct, which expresses an affiliation with real or imagined L2 speakers, there emerges a fully realized sense of integration movement outward into new ways of communicating and being. Dynamic Systems Theory (DST), Ecological-Semiotic Linguistics (E-SL) and Sociocultural Theory (SCT) perspectives also resonate with this sense of shortening distances between social milieus.

Vertical integration: Learning to the core

A complete sense of vertical integration from surface to core is within reach; however, we need to take care in visualizing this image of learning as integration into the self. Vygotsky (1932/1986/1994), as previously mentioned, used 'internalization' to describe the integration of cultural tools and signs encountered on the social plane into individual cognition. Self-Determination Theory offers the integrated/introjected distinction, which serves to distinguish a quality of integration that is sanctioned by the core self. According to Dynamic Systems Theory and Sociocultural Theory, this point of connection between the social plane and the core self is just the beginning of the learning process. Dramatic shifts can occur since learner and context are reciprocally bound together in a dynamic dance of concept growth that may deepen to the extent that the dance is choreographed and sustained. Along with Ecological-Semiotic Linguistics, all three theories share a sense of learning-as-emergence; the individual and his or her context are constantly evolving. Consequently, the Integration Model envisions both outward and inward-directed processes that, under optimal conditions, match a breadth of outward exploration in a spiral-like descent from the surface level to a sense of core integration of one's participation—both virtual and actual—in new symbolic capacities, which involve an array of linguistic and cultural signs. While the language educator is perhaps uniquely associated with such an enterprise, it is easy to see that this view of learning could apply to any academic area, as well as professional development and psychological development, in general.

The Integration Model: Key components

Figure 1 illustrates key components of the Integration Model, which employs a 'learning as digging' geological model to account for an integrated epistemology of development. The metaphor, in addition to evoking the churning sense of mantha, is an important alchemical tool to conjoin (coniunctio) Jung's innatist view of cognition with the social view advanced in Vygotsky's Marxist-empiricist approach.[1] In diverse ways, both thinkers were responding to the radical paradigm shift rooted in Darwin's discoveries. As Sinha (1989) has noted, Darwin's evolutionary theory affronted the dominant Enlightenment rationalism of his time, offering up obvious evidence of a phylogenetic truth governing the development of culture and cognition. Similarly, Matthews and Hua Liu (2008, p. 24) found direct evidence of Vygotsky's affirmation of the geological metaphor:

> one of the most fruitful theoretical ideas genetic psychology has adopted is that the structure of behavioral development to some degree resembles the geological structure of the earth's core. Research has established the presence of genetically differentiated layers in human behavior. In this sense the geology of human behavior is undoubtedly a reflection of 'geological' descent and brain development. (citing Vygotsky, 1981, p. 155)

Inspired by Greek *katabasis*, descent is basic to Jungian depth psychology (Jung, 1911-12/1952/2014, para 374-375), affirmed by Neumann (1994) as an important initiation. In 1909, Jung (1964) recounts his dream of a house in which each floor led level by level from contemporary down to the most primitive roots of his being, a dream that eventually transform into his notion of "unconscious ancestral elements" (Jung, 1925/1989, p. 36). Adapting Jung's geological excavation of the psyche, Singer and Kimbles portray eight strata leading in the following direction from the individual psyche to a 'Central fire': 1) individual, 2) family, 3) clan, 4) nation, 5) larger regional identification, 6) primates, 7) all animals, 8) the Central Fire'. In a similar fashion, Vygotsky layered development from phylogeny to ontogenesis, mediated by a sociocultural stratum. Jung (1954/1974b) shared this acknowledgment of the

---

[1] Though far from being a materialist himself, Jung (1954/1974b) affirmed "the biological structure of the mind" (p. 41), insisting that "one can hardly overestimate the value of strictly scientific biological inquiry" (p. 76).

old adage, 'ontogeny recapitulates phylogeny': "Just as the developing embryo recapitulates, in a sense, our phylogenetic history, so the child-psyche relives 'the lesson of earlier humanity,' as Nietzsche called it" (p. 134).

The Integration Model I am proposing is an attempt to reconnect culture and cogito by means of the aforementioned geological metaphor, which recognizes the interdependent nature of the corresponding elements. The core notion is one of a developmental 'dig' that excavates outward on the cultural and inward on the cognitive plane. The more one churns their way into a new culture, be it academic, professional, or social, the more he or she is put in touch with some inner truth; we find that the Other was refracted inside all along, just operating on a different frequency, a projection, the proverbial fingers that point back for the one that points outward. Both trajectories move from surface to core, though no one can say definitively how this works, or the extent to which the process is situated in individual cognition or the cultural milieu. Giegerich (2012) offers a radical notion of culture, rather than the individual subject, as the bellwether of the soul's logical life: "The works of culture are not self-expressions, not fantasizing in the sense of the unconscious's projection of images onto the screen of the conscious mind. Cultural works are their own origin, *they* produce themselves and come as a 'surprise' to people" (p. 183), gradually working their way down, past the resistance of the culture's status quo, through a process of integration and sedimentation, "ending up as sunken cultural assets in people's inner" (p. 183). His conclusion, based on Hegelian logical negation, is one interpretation. We may just as easily follow the empirically positive evidence of dynamic systems that influence both culture and cognition. In some ways, both logical negation and positive empiricism lend some support to Jung's concept of synchronicity, a connecting principle. Likewise, there is something of a mantha in their relationship.

At the heart of the Integration Model are three modes of learning and four strata of depth. Regarding the former, Self-Determination Theory (Deci & Ryan, 2000) posits that intrinsic motivation is nourished by the provision of competency, autonomy, and relatedness. Because the intrinsic motivation construct is inconsistent with Jungian or sociocognitive epistemologies, and for reasons that will be clarified later on in this chapter, I have made some minor adjustments. The adjusted triad consists of competencies, authentication, and engagement. Competencies are self-evident, requiring no elaboration. Authentication, which builds on van Lier's (1996) work and Jung's theory of individuation, adjusts the notion of autonomy to a predicate, a process that affirms the learner as the final arbiter and alchemist of learning content and experiences with regard to genuine ownership of the learned material. The selection of Engagement, rather than relatedness, affirms the broader imperative of recruiting learner involvement for deeper learning, not just for personal and social well-being inherent in the Relatedness construct. In a similar way, engagement reflects the effort and commitment associated with participation in a Community of Practice. SDT's continuum of motivational orientations from other- to self-regulated varieties is more or less faithfully followed in evaluating the quality of engagement.

As will be discussed in more depth later on in this chapter, the Integration Model is divided into four levels or *strata* of internalization, just like the layers of the earth. Surface Integration, the first level, corresponds to a baseline of a-motivation (total lack of motivation) and extrinsic motivation embodies the essence of peripheral participation in instructed or natural L2 communities. Based primarily on Peircean semiotics, E-SL (van Lier, 2004) sees learning as beginning with direct, iconic sign processing, evolving into indexical, associational cognition, and eventually maturing into a fully symbolic stage at which all three semiotic modes are orchestrated and meaning is fully organized and stabilized. Accordingly, surface-level engagement is characterized by an iconic initiation into a community of practice and the development of an indexical and eventually symbolic orientations to the various affordances, both material and mediated, available in the classroom (in the case of instructed settings) or whichever community of practice into which one seeks membership, though symbolic capability is only meager at this stage. The affordances available to the learner through the course content, the teacher's personal and discursive qualities, the participation structure, the society's bylaws, etc., are subject to initial authentication or rejection by the learner. Due to the strong connection to known cultural identifications, the iconic quality is essential for this process in order to promote ownership.

'Mantle Integration' involves deeper exploration into and interrelation of the symbolic competencies that constitute the community of practice in question, which may promote the deepening of engagement from purely extrinsic involvement to the introjection of external pressures as the individual deepens his or her participation. This exploration, guided by an autonomy-supportive teacher, supervisor, or facilitator, has the potential of achieving a genuine and sustained quality, as predicted in SDT (Deci & Ryan, 2000).

'Outer Core Integration' is a layer that features the emergence of an identity that accommodates both known and new symbolic capacities represented in the academic or social setting of the community of practice in question, though there may be some unevenness between progress within the three processes; consequently, it shares some of the same features of identified regulation since the learner has not yet allowed him or herself to fully forge the tensions that have emerged between what is known and elements of Otherness in the CofP; they remain effectively compartmentalized from one another. Though the door has been opened, the ego is not yet ready to fully welcome the cultural Other, or in Jungian terms, the guest at the door; therefore, outer core integration has a 'darkness before the dawn' quality, anticipating a deeper dive.

Finally, Core Integration connotes the highest qualities of competencies and engagement and a deeper sense of trans-symbolic capability and appreciation of unexpected connections. With regard to authentication, the learner develops the requisite ego-permeability to accommodate complex patterns of meaning construction across a variety of cultural systems. There is something novel, visionary, beyond ties to one's first culture that shines forth in works produced from this level of integration. A glimpse of core integration presents what Marlan (2021), invoking Taoist alchemy, describe as "a new vision of light mysteriously described as inner, invisible and as vivifying fire, mundus imaginales filius, Primordial Man or Golden Flower" (p. 105).

It is important to point out that, like the classic Chutes and Ladders board game, with its random advancements and setbacks, there is never any guarantee that progress through the various levels of integration will follow an even, linear path. All of the paradigms synthesized into the Integration Model, in their own ways, affirm a dynamic alchemy of development. There is a corresponding acceptance of the possibilities of both unexpected leaps forward and major setbacks. Of course, there is also the possibility of pulling out of learning with regard to a particular community of practice at any stage along the way. In fact, we should affirm the learner's legitimate peripheral participation. There are just too many options for learning in a lifetime; one cannot commit to all!

Having introduced the most salient features of the Integration Model, let us consider several hypotheses that naturally flow from the key elements of integration: The Ecology Hypothesis (Hypothesis I), The Integration Hypothesis (Hypothesis II), and the Strata Hypothesis (Hypothesis III). As hypotheses, I do not necessarily limit their exploration to empirical approaches; indeed, they may be considered Sutras. As this is all exploratory, there is just as much to be gained by both imaginative and rational speculation.

Hypothesis I: The Ecology Hypothesis

The Integration Model affirms a holistic connectedness that transcends the cognitive, the personal and the external domains (Kincheloe & Steinberg, 1993; van Lier, 2004). All life is intricately connected, from mind to body to milieu. This is in direct contradiction to the rationalist cogito, a model in which mind is split from body. With regard to the false dichotomy of mind (spirit) and body, Jung commented extensively on this point within a holistic framework:

The distinction between mind and body is an artificial dichotomy, a discrimination which is unquestionably based far more on the peculiarity of intellectual understanding than on the nature of things. (Jung, 1933/2001, p. 85)

We must find out how to get everything back into connection with everything else. We must resist the vice of intellectualism, and get it understood that we cannot only understand. (Jung, 1987, p. 420)

the spirit is the life of the body seen from within, and the body the outward manifestation of the life of the spirit – the two being really one. (1946/1970, p. 195).

We are used to thinking of matter and spirit as of two wholly different and opposite principles. But to the alchemist, the material was filled with a spiritus, and the two were inseparably one. (1939, p. 66)

Jung's holistic psychology extends the connection to the natural world, which he arguably held in higher esteem than the cultural milieu. Nothing for Jung could breathe quite so much oxygen into the work of individuation like a walk in the woods, stone carving on the shores of a lake, and such, especially for Modern Man:

As scientific understanding has grown, so our world has become dehumanized. Man feels himself isolated in the cosmos, because he is no longer involved with nature and has lost his emotional 'unconscious identity' with natural phenomena. (Jung, 1964, p. 85).

Such connections echo the potentially generative encounters with the titanic-elemental explored earlier. Terrence Dawson (2008) highlights of Jung's call for an outward life in youth and a movement inward in the second half of life, though perhaps the need for natural, elemental connection transcends matters of life stages. To be sure, Jung was much more preoccupied with the transformative potential of adult education than with the education of children and adolescents. The Integration Model pushes past these polarities of introspection and engagement, youth, and age, and it does so by way of the transcendent function, rooted in his own acknowledgment of a deeper, a-historical connectedness of all things. This connectedness embraces an expanded notion of ecology, beyond the 'wilderness' sense of the word. The habitat of today's learner is far removed from the idyllic woodsy education of Rousseau's *Emile*, though it may have been precisely this sort of temenos in Mother Nature's womb, freed from the contaminants of the collective, that Jung might have envisioned and to which he held fast in his flight from the unilateral, monotheistic constraints of Modern European Man.

Ecological-Semiotic Linguistics (van Lier, 2004), which was introduced earlier in this chapter, furnishes expanded notions of ecology and habitat beyond the wilderness sense of ecology. Every learning environment—whether natural or instructed—presents a unique array of physical (seating, aesthetics) and semiotic (multi-media, classroom discourse, participation structures) tools or as they are referred to in ecology, affordances. Affordances in the learning context—whether encountered in natural, organizational, or instructed settings— vary in their optimality in promoting integration with new symbolic capacities. Some affordances may be presented or perceived as coercive or socially distant from the self, thus undermining integration.

Like habitats, Communities of Practice do not exist in isolation; they are dynamically interconnected. The same can be said of mind and society. The most minute action or interaction may ripple into the local context and beyond, and global events may cause major shifts in individual cognition, as asserted in Sociocultural Theory and Dynamic Systems Theory; hence, in educational settings, major interventions may result in little learning, whereas minor interventions may result in revolutionary developmental breakthroughs. The three key dimensions of social learning (authentication, competencies, and engagement) are likewise permeable and interconnected; this interrelatedness increases as we progress toward core integration. For example, growth in one's second language (L2) and second cultural (C2) development lends itself to heightened and more authentic engagement in communities where the L2 is spoken as the L1.

Every educational ecology is subject to its own unique manifestations, at both the individual and collective level, of compensation, especially when affordances become polarized. Jung observed this phenomenon among American adolescents during the post-WWII era:

> Look at the rebellion of modern youth in America, the sexual rebellion, and all that. These rebellions occur because the real, natural man is just in open rebellion against the utterly inhuman form of American life. Americans are absolutely divorced from nature in a way, and that accounts for that drug abuse. (Jung in Evans, 1957, p. 35)

In a similar way, Resistance Theory (see Bernal & Solorzano, 2001, for summary) has demonstrated how students are quite capable and agentic in overcoming a unilateral and or autocratic learning context. To this point, Jung added a caveat: "Resistance to the organized mass can be effected only by the man who is as well organized in his individuality as the mass itself" (Jung, 1957/2005, p. 43). Consequently, educational contexts must be co-created through collaborations of educators and their students. Such is the cornerstone of John Dewey's

(1916/2009) notion of a 'democratic education', as well as van Lier's (2004) pedagogical applications of Ecological-Semiotic Linguistics.

As previously discussed, there are essentially three interconnected processes that characterize learning in educational —or any organizational— ecologies, whether conceived microgenetically, in terms of discrete educational interventions or on a more long-term ontogenetic level across an individual's education. The focus on learning within one or another community of practice adds yet another context. Still, within an integrated epistemology, growth within the three processes remains the focus: Competencies, Engagement, and Authentication. Competencies represent the emergent range of knowledge and skills afforded by the CofP in question. Engagement denotes the extent and depth of interaction with peers and expert-others within a given CofP. Engagement, often overlooked in both empiricist and rationalist approaches to learning, is not just a third wheel in integration; it is the glue that holds the process together. As Ryan (1993) states: "The more closely related one feels to socializing others the more likely it is that internalization will occur" (p. 47). Finally, Authentication, denotes the process by and the extent to which we construct genuine personal meaning of participation in a particular CofP through engagement with peers and expert-others. According to the proposed model, 'Core Integration' describes a quality of deep learning characterized by the interaction and internalization of three aforementioned processes, whether encountered in traditional academic or in social settings.

Hypothesis II: The Integration Hypothesis

Mainstream research on individual differences tends to focus myopically on achievement or aptitude as the definitive sources of proof that learning has occurred, but what is either achievement or aptitude worth if there is no sense of an authentic, cited (rather than merely recited) self, multi-competency, or of sustained engagement to back it up? 'Core Integration' describes a quality of deep, dynamic learning characterized by the interaction and internalization of the three modes imbued in either instructed or natural communities of practice: Competencies, Autonomy, and Engagement. Though the three dimensions of integration may not necessarily uniformly transcend the layers, there is no true, transformative Core Integration without the deepest levels of attainment in all three dimensions.

Hypothesis III: The Strata Hypothesis

Like a drill aiming for the center of the earth, integration progresses through four layers that are more or less distinct: surface, mantle, outer core to core. This movement reflects the appropriation of signs encountered in a given CofP from the intersubjective (social) to the intrasubjective (mental) plane. At each stage, each of the three developmental processes takes on its own unique qualities. In order to orient the reader, I have fronted the discussion of each layer with its empirically positive aspects illuminated by the field of geology, and its index to a particular aspect of the CofP into which the learner may or not be integrated, depending on a variety of factors. Below, the reader will find a brief summary of the quality of development within the three essential processes for each given stratum. The focus, thereafter, will center on a holistic discussion of the layer itself, as it has emerged for me in imagination, rational reflection, and praxis.

Surface integration

Geological quality: Light, crusty, and volatile, the surface of the earth is a mere three to five miles thick.

Learning context: Learner is introduced to a new CofP, which may be a primarily social or purely academic variety or somewhere in between (i.e., a club, course, or a professional community, respectively). One is testing the ground, breaking the ice.

AUTHENTICATION: Learner is introduced to new tools and tasks that are either authenticated or rejected. In language learning, there is a tension between primarily first language and cultural identification and issues of personal and ecological authenticity.

ENGAGEMENT: Legitimate peripheral participation (Lave & Wenger, 1991): *Is this where I belong?* Unratified participation limits role to 'hearer', 'indexer.' There may private verbal thinking in relation to the new symbolic system. Classroom discourse varies in appeal to emotions, senses.

COMPETENCIES: There is a focus on phylogenetic (innate) competencies, and a corresponding need to appeal mainly to iconic (sensorial, emotionally appealing) and indexical semiotic mediation (here or there?) semiosis, though symbolic competency will also begin to emerge, though shaped essentially through the first language and cultural lens. In language development, the emphasis is on lexical rather than morphosyntactic acquisition and on buzz words that have 'capital' with the CofP.

Metaphorically, the 'surface' characterization fits well as a model for the learner's initial experiences in a particular community of practice. Remember that we all skirt the periphery of a multiplicity of CsofP, so the qualities of authentication, engagement and competencies likewise have an awkward, superficial feel. It is best not to drill too deep too soon since the learner is testing the ground and the educator-initiator often is trying to break the ice in order to make an iconic connection, what van Lier (2004), adapting Peircian semiotics, referred to as a *firstness* that starts the chain of semiotic development. Similarly, Vygotsky (1986) insisted that there is little possibility of sustained, effective learning unless the task matches up with the learner's 'affective-volitional' disposition. Within Dobson's (2008) stages of transformative learning, learning experiences should be exploratory and non-directed, at first. Sue Congram (2008) suggests a variety of active imagination techniques for such a purpose: making a mandala, authoring a poem and other creative tools may be put to work, but this is not the work of ego or intellect since "symbolic events develop according to their own logic" (Jung, 1935/1976, para. 397, cited in Congram, 2008). The imaginal content that arises may be set aside for subsequent reflection and integration, but, Stage One, as conceived by Darrell Dobson (2008), should limit itself to the generation of symbols through the introduction of polarities. This play of imagination finds favor in Vygotsky's sociocultural theory of mind, though it is framed within a reality principle. Toys and fantasy images are seen as precursors of more abstract cultural tools associated with the development of higher-order competencies (Vygotsky, 1978). As childish as such suggestions may appear, Creative Studies teaches us that even adult learners need this sort of iconic play in order to find a way into a new CofP.

In Vygotskyan terms, the focus of Surface Integration is on experiential concepts that will reflect minimal conceptual control and perhaps a great deal of mistransference from 'known' symbolic competencies. This also makes sense from a Jungian perspective, particularly in the case of younger learners, as suggested in Dobson's assertion:

> if children develop their imagination before they can assess their relation to what they imagine, there is a danger that children will begin to identify with issues and values that have little to do with their own stage of development, and that, in this way, they will begin to live a false life. (2008, p. 62)

The greatest value of school, for Jung, in terms of the development of the child, is its capacity to draw the child out of its fusion with caregivers, a first step that opens up identification with the collective. Though it would, on the surface, appear to contradict Jung's emphasis on individuation, which after all, depends on breaking away from identification, he saw the need for some sort of self-organization to take shape before stepping into the rigorous alchemical work of re-organizing symbol polarizations in the psyche through the transcendent function. As the following quote suggests, one must be rooted before (s)he is uprooted:

> Children are in the collective unconscious until they acquire a small consciousness of their personality, until they say "I," or "me," or their name. They are rooted in the collective unconscious and are uprooted from it by the flood of impressions from the outside. They know everything, but they lose the memory of it. (Jung, Jung, & Wolff, 1982, p. 65)

In the language of Ecological-Semiotic Linguistics, Surface Integration is nestled in the very initial stages of symbolic capability, which is characterized by the firstness of direct emotional, sensorial, iconic connection to the affordances associated with the targeted community of practice. First impressions matter, one might say. Consequently, a great deal of attention needs to be directed to the sensorial and emotive quality of the learning context. In thought and language, the learner, rather than demonstrating the capacity to develop and subordinate concepts and constructs, will try out buzzwords that have capital with the instructor or facilitator without a clue as to what these words even mean.

All of this has the feel of initiation, and it is much more iconic than cerebral. As Jungians point out, Modern Man has lost the art of initiation. This is plain to see in the typical CofP, where there may be little conscious awareness on the part of the teacher-leader of the distance between the learner's way of seeing and that of his or her expert standing within the targeted area of knowledge and skills. This gap grows as younger initiates cope with greater digital distractions and access to an ever-growing array of CsofP competing for their focus and sustained commitment.

If the aforementioned affordances are furnished to the learner, he or she *may* elect to go deeper. We are still on the surface, however, so we are still only at the most exploratory stage. There may be some evidence of Stage 2 of Dobson's stages of transformative learning, with further amplification and reflection of personal and transpersonal archetypal connotations of the learning material, but this material is mainly learner-generated and pre-conceptual; though there is some evidence of learner-directed thinking, it may only reflect the targeted constructs and concepts in the most rudimentary ways.

With regard to the authentication process, the learner is introduced to new tools and tasks that he or she authenticates or rejects. In language learning, there is a tension between primarily first language and first cultural identification, including the grammatical mis transfer mentioned previously. Accordingly, there significant issues of personal and ecological authenticity (van Lier, 1996) emerge.

In matters of engagement, the surface layer evokes the notion of legitimate peripheral participation (Lave & Wenger, 1991). The learner asks himself or herself: Is this where I belong? Giegerich (2008), as alluded to earlier, points to the Jungian notion of shadow-as-guest at the door; the first encounters with the Other: How will the first knock at the door be received? If the iconic quality of the community of practice is inviting enough to evoke a commitment, the learner will participate initially as an ungratified hearer/ indexer of the affordances (s)he encounters, and there may be the rudiments of private verbal thinking in relation to the new symbolic system, evidence that the self and the social milieu have begun to dialogue in a way that leads to meaning construction, and consequently, symbolic capability. With regard to competencies, the learner, at this stage, is armed with the phylogenetic (innate) capacity to make meaning; however, at this stage, (s)he may be more focused on lower levels of semiotic processing— iconic (sensorial, emotionally appealing) and indexical mediation (here or there?)—rather than fully symbolic cognition. For example, in language development, the emphasis may be more on simple lexis (new words and meanings) than on morpho-syntax and rhetorical subordination (i.e., marking words for who does what, when, with or to whom, with what consequences, and according to which laws?).

Mantle integration

Geological quality: Gritty, asphalt-like, hot, flowing, erupting, 1800 miles thick.

Learning context: A quality of participation in CsofP that is more genuine, sustained within the 'zone' of proximal development (ZPD).

   o   AUTHENTICATION: Ecological and personal authentication fully realized. Greater competencies and involvement promote more autonomous exploration. Nurtured by dialogic teaching approaches attuned to need for optimal challenge and feedback.

   o   ENGAGEMENT: Integrative engagement into the community of practice's ecology prefigures exploration into CsofP where content is engaged more experientially than scientifically (field experiences, study abroad). There is more ratified than recited participation, and private speech reflecting CofP surfaces in group tasks.

   o   COMPETENCIES: Socio-institutional and bilingual competencies. Spoken and unspoken rules in the participation structure. In language learning, the focus is on morphosyntax, as well as lexis.

At this stage, ecological and personal authentication should hit a stride. Moving beyond a 'requirement' or a 'badge' or any other extrinsic reward, the learner begins to turn inward the values, tasks, and tools of the community of practice, but not without some important tests. If the setting is instructed (rather than experiential), learners begin to imagine themselves as full participants in the CofP in question. For example, language learners may imagine themselves going abroad or interacting with native speakers in their community; teaching candidates may imagine themselves in 'real' classrooms; and members of societies may consider board service. Identification with a new symbolic system (i.e., second language and culture or professional standards) is the gatekeeper of the integration process; it finds its confirmation in the formation of an expanded sense of oneself as connected to (or identified with) a larger mediational milieu. What is more likely is that the learner will have heightened the iconic connection to the CofP, with a related, introjected need to please and not disappoint the leader or others of perceived prestige within that community.

A more consciously identified subjective stance will affect the quality of engagement in such a way that reflects more ratified than recited participation. Concretely, speech and writing will be less parroted (recited), and private speech reflecting the CofP may surface spontaneously in group tasks. Language learners, for example, may start to use the second language as a semiotic tool to complete learning tasks. Teaching candidates may use the specialized language of their discipline area to discuss pedagogical phenomena. With regard to competencies, learners at this stage have fully accessed the socio-institutional and bilingual competencies they have tacitly learned in navigating the various spoken and unspoken rules and norms that pervade the participation structures of various CsofP to which they have ascribed by this point in their development. In language learning, the focus is on more complex symbolic processing beyond lexis and morpho-syntax.

Outer Core Integration

Geological quality: About 1400 miles thick and constituted by white hot liquid iron and nickel.

Learning context: Self-regulated exploration of new symbolic system that culminates with direct contact.

At this stage, and depending on the context, a figurative or literal sense of culture shock sets in and there may be a falling back to known symbolic competencies. The main goal is holding the tension between familiar and new symbolic competencies, an area that Bhabha (1994), as previously mentioned, refers to as 'Third Space.' Jung's *coniunctio* more generally visualizes the space constituted by a third as the tension of opposites, though Brewster (2017) has proposed a more intercultural iteration of Jung's third, one that centers on "a growth toward deepening human consciousness as regards the issue of racial relationships and racial complexes" (p. 16) and healing through transcendent function.

o   AUTHENTICATION: Emergence of Authorial authentication.
     Development of the concept of aspect and tense allows for sharing of
     narratives, which in turn promotes inscription of an idealized self as
     member of the CofP.

o   ENGAGEMENT: Identified engagement achieved: Genuine sense of
     targeted CofP belongingness. In instructed settings, topos of
     classroom maps both imagined (online) and realized (travel)
     relationship-building in the CofP. Willingness to communicate with
     members of this community may be in evidence at this stage.

o   COMPETENCIES: Internalized competencies: Socio-pragmatics, critical
     awareness variation and one's known ways of being. Cited (less
     recited) CofP discourse. CofP discourse emerges in private verbal
     speech beyond the occasional buzzword.

The learning journey at this stage is likewise arduous and dramatic. If the
setting has been mainly instructional, this is the point at which learners begin
to walk the proverbial walk. Affordances that influence the development of new
symbolic systems may be utilized by the learner in instructional experiences or
direct contact with the members of the CofP [i.e., a target language (L2)-
speaking community]. In fact, in a Vygotskyan sense, they are both vital to
development since they are mutually reinforcing; that is, learning in purely
experiential settings lacks the benefit of more scientific, conceptually mature
or 'schooled' forms of mediation; likewise, instructed settings lacking rich
connection to lived experiences fail to engage the development of higher-order
thinking (Vygotsky, 1932/1994). Majors begin internships in their fields.
Similarly, language learners at this level may decide to study abroad. Following
a honeymoon stage, some form of culture shock invariably sets in and there
may be a falling back on more familiar symbolic competencies. In consideration of
Bhabha's (1994) notion of Third Space and Kramsh's (1988) explorations of the
same in second language acquisition contexts, learners at this stage may or
may not subject themselves to the work of navigating a Third Space in which
they must balance familiar and new symbolic competencies. Developing a
dialogue between one's innate, tacit ways of constructing meaning and other
cultures' (CsofP) symbol systems is no easy task. For example, teaching
candidates, toward the end of the program, often find the realities of practice
teaching not at all what they fantasized in their education courses.

With regard to authorial authentication, this is a journey that takes a great
deal of time in the case of the language learner, whether in world language
contexts, in which the CofP is within a non-dominant culture to which the
learner may not have direct access, or in the case of learning the language of a
dominant culture (second language), the development of past-tense aspect

facilitates more effective sharing of narratives. This linguistic achievement, in turn, promotes inscription of an idealized self as member of the CofP. However, true to the passionate nature of this stage, the learner's initial experiences with more expert members of the CofP may be ego-threatening, so setbacks are quite possible and potentially devastating to the integration process. Educationist Nell Noddings (1991), alluding to an allegedly shared ancestral heritage in storytelling, argues that the narrative work is crucial in reaching African American students. Accordingly, she affirms that teacher autobiography is a crucial tool in promoting involvement; it is the communicator, not necessarily the content that compels. Similarly, in the interest of stabilizing indigenous languages, I proffer narrative language pedagogy as a way to connect children who speak the language of the dominant culture to the stories and lessons about values and identity of their elders (Warford, 2011). Learning at this stage, is essentially a weaving of narratives. As Jung (Evans, 1957) pointed out, empirical science has uprooted us from our history. Nevertheless, even STEM areas might benefit as well from a narrative approach, given that every scientific phenomenon possesses a history, a compelling story to draw learners in. How many more students would retain the basic measures if they knew, for instance, that one foot was set at twelve inches because that was precisely the length of Henry the VIII's foot?

Having achieved identified engagement, a genuine sense of belongingness moves beyond the classroom to both imagined (online) and realized (travel) relationship-building in the CofP. Active engagement is pivotal at this stage since it opens doors to deeper levels of symbolic capability. As previously noted, a certain resiliency is also vital; encounters with more expert members of the CofP may be discouraging, reminding the learner how far they have to go to achieve core integration. Turning to Competencies, it can be said, at this stage, that the learner has progressed dramatically in their symbolic capacities and has begun to process the socio-pragmatic particularities of the CofP under study, which might be thought of as the rudiments of cultural literacy; however, they may find that the more they know, the more they do not know. This may not be so unique to attaining competency in any other CofP, but it is widely accepted that progression in language proficiency is like an inverted pyramid; each new level confronts the learner with more and more tasks to master; more and more active engagement is needed for fine-tuning the sociopragmatic particularities of capable communication in the discourse of the CofP. In language development, learners rarely achieve pragmatic competency or appreciation of linguistic variation in target cultures. When learners speak in the language of the CofP, the target language, their discourse may be more cited (authored) than recited or parroted, though they may fall back on memorized chunks or buzzwords they assume may have capital with the targeted CofP but connote a sense that integration has not yet been fully engaged.

In a general sense, Outer Core integration is a daunting crucible. If the learner has not already figuratively or literally bowed out, this would be the time. They have put so much work into attaining ratified membership of the CofP, and it seems like the further they get, the more there is to master. As the Buddhist proverb goes, 'Chop wood. Carry water.' In other words, one has to find satisfaction in the journey and leave off the fantasy of reaching its end. Truly no area of knowledge, no CofP has a finite set of knowledge and skills; the learner must dig deeper. In Dobson's (2008) final, fourth stage of transformative learning, action must deeply honor, both conceptually and imaginally, what has been integrated in the learning. He suggests mask-making and drama, but I would argue that some sort of regular ritual is more appropriate, given the difficulty of maintaining commitment at this 'darkest before the dawn' stage of integration. I encourage my Spanish students, at this stage, to find a day and time every week to edify their gains in integrating the target language and culture. Having coffee with a native speaker, community involvement with native Spanish speakers by way of literacy tutoring or serving as an aide in a nursing home where the residents are native speakers are several examples of how students have risen to the challenge, steadily registering a record of accomplishments.

A greater particular concern that needs to be addressed at this stage is the experience of English Language Learners (ELLs) and international students. Regarding to the latter, in particular, a study of international students (Senyshyn, Warford, & Zhan, 2000) that measured adjustment to college, suggests that life hit rock bottom just before the final year of undergraduate study, and there was reason to believe that lack of linguistic and cultural proficiency, coupled with a resistance to engaging with college life in another country, contributed to the low morale. The failure of universities to recruit and sustain involvement among the international student community continues to present a significant challenge. Engagement in such contexts may still be fronted or backchanneled due to external pressures or cultural patterns rather than genuinely integrated, particularly if they feel objectified by the institution as a badge or tool of global engagement.

Outer Core also exists on the border, so one must acknowledge the psychopathic side of this errant wandering between two worlds (Hillman, 1975; López-Pedraza, 1990; 2000a). If increased competencies are not matched with authentication, there may be a sense of being everywhere and nowhere, of 'playing the game.' Like Prometheus, the learner is between communities of practice that may have only a vague sense of themselves or of others, a context that fosters a certain amount of contempt or cynicism. The temptation to use inside knowledge to manipulate must be great. The rotgut of innovation culture openly embraces a tactical exploitation of the breadth of knowledge attained at the Outer Core for profit or self-advancement, or for change as a good unto itself. Such manifestations suggest an absence of the inner compass required for deeper individuation at the Inner Core. On a related note, Hillman (1989) warns of the consequences of a psychopathic education rooted in manipulation:

> Descriptions of psychopathy, or sociopathic personalities, speak of their inability to imagine the other. Psychopaths are well able to size up situations and charm people. They perceive, assess, and relate, making use of any opportunity. Hence their successful manipulations of others. But the psychopath is far less able to imagine the other beyond a fantasy of usefulness, the other as a true interiority with his or her own needs, intentions, and feelings. An education that in any way neglects imagination is an education into psychopathy. It is an education that results in a sociopathic society of manipulations. We learn how to deal with others and become a society of dealers. (p. 171)

It is possible that enantiodromia, Jung's notion of being presented with the opposite pole from that to which the learner has ascribed, is initiated at this stage of integration. Jung envisioned this enantiodromia as a sort of unconscious eruption, but if we apply Dobson's (2008) model, active imagination offers a more conscious way of engaging this process. What is more likely is that the full experience of a more stable shift in one's polarities and the resulting self-reorganization must be worked through at the core. Perhaps such an attainment is the result of an accumulation of enantiodromic moments as a systemic 'third' arises from the cognitive dissonance resulting from the distance between what is 'known' and what is demanded in order to attain full, expert membership in the targeted CofP. Dobson's third stage of transformative learning involves Integration and differentiation of attitude. Like the volatile mantle, symbolic material, both in the iconic, Jungian sense, as well as in the Vygotskyan, conscious-conceptual sense, must be tempered and tested. An enantiodromic turning —or a mantha *churning*— of a unilateral attitude into its opposite makes more sense at this later, more integrated stage, though Dobson suggests it might be possible at Stage 2. Perhaps the perceived distance between the established and new CofPs moderates the rate at which one may be prepared for this step.

A unique aspect of this stage of integration, in relation to the theme of enantiodromia, is that an unevenness between the three dimensions may grow more distinctive at this stage. A fusion between a purely cognitive (competency) achievement within engagement in the norms of the targeted CofP at the cost of deeper personal authentication may present itself. In the Hillman (1975) sense, we literally can go "out of our minds" (p. 112) and into the collective unconscious of the community of practice, which may provide the shadow fuel for an eruption of enantiodromia. How many of us know of 'those people' (never us!) who end up over-identifying with this or that CofP. Certainly, we can acknowledge the value of identification as Deci and Ryan (2000) define the construct; the well-being of the individual and the culture depends on homonomy as well as autonomy. And yet, as Jung warned, the yearning for acceptance carries with it no minor threat to one's individuation. Sadly, this dual nature of identification may never be worked through, a tragic circumstance convincingly conveyed by Arthur Miller in his characterization of Willie Loman in Arthur Miller's (1949) *Death of a Salesman*, the tragic tale of a man who gave all to his job at the expense of his own individuation.

I am also struck by another polarity that never quite attains enantiodromia, and it has a particularly Western accent. Consider the catchword in US culture, 'capable.' Here we find an illustration of how the cultural (engagement) and cognitive (competencies) aspects of integration find themselves at odds with individuation (authentication). There is almost no sense of the latter in the term these days. Rather than framing capability as a deeper empathy borne of a rich and worked-through acceptance of all aspects of the Self, as the term might be connoted in depth psychology, mainstream psychology seems myopically fused to a sense of capability as one's competency or ability to 'fit in' socially. Productivity, industriousness, and the all-pervasive 'agency' are terms that constellate with this sense of capability, uncritically worming their way into a variety of psychometric batteries.

Columnist, David Brooks (2015) has contributed some related insight into this phenomenon. Evoking the metaphor of the resume vs. the eulogy, he questions notions of 'success' in our culture, a stance that is at home with López-Pedraza's (1990; 2000a) critique of the contemporary obsession with ego-based and materialistic conceptions of success, which rob us of the psychic nourishment uniquely afforded by 'failure consciousness'. Roughly, the resume-eulogy distinction fits in with the aforementioned distinctions between mainstream society's focus on social and career achievement vs. depth psychology's focus on individuation, a sense of humane capability. He quite boldly confesses his own failing in overidentifying with the former sense of capability. Arguably, he is portraying for us the borderline between Outer and Inner Core Integration, though both the eulogy and the resume are centered on 'what others think of me,' which suggests an obstacle to deeper integration, both in the Jungian sense, and in the sense of integrated or intrinsic motivation, as advanced by Deci and Ryan (2000). This introjected quality applies to one's work within the second as well as the first culture. Even Nixon, on the eve of a major protest, afflicted by his inability to connect with disaffected, rebellious youth, mingled with protesters at the Lincoln Memorial, trying to convey a genuine sense of empathy for their anger, yet he was simultaneously trying to impress upon them a shiny, star-spangled national narrative.[2] How many of us can honestly say that we sustain our involvement in the many CsofP of the collective with full consciousness? By 'full consciousness,' I mean a capacity to hold the good and the bad, to separate truth from dogma? It is far from certain that we are fully conscious of when our deepest intellectual machinery is merely the intricate shadow play of some icon deep among the ancestral spirits of the *prima cultura* or the projected gold of the second, which resonates with Zoltan Dörnyei's (2008, April) notion of an 'ideal' L2 (second language) self.

If the aforementioned conditions are met, a gateway opens to a progression of identification from identification with the collective to identification with the Self. Robert Moore (2003) warns that there is no way to stare into that fiery core self without being blinded by personal or spiritual grandiosity. Rowland (2002) suggests a more generative meeting, and we may assume that this identification with the Self is tempered by the sort of un-Othering that is only possible through reflective engagement in communities of practice:

> Identification's goal is self-realization, not in the conventional sense of the self being identified with the ego, but by making the unconscious archetype of the self the core of one's being. The ego's most fulfilling role is to be the realized self's satellite, orbiting around it as inferior, and yet energized by its starlike powers. (p.33)

As mentioned previously, the Outer Core has a 'darkness before the dawn' feel; the learner is not yet ready to greet the guest at the door.

Core Integration

Geological quality: A dense, spinning solid iron and nickel orb, 800 miles thick. The spinning of this sphere creates a magnetic field that overcomes thousands of miles of distance and matter to resonate with the surface of the earth and beyond. Over time, the poles of this magnetic field shift.

Learning context

Core Integration: The core self accommodates and is transformed by first and second language and cultural (L1, C1, L2, C2) ways of knowing and being and is capable of transferring this process to new linguistic and cultural practices.

---

[2] Source: Means, H. (2017, May 17). The story of the really weird night Richard Nixon hung out with the hippies at the Lincoln Memorial. The Washingtonian: News and Politics: https://www.washingtonian.com/2016/05/17/richard-nixon-kent-state-protests-white-house-lincoln-memorial/

There is an emphasis on developing more differentiated, other-identified ways of being.

- o   AUTHENTICATION: Core authentication: filling out the 'second soul.' The ideal L2 self is integrated into the core.

- o   ENGAGEMENT: Core engagement: A quality of relatedness to the world and greater awareness of L1-C1 'baggage' in one's shadow promotes a global sense of engagement.

- o   COMPETENCIES: Core competencies: More expanded awareness and acceptance of cultural and linguistic variation. Ever-expanding sociopragmatic competencies that reflect a visionary 'Third.'

There is something compelling about the transcendent image of a spinning, polarized orb. The shifting magnetism and its incredibly powerful and easily imaginable effects on nature, man, and culture, likewise point to the transcendent function as I experienced it: an emergent Yin Yang pattern in a mantha churn. Appointing, as we have throughout this chapter, a Kantian-synthetic critique, the limits of our sense and thought meet with the iconic guest at the door, a seemingly impossible, deep connection with something Other that blends the Self-Other binary into which one has been socialized. The spinning, shifting orb at the core of the earth is the perfect metaphor for the kind of integration toward which the model under discussion is aimed, one in which there is a dynamic ebb and flow between action and reflection, from the deepest self to fullest range of cultural expression. There is also the possibility of attaining that third that is not simply the accretion of two poles, but rather their uroboric mantha, turning into one another. The Integration Model envisions a core self that both accommodates and is constantly transformed by the tension between known and new symbolic competencies, the expanded awareness and acceptance of cultural and variation.

Deeper and broader participation in particular communities of practice has extended the array of symbolic competencies, in general, and, if these differentiated ways of being they have the sanction of self, they are integrated (Deci & Ryan, 2000; Jung, 1959/1979). Mikhail Bakhtin (1930s/1981) coined the term 'dialogic heteroglossia' to denote the many voices one encounters through participation in varied social discourses, all in synergy (not syzygy) with the One. At the core level, the chorus of the Many must be worked through logically, conceptually, in harmony with the diverse semiotic toolkit the learner has acquired through his or her social learning experiences. Though the learner has begun the work of organizing these many 'voices' conceptually, it is important to distinguish Outer Core Integration from Core Integration. Vygotsky's (1932/1994) distinction between lower-order *cluster* concepts, as distinguished from true concepts, is of use here. Whereas the former denotes a sort of loose categorization of experiences and ideas, the latter connotes a more subordinated and nuanced systems of symbols. One sees greater conceptual control of learning experiences in the CofP. In Giegerichian terms, there is more logos and less mythos; experiential and imaginal material has been sublated into Notions, though, as we will see, this process does not concede the reduction into the One, demanded by Giegerich, or for that matter, Rationalism, in general.

The symbolically rich *Thirdness* of Core Integration suggests competencies that are not only reflective of the dominant epistemological lens of one's cultural milieu but rather predictive of a further level of cultural differentiation that is emergent, given that one now is sufficiently differentiated from the most iconic, most deeply rooted assumptions of his or her primary cultural milieu. Similarly, reflecting on the distinction Jung (1964) drew between the *psychological* and *visionary* artistry, Rowland (2010, pp. 52-56) has advanced four principles regarding the latter:

1. Art is mainly centered on signs or symbols.
2. Perceptions of visionary/psychological may switch from age to age.
3. Visionary art is compensatory when cultural values are too 'one-sided.'
4. Visionary art informs future direction of culture.

With regard to core engagement, there is a heightened quality of relatedness to the world and awareness of one's own shadow in the form of previously unexamined assumptions and prejudices, thus promoting a more global sense of engagement. Rudyard Kipling (1929) captures this deeper, integrated learning, in his poem 'We and They':

> Father, Mother, and Me
> Sister and Auntie say
> All the people like us are We,
> And every one else is They.
> And They live over the sea,
> While We live over the way,
> But - would you believe it? - They look upon We
> As only a sort of They!

Ironically, these are the words of the very same agent of colonialism who expounded on *The White Man's Burden*, which serves to illustrate just how difficult it is to authenticate breadth and depth of learning. It is also testament to the fact of compartmentalization; that personal authentication, engagement and competencies often do not match up as we approach the crucible of Inner Core Authentication. With regard to Other integration, the Jungian metaphor of the "guest who knocks at our door portentously" (1975, para. 590), yet we are not quite ready to let him in. Inner core integration also conjures a mantha that recalls Raju's (2008) the seven Swargas (macrocosmic) and seven Patalas or chakras (microcosmic), the intersection of which leads to *tadatmyata*, an intuition informed by fusion with the Self, a simultaneous awareness of whole to part and part to whole. "The individual subject, seeing, thus, its own self in an 'other,' rushes forth towards it, and struggles for union with it" (p. 74).

To be the author of one's deepest self requires an inner match for evidence from the expanded sense of the human theater. Core authentication evokes the sense of discovering a 'second soul' as an idealized self, projected onto the targeted community of practice, then later cultivated imaginally and logically in ways that have the sanction of the Authentic Self. Certainly, Kipling was nowhere near that level of authorial integration. Similarly, Jung, who dreamed of the great Christian God shitting on a cathedral, who preached submission of the ego to "the superior power of the 'other'" (p. 4), who made it his life's work to subvert the West's unilateral vision of human psychology, neither succeeded in transcending his monotheistic formation as a Protestant, nor in extinguishing the destructive, Wotanic flames of his Germanic inheritance, which, as we have already discussed, would gravitate toward National Socialism and antisemitism. Such failures, of course, are made all the more poignant by the fact that Jung's written reflections and actions, as we have likewise established, suggest a sense of universality in human conscious, regardless of national, racial, or gender boundaries.

The lesson is that there is no tenable middle ground in core integration; like the core described in geological terms, one must allow the authentication, competencies, and engagement-related work to be spun through on the deepest levels, turned inside-out, Self into Other and back into Self, *ad infinitum*. How many of us can honestly say we have achieved this level of integration? How many of us have risen to high levels of engagement and competency in our chosen field and yet still retain the most dogmatic, iconic clingings of our primary formation in one particular corner of the collective? In terms of deep integration, we often remain authors of a fragmented personal narrative within a compartmentalized Outer Core.

To be sure, there is a great deal of shadow work that must be addressed in order to attain Core Integration. Primarily, there are those persistent, pernicious *ancestral elements*, the turgid and fossilized roots of our cultural complexes. Singer and Kimbles' (2010), as discussed earlier, posit that the cultural complex is "repetitive, autonomous, resist consciousness, and collect experience that confirms their historical point of view" (p. 6). Accordingly, the center must be also able to sustain the tension between the One and the Many, which is not an easy thing to do the further we expand our sociocultural horizons. That said, even Giegerich (2008) recognizes a related heuristic strategy for such purposes: "polytheism requires its own mode of integration and monotheism knows its own form of differentiation and pluralism" (p. 339).[3]

His highest stage of shadow work, what he calls 'accomplished integration,' centers on moving out from the personal: "The idea of personal interiority is recognized as the last refuge, the last stronghold in the ego's fight for self-preservation" (p. 103). At this level, the persistent polarities are worked upon via Jung's *transcendent function*. For Giegerich, this necessitates a *katastrophe*, a complete sacrifice of the ego in order to give birth to "the Shadow's Easter" (p. 104). Identity, itself, is obliterated, and the shadow can no longer be leashed as "my personal problem" (p. 105). In alchemical terms, it represents the *mortifactio* that results when two psychic substances are worked through one another. Jung saw this process as both subjective and rational, the 'Hell' that is a critical confrontation with "all that you no longer are or are not yet capable of" (Jung, 1915-1930/2009, p. 244). Sticking to the mantha image and the productive interaction of Urvashi, I see this as a dialogic rather than a dialectical process, one in which a systemic, dynamic truth, rather than an atomistic, deterministic one is affirmed. As Vygotsky (1932/1994) pointed out, you cannot understand 'water' by separating out the two hydrogen atoms and one oxygen atom; water is a dynamic, interdependent molecular system.

At this stage, having the quality of being un-Othered, the shadow is converted into "the unconsciousness as a whole" (Giegerich, 2008, p. 106), within the terrain of anima, "the landscape of actual psychology" (p.108). As archetypal psychologists are wont to remind us, psychology literally means 'the study of soul.' For Giegerich, all that remains in shadow work is the 'peace' of "the logical form of psychological consciousness" (p.108), but the current model rejects such reductions to the One. In contrast, the directionality propels self narratives outward into the Many, nurtured by participation in a variety of communities of practice, eventually meeting a mantha in the Third, in Jungian terms, or Third Space (Bhabha, 1994; Kramsch, 1988). More than the sum of the parts, there is something organically unique in the combination, and this meaning is emergent, a living thing. In Vygotskyan (1932/1994) terms, just when language has attained its stabilization as *znachenie* (a decoded 'definition'), we see that close up, it is constantly being reworked from arbitrary denotation to shifting connotations, what Vygotsky called the *smysl* (sense) of language. The play of *smysl* on *znachenie*, or signified elements on an arbitrary

---

[3] It is worth noting that Nicolescu (1994) reduces both mono- and polytheism to binary logic: "Why choose between God and Gods? God has at least three faces and all gods are linked by the same logic. Monotheism and polytheism – another fantasy engendered by binary thought. Of course there is, as always, a third possibility (p. 147)."

signifier, reflects a postmodern view of language that subverts the binary, logocentric lens of monotheism, which for Rowland (2002), is inherently Jungian: "for Jung, as in postmodernism, language is not a reliable and transparent window onto meaning, truth and the world" (p. 139).

Regarding post-modernist conceptions of language, Rowland (2002) highlights Derrida's (1997) concept of *différance*, which reflects the Vygotskyan tension of *znachenie-smysl*. Derrida's notion of the signifier as 'God Term,' as she describes it, is roughly synonymous with *znachenie*. Against this logocentrism, binary signifiers slide off the signified under the weight of many grounded meanings (smysl), or différance. According to Rowland, "cultural codes" are reduced to "fragile fictions" (p. 100). The post-structuralist distancing of signified from signifier is essential for truly integrative learning. "They slide over each other, so that meaning is forever slipping away when words are used. As a result, meaning, language and culture have to be rethought as radically unstable" (p. 99). I wonder if 'unstable' may be too strong a term. Perhaps a better term would be 'dynamic' or 'dialogic,' an energy that withstands the phallic negation of the Enlightenment-rooted 'dialectic' construct, as championed by Giegerich? Something of the 'God Term' (signifier) or 'znachenie' One remains, but the Many of smysl undermines of any sort of stable, structural essence. Similarly, Nicolescu (1994), notes:

> From all evidence, words are quanta, shedding bountiful light upon contradictions between spoken and unspoken, sound and silence, actual and potential, heterogeneous and homogeneous, rational and irrational. The contradictory complementarity integrated within us by the Hidden Third. (p. 73)

A general rule of thumb in translation is that there are many possible translations for a source text, all potentially valid. Accordingly, the plurality of the Many arguably is what renders a Hidden quality to the Third. Between one language and culture and another –Spivak's ghostly "in-between"– or for that matter, in the discourse between an analyst and an analysand, there are many possible manifestations of transference.

Yet another way to conceptualize the slippage between signifier and the signified returns us to Irigaray's (1985a, 1985b) mantha of the feminine Many with the Lacanian masculine One in ways that quite literally, from a Vygotskyan perspective, promote smysl (sense) or in her own words, *sensible transcendence*. According to Rowland (2002), Irigaray's notion of transcendence "is material and maternal in order to inject flesh and blood into the symbolic order" (p. 115). In Derridean, post-structuralist terms, one might refer to this sense of immanent meaning as the restoration of the integrity of the signified over the signifier, or *smysl* over *znachenie*. In Jung's alchemical terms, Rowland compares this meeting of the One and Many as the alchemical union of masculine Sol (Sun) and feminine Luna (Moon). One might argue that this conception slips back into the binary, given the distinctions already drawn between the coniunctio and the mantha, but the resulting sense of this is just the opposite: "Alchemy is a grammar of melting, heating, dissolving, coagulating in new combinations. Gender is an integral part of this fiery, fluid process. Mercurius, usually depicted as an active, potent, masculine figure, is also fiery, watery, and feminine" (Rowland, p. 116, citing CW 16, para. 402).

The dialogic churning—or mantha—of signifier into signified (or the reverse) is inherent in the Third, which at a more macro-level, engenders a critical stance that does not just apply to one´s *prima cultura*, but the second as well. In addition to Third Space, Lantolf and Poehner's (2007) notion of symbolic capability offers a more comprehensive sense of this dynamic and situated nature of meaning-making, which appears stable enough to produce something of a higher order, and it reflects Vygotsky's emphasis on the necessity of sustained cultural engagement for the development of more complex cognitions. As previously mentioned, it is impossible to imagine this sort of deep, meaningful transformation without extensive and reflective participation in the collective; this represents a radical shift in thinking from the Classic Jungian tradition or Enlightenment Rationalism.

At the core level, the symbolically capable one walks confidently, capably in both inner and outer worlds, yet constantly questions the values and assumptions of both. In some ways, (s)he conceptually and understands the new CofP often better than its own members, and of course, the same can be said with regard to his sense of the *prima cultura*. (S)he must act on this mastery of both worlds from the place of deepest individuation that Jung so highly prized, though it may remain ever out of reach. Van Lier (1996) speaks of *authentication* rather than authenticity; accordingly, the core level of authorial integration must narrate and constantly re-narrate from the core. Whereas the outer core may narrate in ping-pong fashion between cultural narratives, the inner core, both literally and metaphorically, is always spinning. Its magnetic poles also shift their axis over time- no 'true north' or south! There is soul in this spinning and shifting, and there is logic in it, a *dia*logic of the third. Somehow symbolic capability needs to be spun out of the empiricist Vygotskyan container to be fully realized within a theory of integration.

Symbolic capability, though rooted in more of an empiricist than rationalist epistemology, has more in common with Giegerich's (2012) notion of a logical form of being-in-the world than the traditional, unconscious sense of symbol in the classic Jungian tradition, which would be construed in semiotics as a more primitive, iconic image. Dobson (2008), representing the dominant view among Jungian educationists, insists that pedagogy should entrust itself to the image (active imagination): "The core learning is to gain a trust in the image, to accept the image as your teacher which requires breaking through the ego-controlled attitude that insists there is nothing beyond the ego's horizon" (p. 153). To the contrary, Giegerich contends that we must not only look beyond the ego but through to a distilled logic to which the image points. Perhaps there is a middle ground that can sustain mythos and logos? Pure mythos is in the warm glue of Gaia; it does not want to be moved. On the other hand, logos may be the violent but necessary tool to separate from this stillness, but on its own it is pure madness, or as López-Pedraza (2000a) called it, *puro bla- bla-*. The Western rationalist tradition seems bent on this sort of obliteration of anything concrete, embodied, or for that matter, anything empirically positive or factual. To this point, we recall that purely rational science, for Jung, represented a very particular and peculiar psychic aberration (Evans, 1957). Arguably, it constitutes a major component of the Western cultural complex.

I mentioned earlier that we should not expect to find the reductive, Western One, at the core. The core, after all, is always spinning, churning the totality of the Great Self. Anticipating future critiques of Modernism, Yeats (1920/1994) warned us 'The center cannot hold.' Of course not; it is always spinning, shifting, sending out ripples, subtly recalibrating its poles: this mantha-inspired notion of churning the One into the Many and the Many into the One, with no clear victor, no sublation, seems perfectly at home Jung's energetic view of the psyche. The new physics, or what to theoretical physicists refer to as 'Exotic Physics,' upholds a pull for every push, and vice-versa.

Let us then walk through the door opened by Themis and Prometheus: the masculine vs. feminine, the logos for the eros, polytheism vs. monotheism, heroes against monsters, Titans vs. Olympians, all are, at best, crude expressions of this tension of substance and energy. This perspective reinforces Rowland's (2002) post-structuralist and nonbinary view of the archetype: "The metaphysical residue inherent in archetypes is a creative energy, not a fixed stamp of gender identity. Archetypal images are created in a dialogue between biological inheritance and culture" (p. 108). Within a Marxist-materialist epistemology, Vygotsky likewise centered development along an interaction between phylogenetic, ontogenetic, and sociocultural factors. By situating this energy in a conversation between the biological and cultural, we likewise bypass the binary of innatist (rationalist) vs. sociocultural (empiricist) views of cognition; Vygotsky and Jung now share a place at the same ontological table. Perhaps there is also in this dialogic, dynamic transcendent function a way past the Kantian distinction between phenomena and noumena. As Rowland points out, Jung recognized the noumena as the power (or energy) that fuels the imaginal (dream) realm. If we allow ourselves to see past the Jungian tendency to downplay the concept, we may find further fit with Vygotsky's sociocultural theory of mind, his rich imagery of the ions binding the water molecule. This is precisely what Sloan means by "insight imagination" and Paglia signifies as "imaginative academic critique."

Without flying Eastward, as both Jung and Hillman repeatedly warned, I nonetheless find myself repeatedly drawn, by virtue of the transcendent function, to the Tao symbol that emerged for me in the image of a mantha-churn. There is something of the individual and cultural psyche in this. One might imagine the positive 'light' part pushing itself out of the negative 'dark' part, only to find itself pulled back in, chasing that last part of itself, that tiny dot that stays behind, still fused, yet distinct, in the plurality of the Other (Many). One may imagine great potential energy unleashed in this spin. One may also imagine this spin as ego's destiny to pass through shadow yet never completely and that there are individual as well as transpersonal aspects of this alchemy. In any case, the classic Jungian tradition would hold that each individual must ultimately welcome his or her appointed guest at the door, whether that be purely cultural, gender-based (animus/anima) or for that matter, typological (extroversion/introversion, etc.). Certainly, all three and perhaps more polarities may constellate there in varying proportions and relations. With regard to the latter, Jung warned that failure to integrate one's inferior function (i.e., feeling for a thinker), not only constitutes a failure of individuation; such a blind spot constitutes a clear and present danger (Jung, 1921/1990).

The medieval alchemists conceived the philosopher's stone (*Lapus Lazuli*) as capable of transmuting substances into silver or gold. Jung (1944/1993) discerned in their writings a deeper yearning for psychological transformation in this *Opus Contra Prima Cultura.*[4] Inner Core Integration takes the alchemical work a step further by recognizing the fundamental human striving to expand personal and collective senses of meaning, an individuation that makes full, yet critical use of all the collective has to offer. For reasons we have already established, and as befits an *Opus Contra Prima Cultura*, we would perhaps be better off discarding the Western philosopher's stone and taking up the Vedic mantha, aware of the attending misappropriations of Promethean theft and the dangers of appropriation, in general. The promise of core integration that spans from self to culture seems well worth the risk.

---

[4] Upon reading this, my language department colleague, Marko Miletich, noted: "Perhaps grammar as the philosopher's stone that helps us transform ideas into words and communicate? (9/18/21)." There is certainly an alchemy of words beyond the scope of this project that is worthy of its own focus, particularly in light of related scholarship in Translation Studies, Kugler's psychoanalytics of language, and Ong's discourses on our evolution from oralism to literacy.

Concretely, we visualize a cultural transformation rather than the mere transubstantiation of matter, or the purely inner work to which Jung applied the alchemical texts. However, we should not dismiss the potential for an integrative path that matches depth with breadth. Creating consciousness where it is most resistant, both within and without, has tremendous healing potential for both the individual and her milieu. Though the scars of cultural trauma appear genetically up through the third generation and cultural complexes are highly resistant to conscious work, it is not out of the question that they can be ultimately transformed. With regard to the former, gene expression may be worked through, and we can imagine the rigor of consciousness to which Jung often alluded acting as the alchemical engine of that healing. Regarding cultural complexes, both Jung and Vygotsky, and this truth finds further support in Dynamic Systems Theory, the potential for one individual who has transcended his *prima cultura* to send ripples throughout the collective is not a pipedream. Such is the proverbial butterfly whose seemingly inconsequential wing-flapping eventually produce a tsunami across the ocean, the famous "Butterfly Effect." Whether such powerful transformation is conscious or unconscious (is it not a little of both?), the operations of some unseen synchronistic force or a very empirically real and verifiable cause-effect chain, the truth of this connectedness remains intact.

And we may extend this connection to the full measure of life on the planet. Working to transcend one's *prima cultura*, given Western rationalism's rejection of nature and matter, must also, as van Lier (2004) and contemporary Jungian scholars Like López-Pedraza, Neumann, and Rowland have pointed out, work toward ecological reconnection. Jung may have been speaking both psychologically and culturally when he stated: "Culture means continuity, not a tearing up of roots through 'progress' (1954/1974b, p. 144), though, as mentioned earlier, we can ill-afford to give into the regressive fantasy of 'getting back to the garden,' given that ecological affordances now include cultural as well as natural creations, digital and biological. Furthermore, there is no end product. The gold or silver to be found in this ongoing mantha is a vital reconnection with the engine of mind and milieu. There is no way back to this place without a fundamental negation of what is known and tacit, one's most basic assumptions about what constitutes knowledge, where it comes from and where it is headed. Truly transformative, integrated learning is fundamentally an *Opus Contra Prima Cultura*. The reader must decide, as Rowland (2002) has challenged us, to critique proposals of 'truth' posited here somewhere between personal myth and Grand Theory.

Concluding thoughts

In his critique of the dominant rationalist approach to education, Dobson (2008) points to 'human capital,' factories, and "training [of] employees and consumers" (p. 142). Deeper, more expansive learning is not possible in such a context. Transformative, integrative learning that fully integrates the One cannot thrive where "meaningful personal development is ignored" (p. 142). The brightest student may complete a course of study with resounding academic success and yet not take one baby step beyond their rootedness in familiar (first) symbolic competencies, regressing back to elemental aspects of the Many, in the form of family and community identifications. Beyond the tragedy imbued in extricating personal development from education, as I have pointed out here, the quality of learning, itself, is often quite shallow, and even from a purely pragmatic, economic-necessity standpoint, we are producing students who are crammed with facts, yet have no 'core' capacity to accommodate a broad range of people and situations that are Other. Such views have been noted in the *21st Century Learning Standards* (Boix Mansilla & Jackson, 2011). The erosion of liberal arts, cheered on by tech Titans, further ensures that an integrative education is less and less likely in the academy. The typical institution of higher education invests millions of dollars emphasizing a broad-based liberal arts education, factoring a diverse course of study into its general education requirements. Instinctually, the language educator has some insight into why such attempts fail. It is a failure to respect the embeddedness of tacit, known cultural orientations. In the rhetoric of the One and the Many, we confront a fossilized 'we' (Many) in the 'I' (One) that grudgingly plays the game yet remains committed to withstanding the invitation to try on new lenses. It is common for language majors to spend significant time abroad and yet exercise only a modicum of engagement, as evidenced by meager progress in both linguistic and cultural competencies. For that matter, even accomplished scholars fail to engage outside of their *prima cultura* beyond the most basic level; even the most distinguished members of the professoriate have never allowed themselves to be transymbolically 'repotted and pruned,' so to speak. For that matter, we are surrounded by 'cultivated' types, in the surface sense of prestige and polish, rather than cultivated in the Jungian sense of the cultured man.

In light of what we have explored in this chapter, integrative learning is a mantha crucible that does not suffer ending where one began. We may indeed attain a high level of symbolic capability, but may not be learning of the *integrated* variety. To this point, it is important to point out Jung's distinction between psychological and visionary art: the former denotes art that reflects and is of the dominant culture at a particular time in its history. One who does not go all the way through the integration crucible is not capable of producing *visionary* work, borne of the Third, that *mysterium coniunctionis* which connects us consciously with the *unis mundis*, one world.

Though both within the classical Jungian as well as post-Jungian traditions there is no need for empirical verification, there may be profit in interviewing both apprentices and leaders representing a diversity of communities of practice in order to find out how much of the developmental approach presented here speaks to their experiences within their given CofP. An interesting question to research might center on the progression of authentication, engagement and competency and the extent to which they interrelate through the four strata depicted in the Integration Model. Systematic study of the model's predictions may help to sort fact from figurative with regard to the proposed model, but this is not the sort of work one relegates solely to the dominant domain of ´rats and stats´. Regarding the latter, perhaps the greatest threat to more holistic, integrative approaches to education lies in the decline of liberal arts under pressures from the tech sector, a trend that was discerned by Jünger (1946) decades ago: "As the technician enters this [education] field, he converts all institutions of learning to his interest; that is, he promotes technical training, which as he claims, is the only up-to-date, useful, practical knowledge" (p. 154). On the consequences of this trend for higher education, he notes a pedagogical shallowing that directly counters the depth and breadth of learning depicted in this chapter:

> That dubious adage which says: 'Knowledge is power,' is less valid today than it ever was, for knowledge of that sort is the very opposite of mental power; actually, it completely enervates the mind. Universities decline in the degree that technical progress spreads into them from the secondary schools. The university becomes a technical training center and servant of technical progress. (p.156)

That is not to say there is anything inherently bad about an education in empiricism, though even industry leaders have noted the need for professionals who can think outside of the box, a trope that proponents of liberal arts often find demeaning and even condescending. J. B. Conant (1964) offers some relevant balance here. In response to longstanding battles in the academy between American empirical and the classical European rational approaches to inquiry, he was able to find value in both epistemologies. A balanced, integrative approach calls us in from extremes of empirical or rational measures and affirms the irreducibility of psyche. Psyche is not bound by the One or the Many, or for that matter, any sort of binary. One path points to so many piles of clay, the other to one vacuous abstraction. Turning matter into spirit, as Jung taught, is only one side of the equation; rational introspection owes a debt to the Many. The integration of these tasks promises at least a glimpse of that spinning orb at the center of World and Self.

Figure 6.1: Overview of the Integration Model

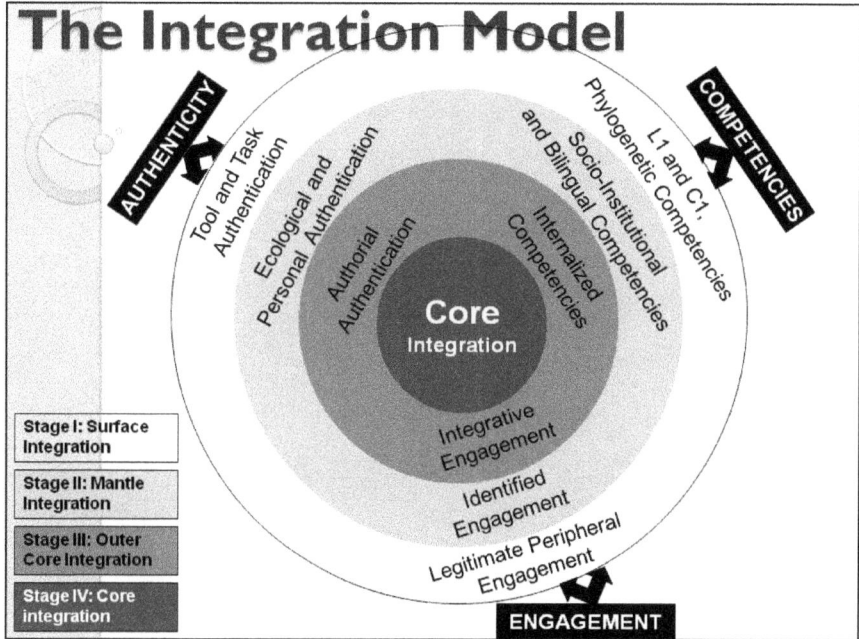

The Integration Model

AUTHENTICITY

COMPETENCIES

Tool and Task Authentication

Ecological and Personal Authentication

Authorial Authentication

L1 and C1, Phylogenetic Competencies

Socio-Institutional and Bilingual Competencies

Internalized Competencies

Core Integration

Integrative Engagement

Identified Engagement

Legitimate Peripheral Engagement

ENGAGEMENT

Stage I: Surface Integration

Stage II: Mantle Integration

Stage III: Outer Core Integration

Stage IV: Core integration

Chapter 7

Alchemies of Creativity and Innovation

In almost every Western enterprise, we are bombarded with the rhetoric of innovation and creativity. In matters of mantha and alchemies of the One and the Many, there is quite a lot to be sorted out (blended) in terms of how to characterize these ubiquitous pursuits. So, what exactly do we mean when we speak of creativity and innovation? When we consider the nature of creativity and innovation in the most literal sense, creativity has a 'first-order' feel to it. Accordingly, the 'spark' of innovation is often portrayed as the issue of the creative act: the Great Mother issues forth the fire of progress through her son. Accordingly, as pointed out earlier, Prometheus's foresight is the issue of Gaia-Themis's ordinance (utterance). Furthermore, there is a precedent for Prometheus adapted from Palamedes, the Carian as "inventor" or "under the goddess's inspiration" (Graves, 1960, p. 9). In light of the longstanding suppression of matriarchal femininities, the parenthetical reference to *the goddess's inspiration* further tethers a gender-based focus to the present discussion.

The Vedic equivalent of this trope requires extensive detective work. Western reductions of mantha around phallocentric stick friction –as with the privileging of Sol over Luna in the Western alchemy of the coniunctio— conveniently focus more on the Pururavas (male) and minimizes the role of Urvashi (female) in articulating that primordial spark. In contrast to Freud's and Jung, Kuiper (1971) sticks to the Vedic traditions, noting that the fire god Agni arises from "the womb of the waters" (p. 94), and, in fact, his sacred gift (fire) cannot be realized without the consecration of birth from the dragon-Asura Vrta (citing Cf. TS. II. 5.2.2-3). Likewise, according to Sir Monier Monier-Williams (1899/1988) the name of his counterpart, Mātariśvan, translates to 'growing in the mother.' Even Jung and Freud's peer Karl Abraham (1913), who arguably perpetuates the classical Greek trope of Father Birth, nonetheless acknowledges that the womblike "cave in which Agni was hidden" (p. 57) constitutes a feminine trope. So, whether we turn westward or eastward, it would appear that the alchemy of creativity and innovation makes use of a similar matriarchal materia prima: womb, water, and word.

The work of differentiating creativity from innovation also necessarily directs us back to the invention of fire. Earlier we explored Karl Kerényi's (1997) critique of Hermes and Prometheus, both of whom are credited with the discovery of fire, with one caveat: whereas Prometheus merely pilfers this critical innovation from the Olympians, Hermes engages with the process, learning how to create fire. Accordingly, we are left with an association between Hermes and creative process, on one hand, and Prometheus's pirated innovation on the other, the latter with all its attending association of intellectual property theft.

What unifies creativity and innovation in ancient Greco-Roman contexts is a shared quality of (re)shaping things of the earth, or *techne*, and its original crafters, immortalized in the ceramic work of Athene[1] and Prometheus, the forges of Hephaestus-Vulcan, Titans (Dactyls and Kabeiroi), and monsters (Cyclopes). Sorting out which god, goddess, titan or monster gets credit (or blame!) for this creation or that innovation is complex work, a question we will revisit later on this chapter within an exploration of what distinguishes crafters from technicians.

A Brief Overview of Research on Creativity and Innovation

The preceding origin myths notwithstanding, let us fast forward to today. It is abundantly evident that engagement with creativity and innovation tends to blur in corporate labs and classrooms. Unpacking backward design in Research, Develop and Disseminate (RD&D)-modeled labs and the teacher ethos of 'beg, borrow and steal' or 'nothing new under the sun,' the question is put to us on the proverbial Prometheus Interactive Whiteboard: is true creativity, the production of something qualitatively new (as opposed to rehashed) even possible? Given the current obsession with innovation and innovativeness driving change for its own sake –to demonstrate some new "update" to spice up the quarterly report— is creativity even relevant anymore?

This chapter explores two relatively young academic disciplines: Creative Studies[2] and Innovation Studies. While these fields may appear fairly interchangeable on the surface, they flow from somewhat distinct epistemological stances regarding the nature of change and progress. Churning these two elements in an interdisciplinary mantha brings us back to their distinct archetypal origins and offers us an opportunity to reexamine alchemies of the One and the Many, Promethean and Theman energies that may play a role in the undercurrents of creativity and innovation. On the surface, it is difficult to raise any credible objections here: how could one possibly find fault in being too creative or too innovative? A deeper look reveals a mixed picture,

---

[1] Athene also was also revered for her weaving.

[2] Not to be confused with "Creativity Studies," an emergent field that focuses on creative economy and the notion of "creative society," which is explored in a variety of business and sociocultural contexts. For more information: https://journals.vgtu.lt/index.php/CS/aimsandscope.

particularly with regard to innovation. Often the human subject and sociocultural implications get lost in creativity and innovation, and the consequences are worth examining more closely. I conclude with some generative directions for both fields of study in light of points discussed, as well as implications for fresh perspectives on how to engage personal and cultural change.

The lines that distinguish study of creativity from the study of innovation are somewhat blurred. Both areas are informed by rich research traditions and an often-overlapping empirical terrain ranging from boardroom discussions, R&D, and publicity campaigns to professional development days for educators. Both areas weather the winds of so many buzzwords, borne of social media hype and catchphrases. Consequently, the current landscape is characterized more by socially constructed connotations than simple dictionary denotations, and connotation no doubt adds velocity to the buzzword breezes. If the reader will indulge the cliché a second time, the places where we talk about creativity and innovation are often *a mile wide and an inch thick.*

There are scholars, however, who ascribe an immeasurable depth and the timeless quality to human creativity. On creativity, E. O. Wilson (2017), for example, proclaims the following:

> Creativity is the unique and defining trait of our species; and its ultimate goal, self-understanding: What we are, how we came to be, and what destiny, if any, will determine our future historical trajectory. (p. 3)

Similarly, on alchemies of creativity, Jungian analyst Stanton Marlan (2021) comments:

> The notion of a creative process at the core of human existence is a way of imagining the question of intentionality, and it predates analytic theory in our earliest attempts to visualize life's energies (p. 59).

In matters of the One and the Many, Marlan locates the drive to create as "beyond the ego" (p. 59). Seen through a Levinian lens, creativity arguably corresponds more to the totality of the Other than of the Self-Same (ego), with the clarification that this "beyond" is both infinitely without –across time, space, cultures— as within, in the classic Jungian sense of the Self.

The modern origins of creativity, including the totality of their myriad brainstorms and widgets, processes, and products, point to Creative Studies. Over time, a more applied Creative Problem Solving branch has developed, one that emphasizes matching the increased momentum of knowledge (re)creation with greater organizational capacity to engage the change process (see Puccio, Mance, Swiatalski, & Reali, 2012). The terms are used somewhat interchangeably here, the reader should bear in mind the more *applied* sense connoted in Creative Problem Solving, which is attributed to publicity guru Alex Osborne and Buffalo State University professor, Dr. Sidney Parnes, co-founders of the International Center for Studies in Creativity. Creative Problem Solving's specific concepts and steps center on making the workforce more fluid in keeping pace with the ever-changing challenges of the Information Age.

Creative Studies' and Creative Problem Solving's open and playful embrace of the imaginal and association with Myers-Briggs confirm the enduring nature of Jungian thought. In terms of the latter, the Myers-Briggs test, inspired by Jung's scholarship on personality types, tends to oversimplify the alchemical intricacies of the preference poles. For Jung, the unused personality style within the various polarities (i.e., introversion/extraversion) is still very much present, if unconscious, prone to erupt to the extent that is not integrated; at the same time, it is highly resistant to conscious integration (Jung, 1954/1991).

The study of innovation originates in Everett Rogers' (2003) Diffusion of Innovations Model (hereafter referred to as DIM), though his approach adapts work conducted nearly a century earlier by Gabriel Tarde, who studied the diffusion of *inventions*, integrating the study of both ecological and social patterns. Rogers' model presents a linear and temporal map of three variable groups: *antecedent* variables, which encompass features of an adopting social system, *process* variables, which denote the efforts of a change agent to persuade adopters to use their innovation, and finally *consequences* variables, which examine the ultimate integration or rejection of the innovation by the adopter. By his own admission, Rogers recognized a source-side bias, one which does not fully appreciate receiver (adopter) side factors, though DIM researchers continue to cast aspersions on *laggards*, those hold outs who undermine the momentum of new ideas and technologies. Innovation studies, beyond the more speculative airport bookstore varieties and their buzzwords, tends to paint with broad strokes with dances of change agents and adopters, innovators and laggards, social networks that are homophilous vs. heterophilous (like-minded vs. polarized).

While somewhat new to the creativity fields, I have dedicated years to quantitative research in educational applications of Rogers' DIM, only to find that the dynamics of change are much more complex and subjective than depicted in conventional models. Consequently, I have turned to Jung and his proteges in order to deepen quantitative approach of innovation studies' measures with humane qualities. Another way to portray this shift is as one of movement from 'how' to 'why' innovations and stakeholders in innovation diffusion behave as they do. Ultimately, both research in creativity and innovation must openly embrace and speculate on this core epistemological question: why do we create and innovate? In answering this question, Jung's legacy invites a multiplicity of hermeneutic tools, from the mythological and metaphysical realm to anthropological and philosophical approaches to the roots of creativity and innovation. As will be evident by the conclusion, the central assertion of this chapter, guided primarily by Jungian thought, is that creativity and innovation are archetypally blended, a complementary mantha of the Many and the One.

Foundations of creativity and innovation

Setting their respective academic areas aside, creativity and innovation share a common sense of urgency in matters of how to manage change, evincing an overall sense of angst in confronting the fast pace of modernity. In his epic poem, *Paterson*, one of the premiere poets of Modernism, William Carlos Williams (1946/1995), offers the right trope for taking creativity and innovation deeper. Imagine the founder of a New Jersey City, a 'Mr. Paterson,' arising from the base of Paterson Falls and contemplating the cascade before him:

the river comes pouring in above the city
and crashes from the edge of the gorge
in a recoil of spray and rainbow mists—
(What common language to unravel?
. . combined into straight lines
From that rafter of a rock's lip.). (p. 7)

Williams' tracing of that one syntactic stream backward to the source is the work of over two hundred pages, but the central idea is one of tension between the individual and the collective: Mr. Paterson is constituted as both a man and a city, a One and a Many. Paterson is perhaps the most eloquent and poignant illustration of Jung's notion of the archetype, this notion that each individual is born with pre-set streams (or in the case of *Paterson*, rivers) through which deep-set biological and cultural patterns are worked out in the individual psyche.

In a similar fashion, Pierre Teilhard de Chardin (1959/2008), the Jesuit Priest-archaeologist credited with the discovery of Peking Man, used the metaphor of a tree to represent the evolution of life on earth, from elemental roots to a biological trunk, culminating with the top branch of hominids. Like Williams, Teilhard de Chardin speaks to the union of the *inner* and the *outer*, the idea that each individual carries the biological and cognitive blueprint of evolution. The following quote suggests that Jung may have influenced his ideas:

The 'mystics' and their commentators apart, how has psychology been able so consistently to ignore this fundamental vibration whose ring can be heard by every practiced ear at the basis, or rather at the summit, of every great emotion? (p. 266)

In social anthropology, Claude Lévi-Strauss (1955) used the term "deep structure" to depict the psychological imprinting of cultural patterns, and as Kugler (2002) points out, he was likely also influenced by Jung's theory of the archetypes. The marginalization of Jung's allegedly mystical thought is unfortunate, given that Jung distinguished himself in both empirical and speculative approaches to science. In fact, As Kugler reminds us, Freud invited him into his psychoanalytic circle precisely due to his scientific credentials. The inconvenient truth of creativity and innovation, indeed of the totality of human scholarship is that all *objective*, empirical matter is filtered through the human subject; the Many through the One. Simply put, subjectivity *is*. Consequently, this in-depth exploration of creative and innovative ways of engaging change necessitates an upstream trip, following one stream along the archetypal channels, back through some iconic Greco-Roman mythologems that pervade Western ways of change.

Seen another way, we are following a spark. Wilson (2017), for example, offers a compelling connection between the earliest stories and fire's invention. His notion of *adaptive radiation*, denotes the various specializations and mutations that have emerged over the course of evolution, and he situates a related biological and cultural shift in human evolution around the concordance of fire and meat consumption. Regarding the latter, the shift to a meat-based diet is attributed to the reduction of jaws and dentition (no longer needed for the consumption of coarse vegetation) and brain augmentation. In matters of cultural change, he argues that the simple gatherings around fire would eventually give rise to Homo Sapiens and the capacity for "internal storytelling" (p. 150), as well as the rudiments of memory, eventually giving rise to "unprecedented creativity and culture" (p. 150). As we will discuss later, this evolutionary perspective of storytelling necessarily centers on a stage of our evolution when a longer lifespan supported the rise of the institution of grandmotherhood, forerunner of bedtime stories and the *consejitos*, or little pearls of *abuelita* (granny) wisdom.

Regarding the first vestiges of creativity, Pierre Teilhard de Chardin (1959/2008) regarded cave paintings as artifacts that affirm

> a power of observation, a love of fantasy, and a joy in creation (manifest as much in the perfection of movement and outline as in the spontaneous play of chiseled ornament)—these flowers of a consciousness not merely reflecting upon itself but rejoicing in so doing. (p. 203)

There is a lot in this quote that resonates with a Jungian approach to creativity. First, there is a sense of 'losing oneself' in the creative process that was fundamental to Jung's (1933/2001) approach to the creative act. There is also a playful, joyful quality portrayed here, as if somehow this primal sense of ecstasy in the act of creation has been lost in modern society, which has arguably given over to the techno-grind of innovation and a corresponding emphasis of product over process. In archetypal psychology, a similar sense is evoked in Hillman's (1989) call for abandoning the Western Ego and surrendering to psyche: "in exchange for fingering the push buttons, finger-painting; instead of Kodachrome, Easter eggs. The primitive barter of stupidity for simplicity— beginning where it's at" (p. 168). López-Pedraza's (2000a; 2000b) Spanish notion of Dionysian *duende* abandon is not far behind this sense of giving oneself over to some other, deeper archetypal richness of the Self.

Imagine your ancestors gathered around the fire. Constituted within this scene are two fundamental images for research in innovation and creativity. With regard to the former, we have a singularity, one of the first innovations: fire, the product *par excellence* of mind working on nature. We can imagine this invention as the product of a first engineer breaking off from the pack to solve the perennial problem of preserving a food source (meat) and surviving cold winters. We can also imagine this invention as the result of communication and co-construction. Mythologically, the image might present itself as Prometheus, the Prodigal Son, proudly introducing the gift of fire to en-lighten Themis's *Agora*-circle. Another way to think on this continuum is that it moves from individual cognition to cultural being, the One to the Many.

Now, zoom out from the fire to the clan circled around it and the earliest manifestations of cultural being come into view: telling stories, managing disputes, creating and improving tools, and problem solving. Certainly, it is conceivable that the perfection of fire-construction would have figured prominently on the agenda for these first creative problem-solving sessions, as evidenced in the emergence of one of the first innovation- the pramantha fire bore's evolution from a mere physical tool to a cultural tool of great archetypal significance. Whether evolution was propelled mainly by individual ingenuity or collaboration, there is no clear evidence one way or the other, though Teilhard de Chardin (1959/2008) asserts that inventions were collective products that were fashioned over extensive periods of time, as opposed to milestones or paradigm shifts. Without losing ourselves in binary distinctions, let us stick with this premise of innovation as closer to the fire and creativity as nearer the encircling community. This is not to say that innovation is not cultural. On matters of distinguishing creativity vs. innovation, Wilson (2017), for example, depicts the latter as rooted in cultural change in response to environmental conditions.

Creativity and the Crafter, Innovation and the Technician

In classic Jungian perspective, the creative is gendered as feminine and matriarchal at the source. Within that assignation, Neumann (1994) notes a plurality that has a shared, collaborative quality, emerging in groups of three or nine women.[3] That said, the crafters, as noted by Gier (2000) are the original polluters, the harbingers of Industrial Age smokestacks and arguably constellate more closely to Western patriarchy and technological innovation, so the association between crafting and the (matriarchal) feminine is not unequivocal. The figure of Hephaestus presents a number of related contradictions. Jünger (1947/2006) recites the misfit Olympian's impressive resume as a craftsman-inventor. In addition to forging Helios's chariot, Hephaestus is credited with producing Eros-Cupid's famous arrows, Achilles' armor, and the chains of fellow artisan Prometheus. Though rejected by his mother Hera and serially cuckolded by Aphrodite, Hephaestus is foster mothered by sea nymphs and though she rejects him as a suitor, Athene shares a rich collaboration with Hephaestus. Prefiguring a whole branch of dystopian science fiction-horror literature and cinema, Hephaestus also fashions two female robot slaves made of gold. Both Jünger (1946) and Stein (2020) ascribe monstrous qualities to Hephaistian creativity. Jünger, for example, notes that the Greeks associate smith work to dwarves, deformed figures, a sign that this sort of work was "considered unlawful and sacrilegious" (p. 291). For Stein, Hephaistian monstrosity centers on potential insult to the (matriarchal) feminine:

> The Hephaistian creator represents a subtle undermining threat to natural feminine creativity in that he forges symbols, that is, representations of the creative processes occurring in the unconscious, and produces art objects that both represent and substitute for "the real thing," i.e., a baby. Hephaistian creativity can appear monstrous to the feminine since it goes contra naturam ("against nature") in a way that threatens to undermine or rechannel the value of purely natural female creativity. Is art more valuable than nature? Hephaistos may be seen as a monstrous offense to feminine naturalism, a state of competitive dissonance in the tones that typically vibrate between feminine consciousness and the Great Mother. (p. 24)

Jünger (1946), veering from the creative camp, actually prefers to cast Hephaestus as a forerunner of the technician-innovator. Technological innovation, for Jünger, is always inextricably linked to the machinery of Titanism, which, as alluded to earlier, he contrasted sharply with transformative, Dionysian

---

[3] There are nine muses, for example. Regarding the matriarchal connection to creative production, Neumann (1994) comments: "'Matriarchal consciousness,' a 'birth giving' consciousness in a very specific sense, forms the bridge between the woman and the creative individual—for example, the male artist, in whom the anima, his female side (and with the matriarchal consciousness), is more strongly accentuated than in the average patriarchal man" (p. xii).

artistry. In the following passage, Jünger elaborates on Titanism's connection to technology and technicism:

> They [the gods] beat down the revolt and the presumption of the Titans. But all technology is of titanic mold, and man the maker, is always the race of the Titans. And so, we meet him first of all in volcanic landscapes. From his titanic kinship stems his love for the enormous, the gigantic, the colossal; his delight in towering works that impress by their quantity and mass, the vastness of their piled-up matter. That trait, incidentally, explains why man the technician so often lacks a sense of beauty and proportion; he is not an artist. (p. 291)

For Jünger (1946), the alleged hubris and myopic obsession of the "gadgeteer" is uniformly denounced in the Greek myths.[4] His negative characterization of the technician resonates in some ways with the mania of Dr. Frankenstein, and it strikes us as a destructive inflation of the One: humane values displaced by quantitative, empirical varieties:

> we must not expect from him any wisdom outside of the technical field. His preoccupation with facts not only prevents him from thinking about himself; it also blocks his approach to that more spiritual wisdom which cannot be reduced to mechanics. (p. 292)

Elsewhere, Jünger analogizes this privileging of empirical over humane values to a distinction between artistic and technological thinking:

> Technological thought, as distinct from merely technical or artistic thinking, demands a steady and deliberate abstract consideration of the cosmos, of nature, and of man, in order that they might be described in purely mathematical terms. By ignoring the irreducibility of the being of things –unique and unrepeatable– modern science found it was possible to unite all things under the concept of quantity. Since measurable quantities can be predicted, they can be controlled. (pp. 13-14)

---

[4] "The view which ancient myths hold a man as a gadgeteer is decidedly unfavorable. It would be even more averse to the modern man of high explosives and the internal combustion engine" (Jünger, 1946, p. 288). "His [the gadgeteer's] restless industry, his busy activity, his eccentric thirst for power make man the gadgeteer hateful to the gods. The majesty of Zeus is fullness of being, quiescent strength. The strength of Prometheus, in contrast, lies in rebellious upheaval, in the urge to cast Zeus from his golden throne, to drive out all gods, and to make himself master of the world" (Jünger, 1946, p. 292). This 'restless industry' may have inspired López-Pedraza's (1990) references to 'Titanic sweat' in the machinery of modernity.

Certainly, there is something of Titanism and Monotheism in this privileging of numerical quantities over humane qualities, and perhaps it is the very source of power driving these trendlines in Modern Western cultural complexes. To this point, Nicolescu (1994) asserts that "The rule of quantity is the rule of binary thought" (p. 87).

None of what we have just described constitutes technē, as envisioned by the Greeks, and Jünger would likely agree with Panikkar's (1995) argument that technē, in the classic sense, is more "cultural craftsmanship" (p. 47) than the labor of of homo technologicus. Modern technology's human space, for Panikkar, may be reduced to technocracy, a project of "rational organization" (p. 47). Artisanship is not the aim of technocracy; rather, Panikkar alleges that the technics of technocracy serves a "technics of dominion" ruled by *kratos*[5] (power) (p. 48). Accordingly, like Zeus's right-hand man, Kratos, one might argue that innovation is autocratically aligned.

Taken to the extreme, technological innovation and the innovator as object and subject are reversed, such that, as Jünger (1946) notes, "It [technology] plugs man in" (p. 125), and a particularly insidious sort of instrumentalism sets according to which "The rights of the individual are turned into the rights of the technically organized person" (p. 140). This dystopian picture, much like the Borg hive, Matrix or similar science fiction tropes, has an unequivocally collectivistic quality,[6] though it is not clear whether Jünger understood this term in a Jungian sense of the Collective Complex or in a strictly anti-Marxist sense, though perhaps the two connotations are not too far apart. In the end, the human is irrelevant in this perspective because technology serves its own goal of *perfection*,[7] and the human object is a means to that end. When we consider this trend toward quantity over quality, it is likely, as Nicolescu (2008), suggests, that perfektion has been fueled by the corresponding rift between science and culture: "In our time, the gulf was widened. Science and culture have nothing more in common; this is why one speaks of science and culture.

---

[5] As in Kratos, Zeus's henchman, who oversees to the rock.

[6] "Technological thinking is obviously collectivistic. But such collectivistic thinking presupposes an individual freed and cleansed from all conflicting considerations, an individual that will abandon itself unreservedly to the collective" (Jünger, 1946, p. 163).

[7] "Perfektion bespeaks a purity and thus a purification of the irrelevant, a purgation of all things other than itself. Jünger insists that as technology approaches these states, it purges nature of life and man of humanity. It perverts the state by turning politics into an order of technical problems rather than an exercise in moral judgment. It destroys the profit motive by subordinating the good of both capitalist and laborer to the good of the machine" (Wilhelmsen, 1946, pp. 17-19).

Science does not have access to the nobility of culture, and culture does not have access to the prestige of science" (p. 13).

While all of this may seem straight out of dystopian science fiction, I recall an interview with a German auto engineer who was asked what his next design would offer consumers. Without a hint of irony, and perhaps a bit of indignation, he retorted to the interview that he takes his directions from the car. *Perfektion*, for Jünger, is timed to Kronos's grinding gears. Similarly, Panikkar (1995) warns of *technochrony*- technocracy's ever-quickening clock. This acceleration of time accentuates a distinction between "cultural organism" and "technocratic organization" (p. 49). Furthermore, the organismic vs. organizational distinction is perhaps relevant to this discussion of creativity vs. innovation. Organizational ecologies take a lot of time to grow, and it also makes sense that project deadlines and such privilege quick-fix innovation over the more rhythmic flow that creativity requires. Accordingly, a distinction between ecological and technological ways of change may likewise emerge in these comparisons of modern manifestations of technē in terms of workplace psychology and cultures. Likewise, creativity and innovation may be further differentiated along these lines of Hermetic process vs. Promethean product.

This notion of an overarching techno-grind subjectivity that transcends the human container is not necessarily a fringe concept. A presence is evoked here that is not property of the ego or the Self; there is something of soul as pure consciousness, freed from all traces of human subjectivity and emotion, artifacts of a bygone era of mythos and metaphysics that were discarded in the wake of the Enlightenment and the Industrial Age that reflects Wolfgang Giegerich's (2007) post-Jungian stance. Giegerich's core criticism of Jung's psychology lies in its focus on the human subject. For Giegerich, the focus of psychology, as handed down in its etymology, is literally the study or "logic" of soul (psyche-logos). Working upon a Hegelian template, Giegerich replaces the human subject with the 'soul,' constituted as a distilled logic of being in the world that drives culture and cognition: myth and metaphysics, grounded in feeling-tinged human subjectivity, are no more. In this way, he alleges that the soul has moved onward and upward into pure consciousness, propelled by the rise of science and technology. In light of Giegerich's psychology, this epistemology of innovation according to which the car drives us is perfectly sensible.

In *classic* Jungian and archetypal psychological circles, innovation is roundly denounced, since it is so tightly tethered to technological varieties. This cynical view resonates with Jünger, portraying innovations as de-natured products of *titanic sweat* (López-Pedraza, 1990). Innovations are, at best, upheld in the classic polytheistic sense as 'inventions' credited to the legendary line of *prōtoi heûretaí*, exalted inventor-innovators from Hephaestus and Prometheus to

Elon Musk. There are also scattered references to a Dionysian sense of innovation in the workplace (Handy, 1995), but this may have more of a sense of innovation connected to creative process; as patron god of arts and theater, it is difficult to imagine any tenable archetypal connection to modern-day conceptions of innovation, especially if we recall the Peter Pan rebels who flew too close to the sun in the dot-com era. Sober Apollo would seem to be a more appropriate match for a sense of creative products with rigor of structure and form, such as constituted by whatever line of intellect rules the day: more heavenly muse, less gut-wrenching *duende*, to borrow from the poet, Federico García Lorca (1933/1997).

In contrast, there is nothing Giegerichian in the intense affect often attributed to creative consciousness, which is arguably very rooted in the human subject; it does not follow Giegerich's cold, deductive logic, which 'sees through' the image to the abstracted Notion behind it. If one considers that cave paintings figure among the first semiotic tools for interpreting and sharing meanings (planning hunts, for example), Teilhard de Chardin's allusion to a cave painting potentially compensates a weakness within Jungian conceptions of creativity: this pervasive allergy to the collective. The classic Jungian soul of creativity is necessarily a deeply personal, often painful sojourn in one's psyche. The *Red Book* (Jung, 1915-1930/2009), a vivid, illustrated account of Jung's descent into his psyche, is certainly the most iconic example of this sort of lonely experience of 'churning' inward, and it also evokes what was for Jung, the necessary withdrawal from the world and working on oneself, individuation, that eventually yields the worthiest creative products. Borrowing from his distinction between psychological and visionary art (see Rowland, 2010), the former may provide a mirror to what is going on in the culture, but the latter gets into the greater stream and scheme that drives its unfolding. Perhaps *visionary* creative products represent healing gifts to the collective that justify our retreat from it, revealing such withdrawal to be the divergence that leads to convergence.

From Innovation to Adaptation

Creativity Studies faces its own polemic in clarifying creativity and innovation. Centered on a lack of clarity regarding which things belong to which construct, Jonathan Vehar (2008), a leading scholar in creativity, has advanced a particularly useful distinction between creativity and innovation. It is of interest that he attributes part of the problem to the inflation of innovation as a "hot business buzzword" (p. 259). On the subject of creativity, Vehar argues that while creativity cannot be taught; creative *thinking* can. He portrays this contrast thusly:

> If one teaches creativity, then by definition, one teaches a phenomenon. While one can certainly teach about the phenomenon of creativity, what is true is that those of us that teach about it are really teaching a creative process to people in a press so that they can create new products. We are not teaching creativity, we are teaching a creative process. (p. 261)

In short, creativity is a basic, innate endowment. Regarding the process-product question that seems to pervade Jungian notions of creativity and innovation, there appears to be less of a product focus, as depicted by Vehar, and more of an emphasis on mental processes, though as the quote suggests, the goal of promoting creativity is directed to *new* products. A third conception of creativity as a sort of personal transformation (citing Ackoff & Vergara, 1981) is a perfect fit with Jungian conceptions.

In the context of innovations, the process-product continuum as a point of distinction becomes more pronounced. 'New products,' we find, inhabit the action side of the creative process. As has been discussed in this chapter, the traditional, linear approaches from the classic Diffusion of Innovations Model or RD&D models are being reconceptualized. All points lead to this 'master-dispatcher' of change, adaptation, which has emerged as a key principle in educational innovation diffusion. In *Educational Innovation Diffusion: Confronting Complexities* (2017), I illustrated how Paul Mort and his graduate assistant Francis Cornell's (1941/2012) 'educational adaptations' construct finds connection with Rogers et al.'s (2005) update of the Diffusion of Innovations Model around research in Complex Adaptive Systems, Activity Theory (citing Karasaviddis, 2009), and two recent statistical studies (Leejoeiwara, 2012; Tang, Chang, & Sheu, 2015) underscore the simple fact that educational innovations are ultimately and dynamically adapted by specific sociocultural dynamics. Rather than following a tidy, linear path from source to receiver, educational innovations are adapted through complex, dynamic 'meaning' shifts that determine how innovations are used. Innovations, at least in educational contexts, are truly adaptations, as Mort and Cornell (1941/2012) proposed. The more an innovation is subject to multiple meanings, and its successful intake would appear to depend on this sort of reinvention, even beyond educational contexts (Rogers et al., 2005), the line between innovation as the fire and its creator vs. the community-receivers is not binary: innovation and creativity are blended, complementary; this is confirmation of the classic Jungian concept of the *coniunctio*: the union of opposites. In light of such trends, Creative Studies scholars may want to revisit Frank Barron's (1955) criterion of "adaptive" for the products of creativity.

Adding it all up, however, we remain trapped in an often confusing, binary process-product distinction between creativity and innovation. Creativity and innovation certainly appear to serve distinct ends. The assertion that innovation has almost attained the phenomenological status of subject means that innovation is no longer a means to researchers' and developers' ends; it has become the end itself and we the means. This 'we' would of course include the entirety of consumer culture and purveyors of innovations.

So, let us hold the assertion that innovation has indeed become the center of it all, the *status quo*, the end to which we are the raw material. On the surface this is a completely absurd notion, yet the creativity fields have grown, in part, to that very perspective. In *Creativity Rising* (Puccio, Mance, Swiatalski, & Reali, 2012), the authors aptly point to the increased velocity of knowledge creation, downsizing, shortened product life cycles and other aspects of what Giegerich's (2007) has referred to as the Absolute Inflation of technological innovations.

Returning to the adaptation principle, there is a tremendous opportunity for the field to adopt a bigger-picture perspective, one that transcends the technology-focused futurism of Prometheus to embrace the larger scope of cultural evolution, which is archetypally represented by Themis. Mythologically speaking, as the mediatrix between the Olympians and the social order, Themis is that caretaker of culture, ruling that part of the modern psyche that can rekindle our ancestors' first communions around the fire. In a sense, the theft of fire afforded humanity with two related gifts, the first being the obvious survival advantage in terms of warmth and a sustained food source and the second being the resulting longevity to which it contributed. The second yielded a time-honored and treasured innovation: grandmotherhood, which made possible the transmission of group wisdom from one generation to the next.[8]

Let us then allow ourselves to imagine a merging of the creativity and innovation fields. Culture and adaptation underscore the connected ways we create and disseminate innovations: whether in creative problem solving or developing and conveying innovations, meaning is interpreted and negotiated through communication on many scales. Teilhard de Chardin (1959/2008) would no doubt affirm this sense of communal creativity and innovation as fundamental to human evolution. Consequently, this is an important evolutionary moment to hold as it returns us to a time when innovation was intrinsically connected to culture, one that contrasts sharply with today's dehumanized, mechanical sense of technological innovation evinced by Jünger and the (Post-) Jungians. Likewise, the UNESCO transdisciplinary conference Declaration One warns against the existential threat posed by

---

[8] New evidence that grandmothers were crucial for human evolution. Smithsonian Magazine: https://www.smithsonianmag.com/science-nature/new-evidence-that-grandmothers-were-crucial-for-human-evolution-88972191/.

"values largely based on mechanistic determinism, positivism, or nihilism" (Nicolescu, 2008, p. 258).

Rather than being driven by innovation mechanics, a healthier way to engage with change calls for cultures of adaptation. This shift starts with a hard look at organizational life and how a factory-focused innovation mindset is so pervasive in the workplace, arguably consuming the work of creative problem solving and RD&D. Rather than compensating the psychopathic, imaginal lacunae increasingly attributed to top CEOs ("Hey, dial up such-and-such; have her take care of that 'vision thing'"), creative consultants, equipped with a rich sense of *adaptation*, might emphasize the part of their work that centers on cultivating generative workplace ecologies. Ironic, is it not, that Amazon, a toxic and arguably Titanic 'churn and burn' mantha[9] of innovation culture that has arguably transformed into a technified mutation of the jungle for which it was named?[10]

The first step in this process of moving toward cultures of adaptation centers on a blended perspective, one that reduces pervasive polarities: creativity vs. innovation, research and development vs. dissemination, diffusion vs. adoption, and for CPS, internal vs. external presses. The solution is simple: first, shift the emphasis away from the product and bust the barriers artificially imposed by linear models of change. In terms of educational innovations, Michael Huberman's (1983) Linkage Model has already opened the door by enfolding the source and end sides of educational innovation dissemination into a sort of trefoil in such a way that invites communication across practitioners, basic and applied researchers. In a similar fashion, Puccio, Murdock and Mance (2006) have proposed a cyclical Creative Problem Solving model that follows four steps: 1) assess, 2) clarify, 3) transform and 4) implement. Implementation, by virtue of the circular arrangement, becomes a starting point for repeating the process in a spiral-like fashion. It has been alleged that the rapid pace of change has compromised institutional memory (Ashworth, 2006), which presents a disruptive factor in the sort of staged system posed by CPS. Jung's (1954/1974b) alleged need to protect *cultural continuity* from the rise of technology and technicism (p. 144) alluded to earlier, resonates with Theman ordinance in matters of preserving coherence in socio-organizational systems, though he is

---

[9] Thanks to Dr. John Fischer, a clinical psychologist, for pointing out the expression, which denotes the practice of working employees to the bone until they burn out and the next is put into the grinder. See realityexpander@gmail.com (2019, October 23); Urban Dictionary, https://www.urbandictionary.com/define.php?term=Churn%20and%20Burn

[10] Williams, R. (2015, August 26). Amazon and toxic workplaces: Are toxic workplaces worth the price for financial gain? See Psychology Today, https://www.psychologytoday.com/blog/wired-success/201508/amazon-and-toxic-workplaces.

certainly more focused on the integrity of the process, rather than the outcome-product. In a similar vein, and within the same mid-twentieth century zeitgeist, Jünger (1946) describes the consequences of substituting critical thinking and liberal arts with empirical, factual knowledge "which has been likened to an ocean on which the ship of civilization proudly sails. But this ocean is a *mare tenebrosum* ("a dark sea"); for a knowledge that has become boundless has become also formless. If to the human mind all things are equally worth knowing, then knowledge loses all value" (Jünger, 1946, p. 155). At the end of the day, those who employ CPS ultimately determine whether their efforts are directed to the promotion of greater creativity among the practitioners engaged in the process or the factory model *perfektion* of the creative product *cum* innovation.

Jung (1959/1979) argued strongly against the conversion of educational institutions around this sort of factory model adrift in a mare tenebrosum in his commentaries on *technicalism*:

> Naturally the present tendency to destroy all tradition or render it unconscious could interrupt the normal process of development for several hundred years and substitute an interlude of barbarism. Wherever the Marxist Utopia prevails, this has already happened. But a predominantly scientific and technological education, such as is the usual thing nowadays, can also bring about a spiritual regression and a considerable increase of psychic dissociation. (p. 181)

And yet, Jung unwittingly played into the rise of technology by failing to appreciate a sense of culture beyond the cultivation of the individual psyche.

Lev Vygotsky's (1932/1996) legacy compensates this blind spot in the classic Jungian path if we are to engage a full discussion of the adaptation principle. Obsessively individualistic, misanthropic conceptions of the creative process do nothing to reverse the trend that Jung, himself, warned against. What does a Vygotskyan model entail? In a manner similar to that depicted in Complex Adaptive Systems theory, it means that we have to take this enfolding further. As we move from linear to spiral-like approaches to change. Vygotsky's sociocultural theory of mind challenges us to take the next step, from time to space: cultural development as dynamic, simultaneous, fluid phase states in constant emergence, dedicated to the constant renewal and vitality of the system. Is it so hard to imagine the communication of change moving in all directions, depending on changing circumstances? From a practical standpoint, would it not make change infinitely more effective to be able to communicate needs up and down, within and beyond the system's channels, depending on emergent factors? This sort of flex system is exactly what was exalted by futurist Alvin Toffler (1990) and by organizational studies scholar Sally Helgesen (1995) in her Web of Inclusion Model; however, we must be careful to hold notions of adaptation with a similar dexterity in terms of temporal focus. In the sense of Michael Kirton's (2003) adaption-innovation continuum, there is a time to hold fast to established principles and a time to push back against them. To this point, the philosopher Alisdair MacIntyre (2007), in applying Aristotelian principles to organizational life, reclaims the virtues of argument, not in the sense of bickering, but rather connoted as vigorous, engaged conversations about the nature of an organization's traditions. Without argument, MacIntyre asserts that traditions fossilize into *institutions*. Selling out to the latest bandwagon is not a viable option; such is tantamount to exchanging the difficult process of internal argument for a product, creativity for innovation. Perhaps for this reason, educational reform scholar Alexander Sidorkin (2017) has proposed dispensing with the entire notion of innovations and replacing it with grassroots, intra-organizational creative resources for the production of new technologies and practices.

A move from innovation to adaptation requires us to replace the old linear Research, Develop, Disseminate model with a more in-folded way of integrating stakeholders and processes. In revising a Diffusion of Innovations in Education Model (DIEM, Warford, 2005), I found it necessary to alter the classic source-receiver chain posited in Rogers (2003). Rogers himself admitted that the development and dissemination of innovations is biased toward the source side. He looked to educational contexts as the perfect setting for exploring the ways new technologies and ideas are re-fashioned in school contexts (Rogers & Jain, 1968).

The revised Diffusion of Educational *Adaptations* Model (DEAM, Warford, 2017), as the revised title suggests, is informed by the shift from innovation to adaptation. Rogers (2003) classic, linear timeline from antecedent to process and consequences variables related to innovation diffusion is freed from the temporal plane. Based on emergent circumstances, any part of the system is in direct contact with the other with which it needs to connect, at any time. The antecedents no longer focus on fixed structures but rater *emergent systems*. Process variables no longer center on pushing adoption but rather active, dialogic fashioning of the innovation between developers and adopters. While the final assessment of the consequences of adoption are left more or less intact, the overall picture is triangular rather than linear, with arrows leading in all directions.

No longer is there any obsession with pinpointing an Omega Point of adoption; adoption is merely a brief stop on the way to emerging into some proximal manifestation. As pointed out earlier, a chalkboard never really leveled off in its adoption curve; rather, it is more likely that its proximal stage as a Promethean interactive whiteboard, phased in somewhere in the top of the diffusion curve. The chalkboard did not disappear; it came back to itself in a more innovative way. In this sense, one may imagine the three sub-systems as a sort of in-folded spiral staircase, as opposed to the conventional diagonal staircase imbued in traditional conceptions of the diffusion curve. Because the emphasis is more on phase states than temporal flow, there are infinite ways the systems can expand or retract, progress or regress, depending on emergent circumstances and shared meanings within a given Community of Practice. With regard to the latter, there is now the possibility for stakeholders to drive the process at all phases. In the sense of Teilhard de Chardin's (1959/2008) notion of connection between the within and without of things, we can imagine systems of change as cells or pulsing flocks, phenomena that are not restricted to linear progressions.

Creative Problem Solving seems to resonate with the circularity of the DEAM and the move from innovation to adaptation. Grivas and Puccio's (2012) FourSight model centers on workstyle preferences across four stages of the creative process: Clarifying, Ideating, Developing, and Implementing, which arrange like a spiral, such that implementation can inform back into new cycles of the four stages. FourSight has the added benefit of addressing both individual and group-based profiles of engaging in the change process, and it is very archetypal. There are 'Early Birds,' indexed by a loss of investment toward later stages of the process. In discussions with colleagues on the Board of the Buffalo Jung Center, there was general consensus that this resonates with the style preference of Jungians- sitting with ideas and problems, as opposed to rushing toward practical solutions. There are also slick Promethean 'Integrators,' who possess a questionably even score across style preferences.

Creativity and Innovation scholars and practitioners may both find profit in deeper archetypal reflection around the figures of Hermes and Prometheus, respectively. The creativity fields find their principles exalted in humble Hermes, the connective soul of creative change. Rather than patenting and leveraging his truly innovative lyre, he gave it freely to his brother Apollo (López-Pedraza, 1991). If mythology were economics, Hermes would be the figurehead of the bartering economy and freeware: creativity and innovation for all.

Prometheus, widely embraced in the innovation sector, has emerged in the Technology Age as somewhat of a player, a misanthropic sort of engineer, and his technical focus on cognition and its creations missed the critical grounding in culture. What was the point of prolonging life if innovations in medical technology and psychiatry yield only prolonged anesthesia and suffering (López-Pedraza, 1990; 2000a)? He does not create, he fabricates; the workshop where he is depicted fashioning us out of clay is not artistry, it is repetition, mimesis, the forerunner of the factory. Economically, Prometheus is all-Titan;

he has gone global and consequently, we are all enslaved by this elusive project that Giegerich (2007) calls 'capital m' Money that seems more and more to make the world go around.

Another potentially useful albeit binary archetypal perspective for creativity and innovation situates Prometheus and Themis within the feminine-masculine *coniunctio*. Themis, evocative of less hierarchical and more connected ways of engaging change associated with feminist epistemologies (Helgesen, 1995), needs that presence that breaks away from the harmony to scout some proximal perspective the system needs. In terms of the adaptation vs. innovation discussion, the Theman heart of creativity lies in nourishing cultures of creativity and a circular process that compensates for the dominant, linear approach to innovation.

We only need to take Prometheus out of the linear innovation conveyor belt and re-imagine this mythical figure in orbit around a complex adaptive system, which is archetypally structured as Themis. Loyal to his mother's oracle, yet constructively engaged in the Zeus Order as a corner of the Athenian clique of crafters (alongside Athene and Hephaestus), Prometheus's tangential and lonely orbit around the Titanic and Olympian circles serves a vital role as the *strange attractor*, connecting his Titanic system of origin to novel, Olympian epistemologies.

The ambivalence of the system, or the Many, in relation to its singularity is captured in the polysemy of the word bold in the West. Depending on the circumstances, bold may connote a sanctioned courage of one individual to act or conversely point to a brazen and punishable act of defiance, more akin to the Irish word *dána*. The unruly *buachaill dána* (bad boy) gets the ruler, and yet mythology is abundant with heroes and heroines who dare to go down the rabbit hole, enter the dark cave, open the box. In the case of grails, egg-laying geese, or waters of life, they are even sanctioned as ways to heal a system that is infirm. Likewise, as mentioned previously, this dynamic would not be complete without the complementation of monstrous encounters. Rather than constituting an opposition to the prized product of the hero or heroine's errand, there is a wisdom in the divergence of sphinxes, gorgons, harpies, and sirens that screams for attention. Moreover, the connection of the feminine to the monstrous suggests that positive change, this moment of mantha known in Dynamic Systems Theory as the bifurcation cascade, requires a dissolving of the fragile patriarchal One into the plurality of the Many. Seen concretely, what worth would an invention have without the dialogic, agora-space of focus groups and such? According to Rogers and colleagues (2005) and working within the framework of Dynamic Systems and Diffusion of Innovations, it is precisely this innovative presence at the periphery that prevents a complex adaptive system form fossilizing into a mere complex system. To borrow from

Kirton (2003), innovation and adaptation are mutually reinforcing in order for a system to maintain its vitality. Arguably, the feminine bond and the masculine breaking away is a rather crude oversimplification of a pattern that has undergone much more sublime reiterations; they no longer the property of chromosomal differences, as Rowland (2002) reminds us, but rather principles that are equally accessible by men and women alike.

It is with the same caution regarding that I would like to posit that creativity and innovation speak vastly different languages. Creativity's emphasis on ecology and relation gravitates toward spoken language, the utterance, something that is shaped in the sharing. In contrast, innovation's entrapment in the alienating world of *perfektion* prefers isolated terms; there is no space in the term for the feminine excess of polysemy to grow. In distinguishing words from terms and working within Panikkar's perspective of cultural disarmament, Coward (1996) warns, "Attempts to teach using words removed from relationship would be judged as doomed to failure" (p. 67). In my translation coursework, Dr. Dávila-Montes would repeatedly remind us of the *puro ladrillo* [pure brick] sense of the term; it "is" the thing to which it points; no room for connotation or interpretation. It may also be argued that creativity thrives in the utterance, in interaction. The innovator's cubicle, in contrast, connotes an isolated, silent place (save for music blaring in earbuds), and the focus is decidedly textual. In matters of innovation, Ong (1977) reminds us of technology's reliance on the (written) word:

> Since writing came into existence, the evolution of the word and the evolution of consciousness have been intimately tied in with technologies and technological developments. Indeed, all major advances in consciousness depend on technological transformation and implementations of the word. (p. 42)

In mythological representation, we might apply to this motif the sense of Prometheus in his workshop and Themis convening panels and focus groups in the modern agora of staff lounges and professional conferences. It may be tempting to assign innovation to the Promethean One and creativity to the Theman Many; however, we have already acknowledged that Prometheus was not quite the misanthrope he is often alleged to be in light of his active and generative collaborations with the Olympians, Athene and Hephaestus, in particular. Furthermore, it is well-known that Jung's most creative output was *manth*ed from deeply private and intense bouts of introspection, as well as that these visions were inscribed in graphic form. It is also worth noting that Jung preferred to "write" all of this down. As far as I know, the *visions* of his posthumous *Red Book* were never *verbalized*.

Concluding thoughts

Having followed William Carlos Williams' iconic river backward to the source, we look downriver where the streams once inhabited by Echo and her river nymph sisters, have evaporated into the ethers as ones and zeros. Where once there was a roar over the falls, even bitstreams have been muted in the slipstreams of technological innovation (No more screeching dial-up!). The creative power of utterance attributed to the Mother Tongue has effectively been digitally silenced or limited to the Titanic babble of widget *perfektion*, or the droning of motherboards. Against this dry silence, we measure the rapid spread of Promethean fire, igniting ever more brilliant and ravenous technologies. In fact, it is getting increasingly difficult to distinguish creativity from this all-consuming innovation culture to which we are all tethered, the Many into the One: identities fused with (gaming) and social media platforms. Having already explored the origins of creativity through the lens of the One and the Many, it is worth considering a similar treatment of innovation. Siegel (May 26, 2020), for example, presents a related challenge within a transdisciplinary studies framework:

> Organizational innovation requires a multi-dimensional approach that addresses at least the level of the individual, the group, the organization (both culture and processes), and the larger business environment. This means that the knowledge of creativity and innovation that needs to be brought to bear on the situation must originate in a plurality of disciplines –individual psychology, group dynamics, organizational theory, strategy, marketing, and so on. The process of creating an environment that is favorable to innovation, and then productizing an idea spans a good number of disciplines. But it is not enough to simply draw on material from a variety of disciplines. (p. x)

A transdisciplinary approach likewise blends the binaries of artistic vs. scientific production, which arguable reflect an analogous binary between creativity and technological innovation. To this point, Nicolescu (2008) comments chiastically:

> True artistic creation and deep religious experiences arise at the moment which bridges several levels of perception at the same time, resulting in a transperception. Transperception permits a global, undifferentiated understanding of the totality of levels of perception. True scientific creation arises at the moment that bridges several levels of representation at the same time, resulting in transrepresentation. Transperception and transrepresentation can explain the surprising similarities between moments of scientific and artistic creation. (p. 15)

This chapter has presented how archetypal perspectives on creativity and innovation research map a way out of this quickening fusion into innovation's techno-grind, challenging us to move from a binary to a more blended perspective. Integrating Jung's coniunctio with the Vedic manth, the admixture of creativity and innovation churns into a Third: adaptation. Polarities like the One and the Many, the Innovator and the Laggard, product and process emerge as less binary and more blended. Accordingly, as regards the creativity vs. innovation binary, we might envision *creative* products and *innovative* processes. The danger of solely focusing on the process in Creative Studies is that we lose sight of the endgame, which should aim beyond decidedly anti-creative obsessions with profit and productivity. As Neumann (1994) reminds us, patriarchy has "led to making modern humankind neurotic, to self-alienation, and to a dangerous loss of the creative vitality of the psyche" (p. 118). Accordingly, DIM, given its obsession with disseminating widgets, needs to cultivate a sense of what innovations *mean* for their targeted users. Perhaps it may draw nourishment from the potential mediational richness of the creativity fields. Of course, such a shift would require that the creativity fields shift their gaze from *quantities* of 'productivity' to *qualities* of engagement in organizational life.

In the interest of reclaiming qualities of technological innovation and creativity, and relevant to the present discussions of mantha, Wilhelmsen (1946) references a blended perspective in the work of Jünger: "When man abstracted the nature of a circle from the wood of the tree, he immediately reintegrated the form with the wood itself because his wheel was to be made of wood" (p. 12). At a time when a techno-Logos has seen through nature and is on to other things (Giegerich, 2007), it is certainly still possible for our approach to progress to rediscover more sane laws of necessity, those centered on ecological and humane values, values that echo the ordinance of Themis across genderations past and those to come. Likewise, we find that it is possible to honor both the One of the inventor-innovator and the Many into which the bold audacity of the One is inextricably tethered in a plurality. Contrary to the current trajectory of creativity and innovation in Modernity, any invention perhaps should ultimately subordinate to the utterance and the agora, not the other way around.

Pratimantha (*Afterthoughts*)

Our mantha-fueled metaphysical dance of the One and the Many ends on a somewhat clumsy endnote: Prometheus's dull-witted brother Epimetheus, the "hindsight" to Promethean foresight. If Prometheus is rooted in *prama(n)tha*, then, switching the *pra-* (fore-) to *prati-* (after-) yields a *pratimantha*, a particular *tāla* (meter) in Indian classical music.[1] In addition to resonating with Jung's primordial rhythm sense of pramantha (1911-12/1952/1995, para. 227], a *pratimantha*, in both its Sanskrit and Greco-Roman resonances, seems apropos. Rather than flying into Promethean visions for the future of Western ways, this work has sought to content itself within the limited scope of Epimethean hindsight. Certainly, in matters of pratimantha, we have scarcely set a rhythm, and we cannot rightly say that we have "done the ma(n)th," so to speak. What we have done is open a few portals into the Many and discerned "spheres" of the One, hopefully to the point that a productive churning has been set in motion.

Reconsidering Titanism

Having seen through reductive denunciations of Titans and Titanism, we have discerned and reclaimed lost narratives of matriarchal feminine power that open a gateway to bold excesses of elemental thinking. For example, technology is not altogether antithetical to ecocritical stances. To this point, Neumann (1994, p. 63) called for conscious reconnection with the Great Mother, from her natural to technological forms. Rather than posing some sort of naïve "return to the Garden," Jünger (1946) challenged us to re-cultivate a sense of awe and to reclaim acts of "conciliation and consecration" (p. 185) in navigating between nature and technological progress. To this point, he comments,

> The technician has lost the age-old awe that restrained man from injuring the earth, from changing the shape of its surface. This awe in the past was very pronounced; its traces are found everywhere in the history of agriculture, and it reaches well into historical times. With the great masterpieces of architecture there is always associated the idea of a colossal presumption – the tower of Babel is a colossal example; even Cologne Cathedral was held to be built with the devil's aid. (p. 185)

---

[1] "The tāla are mantha, pratimantha, yati, ekatdli, and rupaka" (p. 172) in Swami Anyanananda (1963). *A history of Indian music.* Calcutta: Ramarkrishna Vedanta Math.

Jünger also reminds us that we are synchronized to dead, mechanized time.[2] While Giegerich (2007) has convincingly made the case that a techno-Logos has left nature behind, Wilhelmsen (1946), referencing Jünger's philosophy, reminds us that "The zero of nature would be the zero of a technology that had reached both its apotheosis and its death" (p. 16).

Rather than writing off Titanism as vacuous and savage, it makes sense to instead acknowledge the potential value of Titanic moments of awe, be it in nature walks, in conversation, or other such moments of being overtaken by something elemental and sacred. In these places, a deep sense of connecting power of the Theman Many is palpable, from a grain of sand to the face of the Other. Such experiences *are*, and rather than cross over into arcane mysticism, I prefer to leave it to the reader to uphold whatever sense of these moments they may ultimately glean. We should likewise be careful not to romanticize the Many, with its myriad mobs and dehumanizing workplaces. The Promethean One, for its part, has provided the spark without which innovative alchemies of psychological and social integration would not otherwise have been possible. Ever vulnerable to the titanic inflations of monotheistic patriarchy, with their cults of personality, conquest, and colonialism, we also recognize that it is not always the martyr or messiah in matters of human progress.

Reconsidering the Other

In terms of the Other, we have recounted here the West's tragic flaws: wholes of conformity to authoritarian collectives and their corresponding holes of hatred and projection, the traumatic effects of which undermine a sense of psychological and cultural wholeness. To this point, and with an emphasis on the rise of technology and technicalism, Jünger (1946) comments:

> the machine and the social organization are linked together, and one cannot be conceived without the other...It may seem strange that this titanic modern industrial system with its human organization that tries to engulf everything, and whose power we encounter at every step, should have grown from seemingly unconnected trials and errors, from widely scattered inventions, from decidedly humble beginnings. (pp. 116-117)

---

[2] Reconnecting with the sensory, organic world and "the richness and idiosyncrasy of personal existence" makes it possible to transcend "a horizontal and featureless cosmos" and the subjugation of nature's rhythm to dead, mechanized time (p. 14).

There are certainly obstacles of Othering that take precedence over such explorations. We are surrounded by failures of integration from the personal to social level to sufficiently integrate the contrasexual and cultural Other without and the Other within constituted in the Self. Insidious cultural complexes, exacerbated by the fragmented curriculum of the One and the Self-Same, have undermined the West's capacity to withdraw its projections and engage a healthier mantha of the One and the Many. In light of Littau's (2000) feminist revision of excess, perhaps the time has come to revisit Aeschylus's ambivalence about Prometheus's "excessive affection" (l. 123) and to consider a revaluation of Titanic excess in light of matriarchal titanism. Likewise, perhaps we have inadvertently "Othered" Western monotheism. Though we have established the hypocrisy of any attempts to distance polytheism from patriarchy by highlighting the foundations of the latter in the Zeus Order, Elise Jordan (May 11, 2022 e-mail communication) has suggested a path that invites broader discussion of monotheistic femininities like Sophia. On a related note, Clarissa Pinkola Estés (2013) calls our attention to a compelling case study in the defiance of a Marianist congregation in Denver in response to the Diocese-ordered eradication of a prominent mural of the Virgen de Guadalupe. Such occurrences highlight the opposition of the matriarchal Many within the Father-centered One True Church, setting aside the inherent paradox of the Holy Trinity within this monotheistic core.

Eastward Turn Reconsidered

As fraught as it is with possibilities for further (perhaps cringeworthy) failures in this awkward cultural turn, perhaps an Eastward turn is in order. Gier (2000) reminds us that Prometheus's wife, according to the Greek historian Herodotus, was Asia, and we can picture him prostrate on the rock, high up on the Caucasus Mountains, the *limes* of the Western world of that time. Just as the treasures of the Silk Road would eventually usher in both commercial and cultural *manthana* between the West and the East, Eastern symbols offer alchemy that compensates the binary inflations of Western patriarchy. Neumann (1994), for example, points to the Chinese Ming character, which recognizes the blending of sun (masculine) and moon (feminine) consciousness. Likewise, Jung (1954/1991), in spite of his own caution not to mix Western and Eastern consciousness, gleans from the Tao a maturation of the hero figure- as a transformative symbol of individuation:

> But, in the end, the hero, the leader, the savior, is one who left undisturbed did not the new way demand to be discovered, and did it not visit humanity with all the plagues of Egypt until it finally is discovered. The undiscovered vein within us is a living part of the psyche; classical Chinese philosophy names this interior way "Tao," and

likens it to a flow of water that moves irresistibly towards its goal. To rest in Tao means fulfillment, wholeness, one's destination reached, one's mission done; the beginning, end, and perfect realization of the meaning of existence innate in all things. Personality is Tao. (p. 186)

In view of Said's (1979) and Lehti, et al's (2010) important contributions to our understanding of Western fetishization, demonization, and exoticization of the East, I am reluctant to give such symbolic convergences more credence than they deserve. I am likewise conflicted about the title of the book, given my own limited exposure to Asian languages and cultures; I only know that this mantha "speaks" to me and that it will take time and much more exploration before I can say definitively that I "hear" it. Having clarified that reservation, I nonetheless turn to Marlan (2021, citing Shual, 1995), who points out that both Western and Eastern alchemy culminates with the red stone, a symbol that links the Western notion of the philosopher's stone and the Hindi notion of the jewel of Rasa or Rasaratnakara, though the latter is considered to more openly embrace embodied, libido-infused wholeness, a sensuality that recalls the work of Irigaray and other post-Freudian feminist scholars.

A trans-fixed cultural turn

In light of all the hazards of casually crossing geographic and academic boundaries, it also makes sense to fully embrace the connotations of "trans....." To this point, Nicolescu (1994) predicts that "the transdisciplinary era will be an era of translators – those who translate what happens at another level of reality into our own macrophysical language (p. 65)." As a translator with an interest in psychoanalytic studies, I understand translation as transference in the fullest sense, not just in terms of the consulting room but in terms of something much broader. Benjamin (1923/2012), certainly without any awareness of Complex Adaptive Systems and strange attractors and even less of Teilhard de Chardin's notion of radial and tangential trajectories, eloquently speaks to this mystical sense of translation:

> Just as a tangent touches a circle fleetingly and at only a single point, and just as this contact, not the point, prescribes the law in accord with which the tangent pursues its path into the infinite, in the same way a Translation touches the original fleetingly and only at the intimately small point of sense, in order to follow its own path in accord with the law of fidelity in the freedom of linguistic development. (p. 82)

If we overlay Littau's assertions regarding the excess and plurality of languages, beyond the binaries of "source" and "target," a natural channel opens up toward the enrichment potential of reclaiming lost feminine narratives in the patriarchal order. The monstrous mysticism of the sorceresses of Greek mythology compels us to shifting the focus on the hero to that of the magician archetype. Accordingly, it is important to reclaim powerful feminine magicians like Hecate and her proteges Circe and Medea. The alchemy of the witches' brew offers a savory recipe of the Many. In organizational settings, for example, we see patriarchal silos flattened into webs of inclusion, for example.[3]

In the mantha, tired tensions between Mythos and Logos start to snap as we reconsider age-old divisions in the academy. To this point, and apropos of the present discourse on mantha-as-churn, Wilson (2017) writes:

> The more closely we examine the properties of metaphors and archetypes, the more it becomes obvious that science and the humanities can be blended. In the borderland of new disciplines created, it should also be possible to reinvigorate philosophy and begin a new, more endurable Enlightenment. (p. 159)

While tempted to end on a definitive call to action, the research reflected in these preliminary excursions represents only the beginning of a sort of transdisciplinary cultural turn. Concretely, while respecting the scholarship of the consulting room, alleged immutability of these psychoanalytic phenomena strikes us as premature assertions. Following the threads planted in the preceding chapters, it makes sense to turn to the reflections of Raimon Panikkar (1995), a scholar of both the West and the East, on matters of how to navigate through the cultural turn. Indeed, Nicolescu's (2008) notion of transcultural attitudes is constructed on Panikkar's East-West intrareligious dialogue (p. 17).

Panikkar's (1995) mantha of Sanskrit and Christian thought yields the peace of cultural disarmament. In contrast to the sort of hypermasculine Titanic sweat and monotheistic missionary zeal underscored by López-Pedraza, cultural disarmament calls for a *feminine attitude* of reception. This feminine attitude displaces the patriarchal obsession with agency and action, replacing it with one of reception and embrace (p. 7); the goal of transformation is achieved through experiential, rather than through action and transactional means. Recast under the lens of semantic linguistics, the human subject is seen not as an agent but rather as the *experiencer: reception* is privileged over delivery. The "good" he calls for is grace, or in Sanskrit, *gurtas*, and rather than arriving in an Amazon box, it is a good that takes no discernible, finite shape. Invoking the Christian *creatio continua*, he describes this reception as a "gratuitous arising from nothing" (p. 9). When we idiomatically speak of gifts that keep on giving or paying it forward, this is, for Panikkar, the essence of

---

[3] See Helgesen, S. (1995). *The web of inclusion.* Beard Books.

generative cultural change. There is perhaps more Pandora and Themis than Prometheus in this sense of gift. If we listen closely to Panikkar's utterance, there is an undeniable sense of a slow, soul-stirred mantha of eyes and lips in this notion of cultural disarmament; foresight and fore*telling*. Accordingly, it makes sense to meet the challenges of the times with less combustion and more conversation, or in matters of mantha, less burn and more churn.

Nicolescu's dream

In closing, and in spite of my lack of formal psychoanalytic training, I would like to conclude as I began- with a dream. In this case, let us consider a dream vision of the pre-eminent scholar of transdisciplinarity, Basrab Nicolescu (1994). Throughout the book, I have included scholarship from transdisciplinary studies and closing with Nicolescu's dream serves as an invitation for future collaborations between this emergent field and scholarship in the cultural turn, which mainly draws from psychoanalytic and Translation Studies.

Before proceeding into the dream, the following overview of transdisciplinary studies offers a practical foundation for the reader. In distinguishing transdisciplinarity from multi- (keeps discipline structures intact) and inter- (merely transfers methods from one to another discipline) disciplinarity, Nicolescu centers attention on the choice of prefix: "As the prefix "trans" indicates, transdisciplinarity concerns that which is at once between the disciplines, across the different disciplines, and beyond all disciplines" (2008, p. 2).

As summarized by Muntuori (2008), "The transdisciplinary approach does not focus exclusively on Knowing, but on the inter-relationship between Knowing, Doing, Being, and Relating" (p. xi). Just as the new physics suggests that perception may affect the perceived on a quantum level (Siegel, 2020, May 26), we must accept and openly explore this space where our inquiry is alchemically suspended in the same stuff as the objects of our inquiry. Indeed, a true transdisciplinary approach demands that, as knowing subjects, we allow ourselves to be objectified, in a manner of speaking. This dynamic correspondence between subject and object, knower and known, rejects the binary of in vitro knowledge, infusing it with the in vivo alchemy of a hidden third. Similar to the Jungian coniunctio, the tension of opposites, the binary, horizontal pong battle of oppositions finds an ascendant space in between "where that which appears to be disunited is in fact united, and that which appears contradictory is perceived as noncontradictory" (Nicolescu, 2008, p. 7). Accordingly, Nicolescu represents these relations as two corners of an Isosceles triangle, "A" and "non-A" and a peak T for the Hidden Third.

Reflecting on the Third

This notion of the Third, has always sparked the Jungian imagination, and The Hidden Third reminds us of the playful "field of indeterminacy" (Marlan, 2021, p. 34) constituted in the alchemy of Derridean Différance (Marlan, 2021, citing Marlan, 1997), and in post-Jungian circles, Marlan reminds us that the third consistently emerges –as far as it can be manifested— as synonymous with soul. Likewise, in Greco-Roman contexts, we have discerned a sublime feminine plurality at work in groups of three (or in the case of the Muses, multiples of three) feminine mythologems. Additionally, we have explored the third in the context of transcultural and translinguistic identities (Third Space).

A broader way of seeing the Hidden Third, according to Nicolescu, centers on the notion of cosmodernity. He even argues that "The alchemists' Ouroboros anticipated the metamorphosis of modernity into cosmodernity" (p. 92). Characterizing modernity as limited by a binary schism between subject and object, Nicolescu describes cosmodernity as "based on the ternary unification of subject-object-included middle" (p. 83). Though there are subtle differences, one could argue that the Tao, the coniunctio, and mantha are strongly associated with this Hidden Third. Consequently, their importance to the emergence of cosmodernity is certain.

Working with Nicolescu's dream description, I will freely embrace opportunities to illustrate many of the tropes and concepts of this work and frame questions yet to be explored. The dream, which corresponds to Nicolescu's aphorisms on reason, unfolds as follows:

> A dream that's always pursuing me. An oriental market, a bustle of people talking in whispers, the most diverse colors, an atmosphere of celebration and ceremony. It is said with insistence that a woman had an "illumination" – an extraordinary event. Before the crowd – three women. To right and left two women seated in lotus position. In the center the woman who had the experience of illumination suspended vertically in the air, her head towards the ground her feed upwards. Is this, therefore, illumination? (Nicolescu, 1994, p. 38)

As a European male shaped cognitively and culturally in the patriarchal binary, it is easy to dismiss this vision as the sort of exoticizing male gaze (Lehti et al., 2010) that is arguably central to the Western Cultural complex lurking in the frame of this dream (aphorisms on reason). We might imagine this macro-context as the classic Cogito of the One. Set in relation to this visually and auditorily rich scenery, adorned in all the richness of the feminine Many, one almost senses the dreamer's enthrallment; this is such a richer place than the traditional academy; it seems much more inviting for the sort of transdisciplinary flow of ideas he envisions. This is a classic trio of Titanesses, the original Hidden Third, though they also have the seductive, siren-like quality that reminds us of the monstrous feminine. Like Gaia-Themis, the central Titaness pronounces the ordinance. Ironically, however, Nicolescu uses the visual imagery (illumination) that echoes a related intellectual period (the Enlightenment). "Is this illumination?" No. Said another way, this is Theman foretelling, not Promethean foresight. Consequently, we are left with a gendered sense of synethesia: feminine voice that can only be visualized, not heard, by the male dream protagonist. Moreover, it leaves us with the sense that the Hidden Third, recast through the matriarchal feminine, is the Silent (or Silenced?) Third. There is an invitation of sorts in this levitating, inspired woman. Perhaps she is foretelling cosmodernity? Perhaps she is Urvashi, uttering sparks of inquiry that are not quite creativity or innovation, per sé, but some mantha of the two. The classic Anima dream of a male, what is certain is that there is a call to integration.

It is upon all of us to work with Nicolescu's dream and to generate rich transdisciplinary discussions in future journeys around the cultural turn.

References

Abraham, K. (1909). *Traum und mythus*. Leipzig: F. Deuticke.

_____. (1913). *Dream and myth* (W. White, Trans.). New York: The Journal of Nervous and Mental Disease Publishing Company.

Ackoff, R. L., & Vergara, E. (1981) Creativity in problem solving and planning: A review. *European Journal of Operational Research, 7*(1), 1-13.

Aeschylus (1961). *Prometheus bound* (P. Velacott, Trans). New York: Penguin Classics.

Ashworth, M. J. (2006). Preserving knowledge legacies: Workforce aging, turnover, and human resource issues in the US electric power industry. *International Journal of Human Resource Management, 17*, 1659-1688.

Asimov, I. (1961). *Words from the myths*. Boston: Houghton Mifflin.

Bakhtin, M. M. (1981) *The dialogic imagination: Four essays* (M. Holquist, ed.). (C. Emerson & M. Holquist, Trans.). Austin: University of Texas Press, Barrett. (Work originally published in 1930s)

Barron, F. (1955). The disposition towards originality. *Journal of Abnormal and Social Psychology, 51*, 478–485.

Beas, C., & Sánchez, J. (2012). At the far end of the world: Exploring the Chilean Cultural Isolation Complex, In T. Singer (Ed.), *Listening to Latin America: Exploring cultural complexes in Brazil, Chile, Colombia, Mexico, Uruguay and Venezuela*. New Orleans, LA: Spring Journal Books.

Benjamin, W. (2012). The task of the translator. In L. Venuti (Ed.), *The translation studies reader* (3rd. ed., pp. 75-83). Routledge. (Work originally published in 1923)

Berman, A. (2012): Translation and the trials of the foreign (L. Venuti, Trans.). In L. Venuti (Ed.), *The translation studies reader* (3rd. ed, pp. 243-163). Routledge.

Bernstein, J. S. (2014). Intergenerational trauma: Difference, genocide, and holocaust. In G. Gudaitė, G. & M. Stein (Eds.), *Confronting cultural trauma: Jungian approaches to understanding and healing* (pp. 113-130). Durham, NC: Duke University Press.

Bioy-Casares, A. (2006). *Borges*. Barcelona: Destino.

Bernal, D. D. & Solorzano, D.G. (2001). Examining transformational resistance through a critical race and latcrit theory framework: Chicana and chicano students in an urban context. *Urban Education, 36*, 308-342.

Bhabha, H. K. (1994). *Location of culture*. London and New York: Routledge.

Boix Mansilla, V., & Jackson, A. (2011). *Educating for global competence: Preparing our youth to engage the world*. New York: Asia Society and Council of Chief State School Officers.

Borges, J. L. (2012). The translators of The thousand and one nights (R. Allen, Trans.). In L. Venuti (Ed.), *The translation studies reader* (3rd. ed., pp. 92-106). Routledge. (Work originally published in 1936).

Brewster, F. (2017). *African Americans and Jungian psychology: Leaving the shadows*. New York: Routledge.

Brisset, A. (2012). The search for a native language: Translation and cultural identity (R. Gill & R. Gannon, Trans.). In L. Venuti (Ed.), *The translation studies reader* (3rd. ed., pp. 243-163). Routledge.

Brooks, D. (2015). *The road to character.* New York: Random House.

Cameron, J. (Director). (1986). *Aliens* [Motion picture]. Pinewood Studios, UK. Twentieth Century Fox.

Campbell, J. (1991). *The power of myth.* Anchor.

Carotenuto, A. (1985*). Vertical labyrinth: Individuation in Jungian psychology (Studies in Jungian Psychology by Jungian analysts)* (J. Shepley, Trans.). Toronto, CA: Inner City.

Cawdrey, R. (2007). *The first English dictionary 1604.* Oxford UK: Bodleian Library. (Original work published in 1604).

Chamberlain, L. (2012). Gender and the metaphorics of translation. In L. Venuti (Ed.), *The Translation studies reader* (3rd. ed., pp. 254-268). Routledge.

Chomsky, N. (1959). A review of B. F. Skinner's Verbal behavior. *Language, 35*(1), 26-58.

_____. (1965). *Aspects of a theory of syntax.* Boston: MIT Press.

Claremont de Castillejo, I. (1997). *Knowing woman: A feminine psychology.* Boston: Shambala.

Clarkson, A. (2008). The dialectical mind: On educating the creative imagination in elementary school. In R. A. Jones, A. Clarkson, S. Congram, & N. Stratton (Eds.), *Education and imagination: Post-Jungian Perspectives* (pp. 118-141). New York: Routledge.

Conant, J. B. (1964). *Two modes of thought.* New York: Trident.

Congram, S. (2008). Arts-informed learning in manager-leader development. In R. A. Jones, A. Clarkson, S. Congram, & N. Stratton (Eds.), *Education and imagination: Post-Jungian Perspectives* (pp. 160-177). New York: Routledge.

Cooper-White, P. (2015). *A tale of two houses: Küsnacht and Bollingen (part 2).* Atlanta, GA: Jung. Society of Atlanta.

Coward, H. (1996). Panikkar's philosophy of language. Chapter in J. Prabhu (Ed.), *The intercultural challenge of Raimon Panikkar* (pp. 58-70). New York: Maryknoll.

Cowper, W. (1975/1891). Preface to *The Iliad* of Homer. In T. S. Steiner (Ed.), *English translation theory—1650-1800* (pp. 134-140). Amsterdam, ND: Van Gorcum, Assen. (Original work published in 1891).

Creed, B. (1993). *The monstrous feminine: Film, feminism, psychoanalysis.* Routledge.

Cronin, M. (2012). The Translation Age: Translation, technology, and the new instrumentalism. In L. Venuti (Ed.), *The translation studies reader* (3rd. ed., pp. 469-482). Routledge.

Czizer, K., & Dörnyei, Z. (2005). The internal structure of language learning motivation and its relationship with language choice and learning effort. *The Modern Language Journal, 89,* 19-33.

D'Ablancourt, N. P. (2012). Prefaces to Tacitus and Lucian (L. Venuti, Trans.). In L. Venuti (Ed.), *The translation studies reader* (3rd. ed., pp. 31-37). Routledge.

Davison, J. A. (1949). The date of the Prometheia. *Transactions and Proceedings of the American Philological Association, 80,* 66-93.

Dawson, T. (2008). Rousseau, childhood, and the ego. In R. A. Jones, A. Clarkson, S. Congram, & N. Stratton (Eds.), *Education and imagination: Post-Jungian Perspectives* (pp. 52-63). New York: Routledge.

Deci, E. L., & Ryan, R. (1985). *Intrinsic motivation and self-determination in human behavior.* New York, NY: Plenum.

_____. (2000). The "what" and "why" of goal pursuits: Human needs and the self-determination of behavior. *Psychological Inquiry, 11,* 227-268.

_____. Eghrari, H., Patrick, B. C., & Leone, D. R. (1994). Facilitating internalization: The self-determination theory perspective. *Journal of Personality, 62*(1), 119-142.

DeGruy, J. (2005). *Post Traumatic Slave Syndrome: America's legacy of enduring injury and healing.* Milwaukie, OR: Uptone Press.

Deleuze, G. (1988). *Foucault* (S. Hand, Trans.). Minneapolis, MN: University of Minneapolis Press.

_____., & Guattari, F. (1987). *A thousand plateaus: Capitalism and schizophrenia* (B. Massumi, Trans.). Minneapolis, MN: University of Minnesota Press.

Derrida, J. (1985). Des tours de Babel. In J. F. Graham (Ed.). *Difference in translation* (pp. 165-248). Ithaca, NY: Cornell University Press.

_____. (1997). *Of grammatology* (G. C. Spivak, Trans.). Baltimore, MD: Johns Hopkins University Press. (Original work published in 1967)

Dewey, J. (2009). *Democracy and education: An introduction to the philosophy of education.* New York: WLC Books. (Original work published 1916).

Dickey, D. (2018, Oct 22). The shrink as secret agent: Jung, Hitler, and the OSS. Daily Beast. Retrieved 3/15/2020 from: https://www.thedailybeast.com/the-shrink-as-secret-agent-jung-hitler-and-the-oss

Dobson, D. (2008). The symbol as teacher: Reflective practices and methodology in transformative education. In R. A. Jones, A. Clarkson, S. Congram, & N. Stratton (Eds.), *Education and imagination: Post-Jungian Perspectives* (pp. 142-159). Routledge.

Dörnyei, Z. (2003). Attitudes, orientations, and motivations in language learning: Advances in theory, research, and Applications. *Language Learning, 53,* 3–32.

_____. (2008, April). The myth of 'individual differences.' Keynote address presented at the Annual Meeting of the American Association for Applied Linguistics, Washington, DC.

Eco, U. (2001): *Experiences in translation* (A. McEwan, tran.), University of Toronto Press, Toronto, Canada.

Edinger, E. F. (1984). *The creation of consciousness: Jung's myth for modern man.* Toronto, CA: Inner City Books.

Editors. (2008). *Webster's new college dictionary (3ʳᵈ Ed.).* Boston, MA: Houghton-Mifflin.

Ellison, R. (1952*). The invisible man.* New York, NY: Random House.

Evans, R. (1957). Conversations with CG Jung, Part V: Some reactions concerning psychological testing, psychotherapy, mental telepathy, and other personal insights [film transcript]. Gnostic Society Library: http://gnosis.org/Evans-Jung-Interview/evans5.html

_____., Jones, E, & Jung, C. G. (1964). *Conversations with Carl Jung and reactions from Ernest Jones.* Princeton, NJ: D. Van Norstrand Co.

Felton, D. (2012): Monstrosity or disability? Ancient accounts of accelerated ageing, *Folklore, 123*(3), 355-361.

Freud, S. (1953-1966). Moses and monotheism. In S. Freud, *The standard edition of the complete psychological works of Sigmund Freud* (J. Strahey, Trans.), *23*, 1-138.

_____. (1967). *Moses and monotheism* (J. Strahey, Trans.). New York: Vintage. (Original work published in 1939).

García Lorca, F. (1997). Teoría y juego del duende. In *Obras completas*, tomo III, págs. 150-162. Barcelona, SP: Galaxia Gutenberg/Círculo de Lectores. (Original work published in 1933).

Gardner, R.C., & Lambert, W.E. (1972). *Attitudes and motivation: Second language learning.* Newbury House.

Geertz, C. (1973). *The interpretation of cultures: Selected essays.* New York: Basic.

Geller, J. (1999). The godfather of psychoanalysis: Circumcision, antisemitism, homosexuality, and Freud's "Fighting Jew." *Journal of the American Academy of Religion, 67*(2), 355-385.

Gerson, J. (2010). Malinchismo: Betraying one's own. In T. Singer, & S. L. Kimbles (Eds.), *The cultural complex: Contemporary Jungian perspectives on psyche and society* (pp. 35-45). New York: Routledge.

Giegerich, W. (1999). *The soul's logical life.* Frankfort, Germany: Peter Lang

_____. (2007). *Technology and the soul: From the nuclear bomb to the World Wide Web (Vol. II).* New Orleans, LA: Spring Journal Books.

_____. (2008). *Soul-violence.* New Orleans: Spring Journal Books.

_____. (2012). *What is soul?* New Orleans: Spring Journal Books.

Gier, N. F. (2000). *Spiritual titanism: Indian, Chinese, and Western Perspectives.* Albany, NY: State University of New York Press.

Graves, R. (1960). *The Greek myths.* New York: Penguin.

Graziano, A., & Raulan, M. (2020). *Research methods: A process of inquiry* (9th ed.). Pearson.

Grivas, C., & Puccio, G. (2012). *The innovative team.* San Francisco: Jossey-Bass.

Handy, C. B. (1995). *Gods of management: The changing work of organizations.* New York: Oxford University Press.

Harrison, J. (1974/1912). *Themis: A study of the social origins of Greek religion (2nd ed.).* Gloucester, MA: Peter Smith. (Original work published in 1912)

_____. (2010/1912). *Themis: A study of the social origins of Greek religion (3rd ed.).* Gloucester, MA: Peter Smith. (Original work published in 1912)

Helgesen, S. (1995). *Web of inclusion.* New York, NY: Doubleday.

Henderson, J. L. (1984). *Cultural attitudes in psychological perspective.* Toronto, CA: Inner City Books.

_____. (2005). *Thresholds of initiation.* Willamette, IL: Chiron.

Hill, J. (2014). Dreams don't let you forget: Cultural trauma and its denial. In G. Gudaitė, G., & M. Stein (Eds.), *Confronting cultural trauma: Jungian approaches to understanding and healing* (pp. 31-46). Durham, NC: Duke University Press.

Hillman, J. (1975). *Re-visioning psychology.* New York: Harper Colophon.

_____. (1979). *The dream and the underworld.* New York: Harper & Row.

_____. (1989). *The blue fire: Selected writings by James Hillman.* New York: Harper Row.

Homer (1995-2009), *The Iliad* (S. Butler, Trans.). MIT Internet Classics Archive: http://classics.mit.edu/Homer/iliad.html (Original work published in 800 BCE)

Huberman, M. (1983). The role of teacher education in the improvement of educational practice: A linkage model. *European Journal of Teacher Education, 6*(1), 17-29.

Irigaray, L. (1977). *Women's exile* (C. Venn, Trans.). *Ideology and Consciousness I*, pp. 62-76.

_____. (1985a). *Speculum of the Other Woman* (G. C. Gill, Trans.). Ithaca, NY: Cornell University Press.

_____. (1985b). *The sex which is not one* (C. Porter, Trans.). Ithaca, NY: Cornell University Press.

Jensen, G. H. (2004). Introduction: Situating Jung in contemporary critical theory. In J. S. Baumlin, T. F. Baumlin and G. H. Jensen (eds.), *Post-Jungian Criticism: Theory and practice* (pp. 1-30). State University of New York Press.

Jerome (2012). Letter to Pammachius (K. Davis, Trans.). In L. Venuti (Ed.), *The translation studies reader* (3rd. ed., pp. 411-428). Routledge.

Johnson, B. (1985). Taking fidelity philosophically. In J. F. Graham (Ed.), *Difference in translation* (pp. 142-148). New York: Cornell University Press.

Joyce, J. (1922). *Ulysses.* Paris, FR: Shakespeare and Company.

Jung, C. G. (1923). Unauthorized notes on the Cornwall Seminar from M. E. Harding. Retrieved on 4/22/15 from: http://brbl-dl.library.yale.edu/vufind/Record/3684132

_____. (1939). Spiritual exercises of Ignatius Loyola. *ETS (Eidgenössische technische hochschule Zürich /Swiss Federal Institute of Technology). Lecture VII.* Zurich, Switzerland.

_____. (2005). *The undiscovered Self* (R. F. C. Hull, Trans.) Routledge. (Original work published in 1957)

_____. (1963a). *Memories, dreams, reflections* (Recorded & edited by Aniela Jaffé) (R. & C. Winston, Trans.). London: Collins and Routledge & Kegan Paul. (Original work published in 1955)

_____. (1963b). *Mysterium coniunctionis: An inquiry into the separation and synthesis of psychic opposites in alchemy* (R. F. C. Hull, Trans.). CW 14. London: Routledge & Kegan Paul. (Original work published in 1955)

_____. (1964). *Man and his symbols* (Prepared by M-L. von Franz, J. L. Henderson, A. Jaffé, & J. Jacobi). New York: Dell Publishing.

_____. (1970). *Civilization in transition (2nd ed.),* (G. Adler & R. F. C. Hull, Trans.). CW10. Princeton, NJ: Princeton University Press. (Original work published in 1946)

_____. (1972). *Two essays on analytical psychology* (R. F. C. Hull, Trans.). CW 7. Princeton, NJ: Princeton University Press. (Original work published in 1928).

_____. (1974a) *Development of personality* (R. F. C. Hull, Trans.). Princeton, NJ: Princeton University Press. (Original work published in 1921)

_____. (1974b). *Psychology and education*. (R. F. C. Hull, Trans.). CW17. Princeton, NJ: Princeton University Press. (Original work published in 1954).

_____. (1975) *Letters, Vol. 2*. (G. Adler & A. Jaffe, Eds.) (R. F. C. Hull, Trans.). Princeton, NJ: Princeton University Press.

_____. (1976). T*he Tavistock lectures: On the theory and practice of analytical psychology* (G. Adler & R. F. C. Hull, Eds. & Trans.) CW18. Princeton, NJ: Princeton University Press (Original work published in 1935)

_____. (1977). *The symbolic Life: Miscellaneous writings by Jung C.G.* (G. Adler & R. F. C. Hull, Eds. & Trans.). CW18. Princeton, NJ: Princeton University Press.

_____. (1979). *Aion: Researches into the phenomenology of the self* (2nd ed.) (R. F. C. Hull, Trans.). CW9. Princeton, NJ: Princeton University Press. (Original work published in German in 1959)

_____. (1987). *CG Jung Speaking: Interviews and encounters* (R. F. C. Hull, Trans.). Princeton, NJ: Princeton University Press.

_____. (1998). *The Psychology of the Transference* (R. F. C. Hull, Trans.). CW16. Princeton, NJ: Princeton University Press. (Original work published in 1954)

_____. (1989). *Analytical psychology: Notes of the seminar given in 1925* (W. McGuire, ed.). Princeton, NJ: Princeton University Press. (Original work published in 1925)

_____. (1990). *Psychological types* (H. G. Baynes, Trans.) CW6. Princeton: Princeton University Press. (Original work published in 1921)

_____. (1991). *The development of personality: Papers on child psychology, education, and related subjects* (2nd ed.). (R. F. C. Hull, Trans.). CW20. Princeton, NJ: Princeton University Press. (Original work published in 1954)

_____. (1993). *Psychology and alchemy* (R. F. C. Hull, Trans.). CW12. Princeton, NJ: Princeton University Press. (Original work published in 1944)

_____. (1995). *Symbols of transformation* (R. F. C. Hull, Trans.). CW5: London: Routledge. (Original work published 1911-12/1952)

_____. (1997). *Visions: Notes of the seminar given in 1930-1934* (C. Douglas, Ed.). Princeton University Press. (Original works published between 1930-1934)

_____. (2001) *Modern man in search of a soul* (W. S. Dell & C. F. Baynes, Trans.). London, UK: Routledge Classics. (Original work published in 1933)

_____. (2009). *The Red Book: Liber Novis*. London, UK: Philemon Foundation. (Original work written between 1915-1930)

_____. (2014): *Symbols of transformation (CW5)*. R. F. C. Hull (trad.), Routledge. Princeton University Press Bollingen Series. (Original work published 1911-12/1952)

_____., Baynes, H. G., & Baynes, C. F. (2006). *Contributions to analytical psychology*. New York: Harcourt, Brace. (Original work published in 1928)

_____., Jung, E., & Wolff, T. (1982). *A collection of remembrances* (F. Jenson & S. Mullen, eds.). San Francisco: Analytical Psychology Club of San Francisco.

Jünger, F. G. (1946). *The failure of technology: Perfection without purpose.* Der Shattige Wald.

_____. (2006). *Mitos griegos* (C. Rubies, Trans.). Barcelona: Herder. (Original work published in 1947)

Kalinenko, V., & Slutskaya, M. (2014). "Father of the people" versus "Enemies of the people": A split-father complex as the foundation for collective trauma in Russia. In G. Gudaitė, & M. Stein (Eds.), *Confronting cultural trauma: Jungian approaches to understanding and healing* (pp. 95-111). Durham, NC: Duke University Press.

Kalsched, D. (1996). *The inner world of trauma: Archetypal defenses of the personal spirit.* New York: Routledge.

Karasaviddis, I. (2009). Activity Theory as a conceptual framework for understanding teacher approaches to Information and Communication Technologies. *Computers & Education 53*(2), 436-444.

Karbiener, K. (2003). Introduction to M. Shelley, *Frankenstein.* (Original work published in 1818)

Kawai, H. (1996). *Buddhism and the art of psychotherapy.* Texas A&M University Press.

Kerényi, K. (1978). *Athene: Virgin and mother in Greek religion* (M. Stein, Trans.). Zurich, SW: Spring Publications.

_____. (1997). *Prometheus: Archetypal image of human existence* (2nd Ed.) (R. Manheim, Trans.). Princeton: Princeton University Press.

Kimbles, S. (2014). *Phantom narratives: The unseen contributions of culture to psyche.* Routledge.

Kincheloe, J. L., & Steinberg, S. R. (1993). A tentative description of post-formal thinking: The critical confrontation with cognitive theory. *Harvard Educational Review, 63,* 296-320.

Kipling, R. (1929). *Rudyard Kipling's verse: 1885-1926. Inclusive Edition.* Garden City, NJ: Doubleday, Doran & Co.

Kirsch, T. (2010). Cultural complexes in the history of Jung, Freud and their followers. In T. Singer, & S. L. Kimbles (Eds.). *The cultural complex: Contemporary Jungian perspectives on psyche and society* (pp. 185-196). Routledge.

Kirton, M. J. (2003). *Adaption-innovation: In the context of diversity and change.* New York, NY: Routledge.

Kramsch, C. (1988). *Language and culture.* Oxford: Oxford University Press.

Kristeva, J. (1982). *Powers of horror: An essay on abjection* (L. S. Roudiez, Trans.). Columbia University Press.

_____. (1986). *The Kristeva reader* (T Moi, Ed.). Oxford, UK: Basil Blackwell.

Kugler, P. (2002). *The alchemy of discourse: Image, sound, and psyche.* Einsiedeln, CH: Daimon-Verlag.

Kuhn, A. (2012). *Zeitschrift für vergleichende Sprachforschung Auf Dem Gebiete Des Deutschen, Griechischen Und Lateinischen (Vol. II).* Berlin: F. Dümmler. (Original work published in 1853)

_____. (2015). *Die herabkunft des feuers und des göttertranks. Ein beitrag zur verglei- chenden mythologie der indogermanen.* Wolcott, NY: Scholar's Choice. (Original work published in 1859)

Kuiper, F. B. J. (1971). An Indian Prometheus? *Asiatische Studien: Zeitschrift der Schweizerischen Asiengesellschaft, 25*, 85-98.

Lacan. J. (2007). *Écrits: The first complete edition in English* (B. Fink, trans.). W. W. Norton & Company.

Lantolf, J. P., & Poehner, M. E. (2007). *Language proficiency or symbolic capability: A dialectical perspective.* CALPER Working Paper Series. Center for Advanced Language Proficiency Education and Research, The Pennsylvania State University. Available at: http://calper.la.psu.edu/pubs.php

Lave, J., & Wenger, E. (1991). *Situated learning: Legitimate peripheral participation.* New York, NY: Cambridge University Press.

Leejoeiwara, B. (2012). Modeling adoption intention of online education in Thailand using the extended decomposed theory of planned behavior (DTPB). *Australian Journal of Management, 11*, 13-26.

Lefkowitz, M. R., & Fant, M. B. (2005). *Womens' life in ancient Greece and Rome: A sourcebook in translation* (2nd ed.). Baltimore, MD: Johns Hopkins.

Lehr-Rottmann, E. (2014). Collective trauma and individual development: The case of Germany. In G. Gudaitè, G., & M. Stein (Eds.), *Confronting cultural trauma: Jungian approaches to understanding and healing* (pp. 61-75). Durham, NC: Duke University Press.

Lehti, A., Johansson, E. E., Bengs, C., Danielsson, U., & Hammarström, A. (2010). The Western Gaze: An analysis of medical research publications. Concerning the expressions of depression, focusing on ethnicity and gender. *Health Care for Women International, 31*(2), 100-112: https://doi.org/10.1080/07399330903067861

Levinas, E. (2006). *Humanism of the Other* (N. Poller, Trans.). Urbana and Chicago, Il: University of Illinois Press. (Original work published in French, in 1972)

van Lier, L. (1996). *Interaction in the language curriculum: Awareness, autonomy, and authenticity.* London: Longman.

_____. (2004). *The ecology and semiotics of language learning: A sociocultural perspective.* Boston: Kluwer Academic.

Lévi-Strauss, C. (1955). The structural study of myth. *The Journal of American Folklore, 68*(270), 428–444.

Littau, K. (2000). "Pandora's tongues." *TTR: Traduction, terminologie, redaction, 13*(1), 21-35.

López-Pedraza, R. (1990). *Cultural anxiety.* Einsiedeln, SW: Daimon.

_____. (1991). *Hermes y sus hijos.* Barcelona, Spain: Anthropos.

_____. (1996). *Anselm Kiefer: The psychology of* After the Catastrophe. George Braziller.

_____. (2000a). *Ansiedad cultural: Cuatro ensayos de psicología de los arquetipos (2nd Ed.).* Caracas, Venezuela: Festina Lente.

_____. (2000b). *Dionisos en exilio.* Barcelona: Festina Lente.

_____. (2002). *Sobre héroes y poetas.* Barcelona: Festina Lente.

_____. (2005). *Artemisa e Hipólito: Mito y tragedia.* Caracas, Venezuela: Festina Lente.

MacIntyre, A. (2007*) After Virtue (3rd Ed.)*. South Bend, IN: University of Notre Dame Press.

Maidenbaum, A. (2013). Carl Jung and the question of antisemitism: Struggling with accusations. *Jewish Currents*: https://jewishcurrents.org/carl-jung-and-the-question-of-antisemitism

Marlan, S. (1997). Fire in the Stone: An inquiry into the alchemy of soul-making. In S. Marlan (ed.) *Fire in the stone*. Wilmette, IL: Chiron, pp. 7-41.

_____. (2005). *The black sun: The alchemy and art of darkness*. College Station, TX: Texas A & M Press.

_____. (2021). *C. G. Jung and the alchemical imagination: Passages into the mysteries of psyche and soul*. Routledge.

Matthews, R. S., & Hua Liu, C. (2008). Education and imagination: A synthesis of Jung and Vygotsky. In R. Jones, A. Clarkson, S. Congram, & N. Stratton (Eds.) *Education and imagination: Post-jungian perspectives* (pp. 1-15). Routledge.

Mays, C. (2005). *Jung and education*. Lanham, MD: Rowman and Littlefield Education.

McDonald, A. A. (nd.) *A practical Sanskrit dictionary*. Digital Dictionaries of South Asia: dsal.uchicago.edu

McGuire, W., & Hull, R. F. C. (1977). *Jung speaking: Interviews and encounters*. Princeton, NJ: Princeton University Press.

Michan, P. (2014). Reiterative disintegration: Historical and cultural patterns and the contemporary Mexican psyche. In G. Gudaitė, G., & M. Stein (Eds.), *Confronting cultural trauma: Jungian approaches to understanding and healing* (pp. 77-94). Durham, NC: Duke University Press.

Miller, A. (1949). *Death of a salesman*. New York: Viking.

Miller, M. (2018). *Circe*. Boston, MA: Little, Brown & Co.

Mlynowski, S., Myracle, L., & Jenkins, E. (2015). *Upside-down magic*. New York: Scholastic.

Mogenson, G. (2005). Interiorizing psychology into itself. In W. Giegerich, D. L. Miller, & G.

Mogenson (Eds.), *Dialectics and analytical psychology* (pp. 61-76). New Orleans: Spring Journal Books.

Monier-Williams, M. (1883). *Religious thought and life in India*. London: J. Murray. Retrieved from sanskritdictionary.com

_____. (1988). *A Sanskrit-English dictionary: Etymologically and philologically arranged with special reference to cognate Indo-European languages*. Columbia, MO: South Asia Books. (Original work published in 1899). Retrieved from: sanskritdictionary.com

Moore, C. (2015). "PROMĒTHEIA" ("FORETHOUGHT") until Plato. *The American Journal of Philology, 136*, 381-420.

Moore, R. L. (2003). *Facing the dragon: Confronting personal and spiritual grandiosity*. Asheville, NC: Chiron Publications.

Morgan, H. (2010). *Exploring racism: A clinical example of a cultural complex*. In T. Singer and S. L. Kimbles (Eds.), *The cultural complex: Contemporary Jungian perspectives on psyche and society* (pp. 212-222). New York: Routledge.

Morgan, M. H. (1890). De ignis sliciendi modis apud antiquos. *HSCPh*. 32-34.

Mort, P., & Cornell, F. (2012*). American schools in transition; how our schools adapt their practices to changing needs.* Whiteish, MT: Literary Licensing, LLC. (Original work published in 1941)

Muntuori, A. (2008). Foreword: Transdiciplinarity. In B. Nicolescu (ed.), *Transdisciplinarity: Theory and practice* (pp. ix-xvii). Hampton Press.

Nabokov, V. (2012). Problems of translation: "Onegin' in English. In L. Venuti (Ed.), *The translation studies reader* (3rd. ed., pp. 113-125). Routledge. (Original work published in 1955)

Narten, J. (1960). Das vedische Verbum math. *Indo-Iranian Journal, 4,* 121-135.

Neumann, E. (1994). *Fear of the feminine and other essays on feminine psychology* (E. Matthews, E. Doughty, E. Rolfe, & M. Cullingworth, Trans.). Princeton University Press.

_____. (2015). *The Great Mother: An analysis of the archetype.* (R. Manheim, Trans.) Princeton University Press. (Original work published in 1955)

Nicolescu, B. (1994). *The hidden third* (W. Garvin, Trans.). Quantum Prose.

_____. (2008). In vitro and in vivo knowledge— Methodology of transdisciplinarity. In B. Nicolescu (ed.), Transdisciplinarity: Theory and practice (pp. 1-21). Hampton Press.

Noddings, N. (1991). *Stories lives tell: Narrative and dialogue in education* (with Carol Witherell). New York: Teachers College Press.

Noels, K. A. (2001). New orientations in language learning motivation: Towards a model of intrinsic, extrinsic, and integrative orientations and motivation. In Z. Dörnyei, & R. Schmidt (Eds.). *Motivation and second language acquisition* (pp. 43-68). Hawaii: University of Hawai Press.

Noels, K.A., Clement, R., Pelletier, L.G. (2001a). Intrinsic, extrinsic, and integrative orientations of French-Canadian learners of English. *Canadian Modern Language Review* 57(3), 424-442.

_____., Clément, R., Pelletier, L. G. (2001b). Perceptions of teachers' communicative style and students' intrinsic and extrinsic motivation. *The Modern Language Journal, 83,* 23-34.

_____., Pelletier, L. G., & Vallerand, R. J. (2000). Why are you learning a second language? Motivational orientations and self-determination theory. *Language Learning, 50,* 57-85.

Ong, W. J. (1977). *Interfaces of the word: Studies in the evolution of consciousness and culture.* Ithaca, NY: Cornell University Press.

Ovid (1994-2009). *Metamorphoses* (S. Garth, J. Dryden, A. Pope, J. Addison, & W. Congreve, Trans.). MIT Internet Classics Archive: http://classics.mit.edu/Ovid/metam.html (Original work published in 1 A.C.E.)

Paglia, C. (2006). Erich Neumann: Theorist of the Great Mother. *Arion, 13*(3), 1-14.

Panikkar, R. (1995). *Cultural disarmament: The way to peace* (R. R. Barr, Trans.). Louisville, KY: Westminster John Knox Press.

Panofsky, E. (1962). *Studies in iconology.* New York, NY: Harper Torchbooks

Peperzak, A. (1993). *An introduction to the philosophy of Emmanuel Levinas.* Purdue University Press.

Pinkola-Estés, C. (2013). *Untie the strong woman: Blessed Mother's immaculate love for the wild soul.* Louisville, CO: Sounds True.

Plato (1994-2009). *Phaedrus* (B. Jowett, Trans.). MIT Internet Classics Archive: http://classics.mit.edu/Plato/phaedrus.html (Original work published in 360 BCE)

Pollina, L. (2009/2013). Untitled [Graphite on paper]. *The omega point project and the noosphere.* Retrieved from: http://lorypollina.com/omegapointproject.shtml (Original project completed in 2009)

Popovic, V. B., & Popovic, M. (2014). Liminality: Discourse as cultural trauma. In G. Gudaitė, G. & M. Stein (Eds.), Confronting cultural trauma: Jungian approaches to understanding and healing (pp. 161-179). Durham, NC: Duke University Press.

Pound, E. (2012). Guido's relations. In L. Venuti (Ed.), *The translation studies reader* (3rd. ed., pp. 84-91). Routledge. (Original work published in 1929)

Puccio, G., Mance, M., Swiatalski, L. B., & Reali, P. D. (2012). *Creativity rising: Creative thinking and problem solving in the 21st Century.* Buffalo, NY: ICSC Press.

_____., Murdock, M. C., & Mance, M. (2006). *Creative leadership: Skills that drive change.* Thousand Oaks, CA: Sage Publications.

Rafael, V. L. (2012). Translation, American English, and the national insecurities of empire. In L. Venuti (Ed.), *The translation studies reader* (3rd. ed., pp. 451-468). Routledge.

Raju, K. V. (2008). Levels of being and reality –Ancient Indian perspective In B. Nicolescu (ed.), *Transdisciplinarity: Theory and practice* (pp. 67-75). Hampton Press.

Robinson, D. (1991). *The translator's turn.* Johns Hopkins University Press.

Rogers, E. M. (2003). *Diffusion of innovations* (5th ed.). New York: The Free Press.

_____., & Jain, N. (1968). Needed research on diffusion within educational organizations. (ERIC Document Reproduction Service No. ED 017 740)

_____., Medina, U. E., Rivera, M. A., & Wiley, C. J. (2005). Complex Adaptive Systems and The Diffusion of Innovations. *The Innovation Journal: The Public Sector Innovation Journal, 10,* 1-26.

Roth, R. (1855). *Atharva Veda Sanhita.* Berlin: Dümler.

Rowland, S. (2002). *Jung: A feminist revision.* Malden, MA: Blackwell.

_____. (2010). *CG Jung in the humanities: Taking the soul's path.* New Orleans, LA: Spring Journal Books.

_____. (2020). *Remembering Dionysus: Revisioning psychology and literature in C. G. Jung and James Hillman.* New York: Routledge.

Roy, M. (2010). When a religious archetype becomes a cultural complex: Puritanism in America.

In T. Singer and S. L. Kimbles (Eds.), *The cultural complex: Contemporary Jungian perspectives on psyche and society* (pp. 64-77). New York: Routledge.

Ryan, R. M. (1993). Commentary on the Fortieth Nebraska Symposium on Motivation. In J. Jacobs (Ed.), *Nebraska symposium on motivation: Developmental perspectives on motivation* (Vol. 40, pp. 255-268). Lincoln, NE: University of Nebraska Press.

_____., Huta, V., Deci, E. L. (2008). Living well: a self-determination theory perspective on eudaimonia. *Journal of Happiness Studies, 9,* 139-170.

Said, E. (1979). *Orientalism.* New York: Vintage.

Salvo, D. (2020, October 6). *Hybrid identities in Greco-Roman mythology.* Unpublished videoconference interview.

Schellinski, K. (2014). Horror inherited: Transgenerational transmission of collective trauma in dreams. In G. Gudaitė, G., & M. Stein (Eds.), *Confronting cultural trauma: Jungian approaches to understanding and healing* (pp. 11-29). Durham, NC: Duke University Press.

Schleiermacher, F. (2012). On the different methods of translating (S. Bernovsky, Trans.). In L. Venuti (Ed.), *The translation studies reader (3rd. ed., pp. 43-63),* Routledge. (Original work published in 1813)

Schumann, J. (1978). *The pidginization process: A model for second language acquisition.* Rowley, MA: Newbury House.

Scott, R. (Director). (1979). Alien [Motion picture]. London, UK. Twentieth century fox home entertainment.

_____. (Director). (2012). *Alien: Prometheus* [Motion picture]. Toronto, CA. Twentieth century fox home entertainment.

_____. (Director). (2017). *Alien: Covenant* [Motion picture]. Milano, NZ. Twentieth century fox home entertainment.

Semetsky, I., & Ramey, J. (2013). Deleuze's philosophy and Jung's psychology: Learning and the unconscious. In I. Semetsky (Ed.), *Jung and educational theory* (pp. viii-xii). West Sussex, UK: Wiley-Blackwell.

Senyshyn, R. M., Warford, M. K., & Zhan, Z. (2000). Issues of adjustment to higher education: International students' perspectives. *International Education, 30,* 17-35.

Seo, J. E. (2018). Fellowship beyond kinship: Sympathy, nature, and culture in Mary Shelley's Frankenstein. *English Language and Literature, 64*(2), 203-217.

Shelley, M. (1818). *Frankenstein: A modern Prometheus.* New York, NY: Barnes and Noble Classics.

Shual, K. (1995). *Sexual magick.* Oxford: Mandrake Press.

Shuttle, P., & Redgrove, P. (1978). *The wise wound: Eve's Curse and Everywo*man. Front Richard Marek Publishers.

Sidorkin, A. M. (2017). Human capital and innovations in education. In A. Sidorkin and M.

Warford, *Reforms and innovations in education* (pp. 127-139). Amsterdam: Springer.

Siegel, E. (May 26, 2020). Observing the universe really does change the outcome, and this experiment shows how. Forbes: https://www.forbes.com/sites/startswithabang/2020/05/26/observing-the-universe-really-does-change-the-outcome-and-this-experiment-shows-how/?sh=216e109367af

Silva-Corvalán, C. (2001). *Sociolingüística y pragmática del español.* Georgetown University Press.

Simon, S. (2012). Translating Montreal: The crosstown journey in the 1960s. In L. Venuti (Ed.), *The translation studies reader* (3rd. ed., pp. 429-450), Routledge.

Singer, J. K. (1976). *Androgyny: Toward a new theory of sexuality.* New York, NY: Anchor/Doubleday.

Singer, T. (2010a). Cultural complexes in analysis. In M. Stein (Ed.) *Jungian psychoanalysis: Working in the spirit of C. G. Jung* (pp. 22-37). Chicago, IL: Open Court. Reprinted online at: https://aras.org/sites/default/files/docs/00042SingerKaplinsky.pdf

_____. (2010b). The cultural complex and archetypal defenses of the group spirit: Baby Zeus, Eliane Gonzales, Constantine's Sword, and other holy wards (with special attention to "the axis of evil"). In T. Singer, & S. L. Kimbles (Eds.). *The cultural complex: Contemporary Jungian perspectives on psyche and society* (pp. 13-34). Routledge.

_____., & Kimbles, S. L. (2010). Introduction. In T. Singer, & S. L. Kimbles (Eds.), *The cultural complex: Contemporary Jungian perspectives on psyche and society* (pp. 1-9). New York: Routledge.

Sinha, C. (1989). Development and the social production of mind. *Cultural Dynamics, 2,* 188- 208.

Skinner, B. F. (1977). Why I am not a cognitive psychologist. *Behaviorism, 5,* 1-10.

Sloan, D. (2008). *Insight imagination: The emancipation of thought and the modern world.* Oxford, UK: Barfield. Press. (Original work published in 1983)

Sommers, C. (2017, March). The godly and the grotesque: the monstrous body in antiquity and beyond. Presentation delivered to NEMLA, Baltimore, MD.

_____. (2020, September 17). *The Monstrous.* Unpublished videoconference interview.

Spivak, G. C. (2012). The politics of translation. In L. Venuti (Ed.), *The translation studies reader* (3rd. ed., pp. 312-330). Routledge.

Stein, M. (1978). Translator's afterthoughts. In K. Kerényi, *Athene: Virgin and mother in Greek religion* (pp. 71-79). Zurich: Spring Publications.

_____. (2020). *Myth and psychology.* Chiron Publications.

Stevenson, J. (1842). *Translation of the Sama Veda.* London: Oriental Translation Fund of Great Britain and Ireland.

Swami Anyanananda (1963). *A history of Indian music.* Calcutta: Ramarkrishna Vedanta Math.

Tang, H.-W. V., Chang, K., & Sheu, R.-S. (2015). Critical factors for implementing a Programme for international MICE professionals: A hybrid MCDM model combining DEMATEL and ANP. *Current Issues in Tourism.* Taylor and Francis Online. Retrieved on 8/2/15 from: http://www.tandfonline.com/doi/abs/10.1080/13683500.2015.1053848?journalCode=rcit20#.Vcqspq3YGSc

Teilhard de Chardin, P. (2008). *The phenomenon of man.* New York: Harper Perennial. (Original work published in 1959)

Toffler, A. (1990). *Powershift: Knowledge, wealth, and violence at the edge of the 21st Century.* New York: Bantam Books.

Toury, G. (2012). The nature and role of norms in translation. In L. Venuti (Ed.), *The translation studies reader* (3rd. ed., pp. 483-502). Routledge. (Original work published in 1995)

Tremblay, M. (1969). L'Intelligence de rire de soi-même. *L'envers du décor, 1*(II) 1 noviembre: 3.

Turner, V. (1969). *The ritual process: Structure and anti-structure.* Chicago, IL: Aldine.

UNESCO. (2008). Appendix 2: Venice Declaration. In B. Nicolescu (ed.), *Transdisciplinarity: Theory and practice* (pp. 257-259). Hampton Press. Original work published March 7, 1994)

Vehar, J. (2008). Creativity and innovation: A call for rigor in language. *Proceedings of the International Conference on Creativity and Innovation Management, 2,* 259-277.

Venuti, L. (2012). Genealogies of translation theory: Jerome. In L. Venuti (Ed.), *The translation studies reader* (3rd. ed., pp. 483-502). Routledge.

Vergados, A. (2012). Hesychius, s.v. στορεύς (σ 1933). *Glotta, 88,* 224-231.

Verspoor, M., De Bot, K., & Lowie, W. (2011). *A dynamic approach to second language development.* Benjamins.

Von Franz, M. L. (2000). *The problem of the puer aeternus.* Toronto: Inner City Books. (Original work published in 1970)

Vygotsky, L. S. (1978). *Mind in society: The development of higher psychological processes.* Luria, Trans.) Cambridge, MA: Harvard University Press.

_____. (1981). The instrumental method in psychology. In J. V. Wertsch (Ed.), *The concept of activity in Soviet psychology* (pp. 139-143). Armonk, NY: M E. Sharpe. (Original work published in 1928)

_____. (1986). *Thought and language* (Rev. Ed.) (A. Kozulin, Trans). Cambridge: MIT Press. (Original work published in 1932).

_____. (1994). *Thought and language* (3rd Ed.) (A. Kozulin, Trans). Cambridge: MIT Press. (Original work published in 1932).

Warford, M. K. (2005). Testing a diffusion of innovations in education model (DIEM). *The Innovation Journal: The Public Sector Innovation Journal 10*(3), 1-41.

_____. (2011). Narrative language pedagogy and the stabilization of indigenous languages. *Reading Matrix, 11,* 76-88.

_____. (2017). Educational innovation diffusion: Confronting complexities. In A. Sidorkin and M. Warford, *Reforms and innovations in education* (pp. 11-36). Amsterdam: Springer.

_____. (2019). Traducción, transferencia y la ética del Otro. Centro Jung de Buenos Aires. Retrieved on 5/31/23 from https://www.centrojung.com.ar/jung_lenguaje_traduccion_mark_warford.htm

Webster, N. (1789): *Dissertation on the English language.* Isaiah Thomas.

West, M. L. (2007). *Indo-European poetry and myth.* Oxford University Press.

Wilhelm, R. (1931/1962). *The secret of the golden flower: A Chinese book of life* (R. Wilhelm, trans., C. G. Jung, foreword and commentary. Harcourt, Brace and World.

Wilhelmsen, F. D. (1946). Introduction. In F. G. Jünger, *The failure of technology: Perfection without purpose* (pp. 9-21). Der Shattige Wald.

Williams, W. C. (1995). *Paterson (rev. ed.).* New York: New Directions. (Original work published in 1946)

Wilson, E. O. (2017). *The origins of creativity.* New York: Liveright.

Wilson, H. H. (1949). *Translation of the Rigveda: A collection of ancient Hindu hymns (Vol. I).* Bangalore: The Bangalore Printing and Publishing Company, Ltd. (Original work published in 1850)

Wisdom Library (2021, February 27). Agnyadheya, Author: https://www.wisdom lib.org/definition/agnyadheya

Wood, M. (2000). *Conquistadors.* Berkely, CA: University of California Press.

Wood, R. (1986). *Hollywood from Vietnam to Reagan.* Columbia University Press.

Yeats, W. B. (1994). *Michael Robartes and the dancer. Manuscript Materials* (T. Parkinson & A. Brannen, eds). Ithaca, NY: Cornell University. (Original work published in 1920)

Zeiser, K. L., Taylor, J., Rickles, J., Garet, M. S. (2014, September). *Evidence of deeper learning outcomes* (Report 3). Washington, DC: American Institutes for Research.

Zoja, L. (2010). Trauma and abuse: The development of a cultural complex in the history of Latin America. In T. Singer, & S. L. Kimbles (Eds.), *The cultural complex: Contemporary Jungian perspectives on psyche and society* (pp. 78-89). New York: Routledge.

Appendix

Author's notes on (Pra)ma(n)tha-Prometheus investigation

Bhrigu	Kuhn affirmed a connection between the Vedic Bhrigu and the Greek Prometheus (Jung, CW5, 208).
Manthá (n.)	noun (feminine) a vessel for butter (Monier-Williams, Sir M. (1899/1988) "n. an instrument for kindling fire, by friction" (Sanskritdictionary.com) Churning or "churning stick" (Sanskritdictionary.com). "the whisking of milk and butter, the mixing of a potion" ["das Quirlen von Milch und Butter, das Anrühren eines Trankes"], etc., cf. manthä- "stirred potion" [rührtrank] (Narten, 1960, p. 121, citing e.B.).
Manthara (n.)	Stick used for churning butter (Kuhn, 1859/2015).
Math (n.)	"a violent snatching" ["*ein gewaltsames Entreißen*"] (Narten, 1960, p. 123; connotations of wind-as-robber: Mätarisvan (Narten, 1960, p. 127)
Nir-math (v.)	"Tearing out, robbing" ["*herausreißen, -rauben*"] (p. 129)
Ma(n)th (v.)	Rub, whisk, shake, reduce, detach (Narten, 1960, p. 121, citing PW). Math as "zero-grade formation" (Narten, 1960, p. 122).
Manthana (n.)	The Vedic sacrificial ceremony that reenacts the birth of the fire god, Agni, through the union of a fire stick and a bored piece of wood. Jung (CW5, para. 210), mistakes the corresponding tools for their mythologems. The two components (my corrections in parentheses) consist of a masculine boring tool called the *uttararani* (which symbolizes the Sun King *Pururavas*) and a feminine receptor stick called the *adhararani* (which symbolizes the moon nymph *Urvashi*).
Manth mi (v.)	Jung, CG, CW5, para. 208: "to shake, to rub, to bring forth by rubbing" Related to Greek verb to learn: μ (citing Kuhn, 1853/2012, p. 395 and IV, p. 124).
Ma(n)thani (v.)	To rub, break off, or rob (Jung, CW5, para. 248).
Manth (v.n.)	Theft of fire ascription as inappropriate for mantha (Narten, 1960, p. 133) "the whisking of milk and butter, the mixing of a potion, etc., cf. manthä- 'stirring potion'" (Narten, 1960, p. 121, citing e.B.). Narten deems these meanings insufficient to account for the myth of Mätarisvan's bringing the fire from the gods for the benefit of mankind (p. 127). Buried in a footnote to CW5 para. 209, Jung resorts to a somewhat eccentric churn and burn through various philologists extends mantha into everything from "mangle" [mengeln] to nouns like "mint" and a priapic "chin" and "mind." Mantha is ultimately ascribed to a primordial, presexual stage of the libido.
Math (v.)	Narten (1960): Math as "a violent snatching away" ["*ein gewaltsames Entreißen*"] or robbery [rauben] (Narten, 1960, p. 123). Snatch or rob, as in wolves stealing sheep, Asuras or Maruts* stealing (portions of) sacrificial animals and other sacrificial food (butter); also tear, as in "rip" (Narten, 1960, pp. 121-125).
Mätarisvan	Wind god alleged to have robbed sacred fire from the Heavens for the benefit of the Bhrigu, a race attributed to the fire-god, Agni. Generally

	considered by Roth and Kuhn to be a prototype for Prometheus; as related by Jung (CW5, para. 208).
Manthu and Pramanthu	Graves (1960): "The brothers Pramanthu and Manthu, who occur in the Bhagavata Purana, a Sanskrit epic, may be prototypes of Prometheus and Epimetheus ('afterthought')" (p. 9). A. Nicholson casts doubt on such connections (personal communication, June 26, 2021).
pra + ma(n)th	"to stir vigorously," "to churn vigorously," "to harass," "~~to steal~~" (A. Nicholson, personal communication, June 26, 2021).
Pramatha	"m. 'Tormentor,' Name of a class of demons attending on iva" (Monier-Williams, 1883, p. 238 found on: sanskritdictionary.com). "'Pramathas' are type of nondivine forces which we call the beings of falsehood that belongs to the subtle physical/vital world, and they impair/ harass any divine work going on in this terrestrial world. They are very low level (not like intelligent asura) beings of falsehood" (S. Joshi, personal communication, June 28, 2021).
*Pra*math (*vi*math)	Rob or tear *away (forward)* (Narten, 1960, p. 129).
pramantha	Fire drill, such as that depicted in Thurii, in the hands of Zeus Prometheus (Graves, 1960, p. 9; Kuhn, 1859/2015) though Jung (CW5), working from Kuhn's analysis, suggests that the Thuric " -μ s" is not directly tied to *pramantha* but rather constitutes a cognomen (nickname) (para. 208). Ultimately, Jung holds the Promethean connection to pramantha in doubt. He also lavishes on the phallic and sexual connotations of a "fire stick," injecting mainly Germanic archetypal associations (para. 212). Accordingly, and working from Abraham and Kuhn, Jung takes up the *bohrer* (drill), ascribing a "masculine firestick" (para. 208) aspect to the pramantha. Adding related images from the Australian Wachandi to plant a "a widespread tendency to equate fire-making with sexuality" (para. 213), the archetypal sacred marriage: the Greek *hieros gamos* (para. 214).

Index

P

www.ingramcontent.com/pod-product-compliance
Lightning Source LLC
Chambersburg PA
CBHW072120020426
42334CB00018B/1659